# Gyascutus

## STUDIES IN
## ANTEBELLUM SOUTHERN
## HUMOROUS AND SPORTING WRITING

Edited by JAMES L. W. WEST III

# GYASCUTUS
## STUDIES IN
## ANTEBELLUM SOUTHERN
## HUMOROUS AND SPORTING WRITING

GYASCUTUS is a collection of primary and secondary materials dealing with the humorous, realistic, and sporting writing of the Old South. The volume includes important essays — published here for the first time — on George Washington Harris, William Tappan Thompson, William Trotter Porter, and Augustus Baldwin Longstreet.

Also of interest is the group of primary materials, by major figures, that are resurrected and republished in this collection. Included are previously unreprinted sketches by Harris and Johnson Jones Hooper, a series of comic "Far West" letters by Thomas Bangs Thorpe, and a new burlesque sermon believed to have been written by William Penn Brannan.

Contributors to GYASCUTUS are Noel Polk, Herbert P. Shippey, Leland H. Cox, Jr., Alan Gribben, Stephen E. Meats, William J. Starr, A. S. Wendel, and Edgar E. Thompson.

JAMES L. W. WEST III, editor of this collection, is Associate Professor of English at Virginia Polytechnic Institute and State University.

# Gyascutus

NEW SERIES • VOLUME V-VI

**COSTERUS**

*Essays in*
*English and American*
*Language and Literature*

1978

# Gyascutus

## STUDIES IN
## ANTEBELLUM SOUTHERN
## HUMOROUS AND SPORTING WRITING

Edited by

## James L. W. West III

ATLANTIC HIGHLANDS, N.J. – HUMANITIES PRESS, Inc.

The illustrations on the divisional half-titles of this book are by F.O.C. Darley, one of the most famous American illustrators of his time. Darley executed engravings for many of the best-known volumes in this genre, including *The Big Bear of Arkansas*, *A Quarter Race in Kentucky*, *Adventures of Captain Simon Suggs*, and *Streaks of Squatter Life*. The engravings on the divisional half-titles of this volume are reproduced from an 1852 Getz & Buck reprinting of William Tappan Thompson's *Chronicles of Pineville*.

On the cover:
"Bob Herring's Camp-fire," an engraved illustration from T. B. Thorpe's *The Hive of "The Bee-Hunter,"* (New York: D. Appleton and Co., 1854), facing p. 33.

© 1978 by James L.W. West III
All rights reserved
Printed in the Netherlands
ISBN: 90–6203–522–1
Library of Congress Catalog Card Number: 78–70703

TO THE STUDENTS,
PAST, PRESENT, AND FUTURE,
OF ENGLISH 845

# Contents

# Preface

No one has ever set down a good working definition of the Gyascutus. We do know that the creature was a near relative of the Whang-Doodle and a distant cousin of the Snipe. We are also sure that it had between two and five legs, and that its color varied from a dark, lush green to a bright, glowing orange depending on the season. The Gyascutus came in three-toed and five-toe. varieties; a cloven-hoofed edition was even known to exist in some regions of the South. Certain members of the species were furry, but others had scales: one mutant variety, sporting a whistle on the end of its tail, was sighted in Georgia as late as 1880. The Gyascutus was found during the last century wherever tall tales were told; often it visited campfires like Bob Herring's, which is pictured on the cover of this volume. And the beast also appeared occasionally in literature, usually in the comic and sporting writing of the Old South. We see the Gyascutus infrequently today, however, and so it is difficult for a modern writer to set down its characteristics.

It has also been difficult for modern literary historians to characterize a group of Southern humorous, realistic, and sporting writers who flourished more or less contemporaneously with the Gyascutus. These authors, some of whom are treated in this collection, are Augustus Baldwin Longstreet, William Tappan Thompson, Thomas Bangs Thorpe, Johnson Jones Hooper, Henry Clay Lewis, George Washington Harris, and several related figures. Scholars and critics have never been able to fit the writings of these authors comfortably into the various schemata which have been devised to accomodate the literature of pre-Civil War America. These writers were too Southern for Professor Spiller and his associates on the *LHUS* project and were not quite respectable enough for Professor Hubbell in *The South in American Literature*. Perhaps as a result, there has been a tendency to picture them collectively as an odd mutation, even as an aberration, that began in the early 1830s, flourished briefly in the 1840s and 1850s, and was killed off by the Civil War. The genre is usually depicted as beginning almost *de novo* with Longstreet's *Georgia Scenes* in 1835, and ending for good with Harris' *Sut Lovingood* in 1867. Thus neatly delimited, the writers in this genre have been tagged with various labels — "Southwest Humorists" or "The Big Bear School of Humor," for example.

If this brief preface has a message, it is that we should not be so insistent about regarding these writers as a discrete group during their own time, and that we should not shut them off from their literary forbears and descendants. They are most successfully viewed as part of a continuum of realistic writing stretching back into eighteenth-century English and American literature and reaching forward to the late nineteenth-century local colorists and even into the twentieth century with such authors as William Faulkner and Andrew Lytle. Some of these relationships, to be sure, have been recognized. For instance, the connections between early American folklore and antebellum Southern humor have been investigated, and the obvious debt owed to the genre by Faulkner and other modern Southern writers has been studied. But additional areas remain unexplored: no one has examined in depth the cross-fertilization between Southern humorous writing and the literature of the turf and chase, for instance. Thorpe and Harris spring as much from the tradition of gentlemanly British sporting writing as they do from the ring-tailed roarer school of frontier American folklore. Likewise, no one has yet dealt successfully with the complex interrelationships between antebellum Southern humor and the postbellum writings of such figures as Richard Malcolm Johnston and Joel Chandler Harris. Finally, to suggest only one more possible approach, no one has carefully examined the manner in which these sketches were presented to nineteenth-century readers. This writing was not limited to big national outlets like the New York *Spirit of the Times*, the St. Louis *Reveille*, and the New Orleans *Picayune*. Rather, examples of the genre were published nearly everywhere, in struggling literary journals and one-horse newspapers, not only in the antebellum South, but in the North and Midwest as well.

The humorists, realists, and sporting writers of the Old South are important figures who deserve serious attention from modern students of American literature – the kind of attention that they are given in this volume. Included here are critical assessments of some of the writings in the field together with historical studies of the careers of certain figures in the genre. Of special interest are the unknown writings by these authors which are resurrected and republished here. One must not assume that this vein of literature has been mined out – that all of the significant sketches and collections have been discovered and reprinted. On the contrary, these diggings have only been lightly worked. Almost any researcher who exercises a little common sense and diligence can discover unknown and important writings very quickly.

This preface, then, is addressed to present and future students of this genre. No major scholarly book has appeared in this field in the past decade. There is only one truly satisfactory biography – W. S. Hoole's study of Hooper. There is no edition of the letters of a major figure yet in print. There is no properly-done edition of a major book in the genre (and the textual problems are fascinating). My friends, to work! The field is open; treasures await you. Who knows? Perhaps one of us will discover, in a Tennessee attic, the lost manuscript of *High Times and Hard Times*. That would be a prize indeed.

JAMES L. W. WEST III
Virginia Polytechnic Institute
and State University

# Essays

# The Blind Bull, Human Nature:
# Sut Lovingood and the Damned Human Race

*by*

## NOEL POLK

so that they are without excuse:

21 Because that, when they knew God, they glorified *him* not as God, neither were thankful; but became vain in their imaginations, and their foolish heart was darkened.

22 Professing themselves to be wise, they became fools,

23 And changed the glory of the uncorruptible God into an image made like to corruptible man, and to birds, and fourfooted beasts, and creeping things.

24 Wherefore God also gave them up to uncleanness through the lusts of their own hearts, to dishonour their own bodies between themselves:

25 Who changed the truth of God into a lie, and worshipped and served the creature more than the Creator, who is blessed for ever. Amen.

\* \* \* \*

28 And even as they did not like to retain God in *their* knowledge, God gave them over to a reprobate mind, to do those things which are not convenient;

29 Being filled with all unrighteousness, fornication, wickedness, covetousness, maliciousness; full of envy, murder, debate, deceit, malignity; whisperers,

30 Backbiters, haters of God, despiteful, proud, boasters, inventors of evil things, disobedient to parents,

31 Without understanding, covenant breakers, without natural affection, implacable, unmerciful:

32 Who knowing the judgment of God that they which commit such things are worthy of death, not only do the same, but have pleasure in them that do them.

Romans I

## I. Butchers

It is not quite correct to say that George Washington Harris is a neglected American literary figure. Indeed, he is not; in proportion to the quantity of his work, he is perhaps among the most frequently studied figures: four separate published editions of his works, including two of the *Yarns*, one published monograph-length study, at least three dissertations, and a spate of articles[1] form, quantitatively, a rather substantial body of scholarly materials on Sut Lovingood and his creator. It is correct, however, to suggest that Harris' work has been badly misunderstood, even by the most ardent Sutophiles. They have

1. Twentieth century editions of Harris' work are: Edd Winfield Parks, ed., *Sut Lovingood Travels with Old Abe Lincoln* (Chicago: The Black Cat Press, 1937); Brom Weber, ed., *Sut Lovingood* (New York: Grove Press, 1954); M. Thomas Inge, ed., *Sut Lovingood's Yarns* (New Haven: College & University Press, 1966); and Inge, ed., *High Times and Hard Times* (Nashville: Vanderbilt University Press, 1967), based on Inge's dissertation, listed below. Perhaps the biggest need in the Harris field right now is a reliable, scholarly text of his work. I have not examined a copy of *Sut Lovingood Travels with Old Abe Lincoln,* since apparently only 150 copies were printed; but the two editions by Inge and the one by Weber are highly unreliable.

Critical work, besides the introductions to the editions named above, include Milton Rickels' monograph in the Twayne series, *George Washington Harris* (New York: Twayne, 1965), and his article, "The Imagery of George Washington Harris," *American Literature*, 31 (May 1959), 173-87; three articles by Donald Day taken directly from his dissertation, "The Life of George Washington Harris," *Tennessee Historical Quarterly*, 6 (March 1947), 3-38; "The Humorous Works of George W. Harris," *American Literature*, 14 (January 1943), 391-406; and "The Political Satires of George W. Harris," *Tennessee Historical Quarterly*, 4(December 1945), 320-38; and Inge's "Sut Lovingood: An Examination of the Nature of a 'Nat'ral Born Durn'd Fool,' " *Tennessee Historical Quarterly*, 19 (September 1960), 231-51.

Dissertations are Day's "The Life and Works of George Washington Harris," (University of Chicago, 1942), still the best and most reliable biographical account of Harris; Inge's "The Uncollected Writings of George Washington Harris: An Annotated Edition," (Vanderbilt, 1964); and Ormond Plater's "Narrative Folklore in the Works of George Washington Harris," (Tulane, 1969).

*The Lovingood Papers*, edited by Ben Harris McClary (Athens, Tennessee: The Sut Society, 1962; Knoxville: University of Tennessee Press, 1963, 1964, 1965), did a great deal during its brief life to encourage work on Harris, especially the search for new Harris sketches, and is still worth consulting. A more complete list of work on Harris may be found in the Appendix to *High Times and Hard Times* and in the annual checklist of writings about Southern literature in the Spring number of the *Mississippi Quarterly*.

emphasized the comedy of the *Yarns*, and rightly so, for Harris' is possibly the most artistically complex sense of humor in American literature before Faulkner, saving *perhaps* only Melville; and they have, again rightly, stressed the brilliance of Harris' language. They tell us that the *Yarns* is after all only the crowning achievement of a very minor literary tradition, and having dismissed Harris as a "humorist," albeit a fine one, they feel that they have dealt with him sufficiently. Thus, it would seem to me, they have admired the comparatively superficial qualities of the *Yarns* and have missed the profounder riches.

It is an odd way to measure literary merit — that is, to divide writers into "backwoods humorists" and "everybody else" — since it is an approach from categories which stresses similarities among books and overlooks crucial differences. And so the emphasis in Harris criticism has been on Sut's victims, for the most part as complete an assortment of stereotyped hypocrites and fools as can be found between the eyebrows of any book, instead of on the book's supreme creation, Sut Lovingood himself. Sut has been seen basically as an irresponsible prankster who, like his literary forbears and peers in the humor "tradition," hates hypocrites, reformers, Yankees, and all forms of authority, and who plays his "pranks" in order to avenge himself for some real or imagined hurt. Sut's actions, no matter how petty and mean, are approved as justified, even if some of his defenders are more than a bit squeamish about them: Sut is "right" primarily because his victims are so completely "wrong." The book, and Sut's role in it, have been greatly oversimplified, because most critics have failed to consider Sut as a character in his own right. M. Thomas Inge, for one example, thinks Sut merely "an unintentional reformer of sorts,"[2] and Milton Rickels, for another, contends that Harris "was always more interested in Sut as symbolic point of view than as a realistic construction."[3] Both views are simply wrong.

2. "Sut Lovingood: An Examination of the Nature of a 'Nat'ral Born Durn'd Fool," p. 245.
3. *George Washington Harris*, p. 48.

At least part of the reason for this failure to understand the character of Sut is the inexplicable fact that, for all of the emphasis on comedy in the *Yarns*, practically no one has approached the book with a sense of humor. Both Inge and Rickels, again using the two most prominent commentators as examples, tend to take Sut literally; they disregard the fact that he is, supremely, a story-teller, that like any good raconteur he is always mindful of his audience, and that much of the elaborated detail of his stories, including the tall-tale exaggeration, is his response to his auditor's laughter, calculated to create a desired effect — usually laughter, but frequently something else. In "Sut Lovingood's Daddy, Acting Horse," for example, Sut names the members of his family, calling his own five times in a wonderfully comic display of bumptiousness; when a "tomato-nosed" man falls into the trap Sut has set, and points out the repetition, Sut responds immediately: "Yas, ole Still-tub, that's jis the perporshun I bears in the famerly fur dam fool, leavin out Dad in course."[4] Rickels' analysis of this fine bit of business is straightfaced and sober: Sut "is five times the fool any other member of the family could claim to be, excepting his dad. . . ."[5] Likewise, Inge accepts Sut's definition of himself as a "natural born durn'd fool" with the same straight face: "Sut frankly accounts for most of his difficulties by the simple fact that he is such a nat'ral born durn'd fool'."[6] Inge believes that Sut feels himself delimited by his lack of education:

> Sut has no education, and recognizes this deficiency. . . . He is frustrated at being unable to express himself, through lack of training. . . . He fails to realize, then, how brilliantly colorful and original his language is in metaphors, similes, and "kinetic" action. His lack of an awareness of his own abilities as a story teller, in fact, add to the quality of his humor.[7]

4. George Washington Harris, *Sut Lovingood. Yarns Spun by a "Nat'ral Born Durn'd Fool.*["] *Warped and Wove for Public Wear.* (New York: Dick & Fitzgerald, 1867), p. 21. Subsequent citations will be to this edition.

5. *George Washington Harris,* p. 97.

6. "An Examination . . . ," p. 240.

7. Ibid., p. 237.

This is a serious misreading of Sut's character which is contradicted at every point by the evidence of the book. Sut of course has no education but experience, but he knows enough to know that "ove all the fools the worild hes tu contend wif, the edicated wuns am the worst; they breeds ni ontu all the devilment a-gwine on" (p. ix). He may in fact fail to realise how "brilliantly colorful his language is," but he shows no lack of confidence in his ability to express himself (cf. his exchanges with George on this subject, pp. 114-116, 134). And how in the world Mr. Inge can doubt Sut's awareness of his abilities as a story-teller is simply beyond me.

Much of the misunderstanding of Sut centers around his description of himself as a "natural born durn'd fool." Rickels suggests that "Harris' conception of his fool . . . is not the antic simpleton but the wise fool; Sut is the ironic hero who perceives the human condition and knows he himself is a fool to communicate his perceptions. . . ."[8] This is all right, so far as it goes, and perhaps even accurate. But the initial insight is distorted as it is developed throughout Rickels' chapter on the fool.[9] At the end of "Sicily Burns's Wedding," for example, Sut opines that if his long legs don't fail him, he "may turn human sum day, that is sorter human, enuf tu be a Squire, ur school cummisiner" (p. 97). This seems simple enough, one of many cheap shots Sut takes throughout the *Yarns* at various pomposities. It is of course not without its implications, but Rickels misses the point when he again takes Sut literally, completely overlooking his rather obvious comic irony: "To become 'sorter human,' " he straightfacedly suggests, "is not plaintive longing, but the ironic man's disdainful scorn for unrealized and, to Sut, unrealizable humanity. *Sut has chosen not to try to become human.*"[10] This becomes the erroneous premise for an argument about Sut's character: "After rejecting the human condition," Rickels continues, "Sut also rejects the religious life . . . . He has

8. *George Washington Harris*, p. 96.
9. Ibid., pp. 95-106.
10. Ibid., p. 97. Italics supplied.

no fear of the hereafter, for he has no soul."[11] From this point
he argues that by making Sut soulless Harris has "freed him
from any transcendental significance,"[12] though in order to do
so he has to avoid dealing with Sut's statement to the contrary
— "I feels like I'd be glad *tu be* dead, only I'se feard ove the
dyin" (pp. 106-107). Then, finally, Rickels contends that Sut,
"in another of his characteristics, his mindlessness,"[13] person-
ifies the anti-authoritarian and anti-rational feelings Harris
expresses in his work. From being a wise fool to being mindless
is a long and contradictory progression; but it is necessary for
Sut to be mindless, apparently, in order for him to be a backwoods anarchist, opposed to both order and reason: "For Sut,"
Rickels has earlier argued, "every practical joke is a delight because it is a conspiracy against all order."[14]

This argument, built upon a number of errors and erroneous assumptions, gives Harris little credit as a thinker and
even less as an artist. Simply, Sut is not mindless, and *he is no
fool*. His repeated description of himself as a "nat'ral born
durn'd fool" is the ironic self-deprecation which is part and
parcel of any humorist's equipment ("Aw, you boys know what
a useless old son of a bitch I am"), and which neither he nor
Harris expects the reader to take literally: the few characters in
the *Yarns* who do are scorned and ridiculed for their lack of
comprehension. But more than that, it is also one of the devices
by which Harris stresses the differences between Sut and his
victims and emphasizes the moral nature of the *Yarns*. Certainly
Harris was aware of the literary tradition of the Fool, and certainly he was capitalizing upon it; but he was also using another
aspect of that tradition, the one personified by Socrates. It is
not difficult to see Sut as a kind of backwoods Socrates, prick-
ing holes in ballooned egos, bringing hypocrites and fools to
their knees before their peers. Indeed, Socrates encounters the

11.  Ibid.
12.  Ibid., p. 98.
13.  Ibid.
14.  Ibid., p. 84.

self-assured and smug sophists, Sut the self-assured and smug preachers, sheriffs, lawyers, and Yankees. Both Sut and Socrates continually expose fools and frauds for what they are, and both are therefore continually in trouble with civic and religious authorities. And both, I would suggest, have the same purpose in life. Sut's goal in "Old Skissum's Middle Boy," for example — to awaken the fat, lethargic, and constantly sleeping boy — is nothing more or less than Socrates', as he explains it in the *Apology*. And though I have found no specific evidence to prove that Harris read Plato, surely "Old Skissum's Middle Boy" is, must be, Harris' allegorical treatment of this passage in the *Apology*:

> . . . for the state is like a big thoroughbred horse, so big that he is a bit slow and heavy, and wants a gadfly to wake him up. I think the god put me on the state something like that, to wake you up and persuade you and reproach you every one, as I keep settling on you everywhere all day long. Such another will not easily be found by you, gentlemen, and if you will be persuaded, you will spare me. You will be vexed, perhaps, like sleepers being awaked, and if you listen to Anytos and give me a tap, you can easily kill me; then you can go on sleeping for the rest of your lives. . . .[15]

Perhaps it is even worth suggesting that the hornets which appear and reappear throughout the *Yarns* are Harris' symbolic "gadflies."

I do not wish to make more of this than can reasonably be made, but it does provide a useful vantage from which we can more easily understand what Sut means when he calls himself a "nat'ral born durn'd fool." It is not only self-deprecation: it is also his way of emphasizing the eagerness of his neighbors to delude themselves into thinking that they are something they are not, that they do not "know themselves." All the characters in the *Yarns* act horse or fool in one way or another, and do so while asserting their righteousness, their respectability, and their

15. W. H. D. Rouse, trans., *Great Dialogues of Plato*, ed. Eric H. Warmington and Philip G. Rouse (New York: New American Library, 1956), pp. 436-37.

general superiority to all other creatures. But Sut, like Socrates, does know himself, thoroughly, and is under no delusion about himself or society; he is, in short, wise precisely because he does not pretend to know anything he does not know or be anything he is not.

Sut, then, is not a fool, and he is by no means, as Edmund Wilson, Sut's harshest critic, would have it, a "peasant squatting in his own filth."[16] It is his lazy and worthless Dad who so squats, and it is one indication of Sut's strength of mind and character that he has been able, with no more of this world's goods than his Dad, to escape and overcome the poverty and filth, both real and metaphorical, upon which his Dad tried to rear him. Sut's wisdom is heired from an incredible background of poverty and deprivation; perhaps because of that background, certainly not in spite of it, he is a singularly perceptive student of human nature: and though his vision of the world is understandably dark, it is persistently realistic and toughminded.

Sut's vision is summed up in two philosophical set-pieces which express in no uncertain terms his profound pessimism about "univarsal onregenerit human nater." The first, Milton Rickels suggests, is a kind of Great Chain of Being:[17]

> Whar thar ain't enuf feed, big childer roots littil childer outen the troff, an' gobbils up thar part. Jis' so the yeath over: bishops eats elders, elders eats common peopil; they eats sich cattil es me, I eats possums, possums eats chickens, chickins swallers wums, an' wums am content to eat dus, an' the dus am the aind ove hit all. Hit am all es regilur es the souns frum the tribil down tu the bull base ove a fiddil in good tchune, an' I speck hit am right, ur hit wudn't be 'lowed. (p. 228)

The second expresses among other things an attitude toward Innocence, in any form, that out-Claggarts Claggart:

> I hates ole Onsightly Peter, jis' caze he didn't seem tu like tu hear me

16. " 'Poisoned!' " *New Yorker*, 31 (7 May 1955), 150.
17. *George Washington Harris*, p. 100.

narrate las' night; that's human nater the yeath over, an' yere's more univarsal onregenerit human nater: ef ever yu dus enything tu enybody wifout cause, yu hates em allers arterwards, an' sorter wants tu hurt em agin. An' yere's anuther human nater: ef enything happens sum feller, I don't keer ef he's yure bes' frien, an' I don't keer how sorry yu is fur him, thar's a streak ove satisfackshun 'bout like a sowin thread a-runnin all thru yer sorrer. Yu may be shamed ove hit, but durn me ef hit ain't thar. Hit will show like the white cottin chain in mean cassinett; brushin hit onder only hides hit. An' yere's a little more; no odds how good yu is tu yung things, ur how kine yu is in treatin em, when yu sees a littil long laiged lamb a-shakin hits tail, an' a-dancin staggerinly onder hits mam a-huntin fur the tit, ontu hits knees, yer fingers *will* itch tu seize that ar tail, an' fling the littil ankshus son ove a mutton over the fence amung the blackberry briars, not tu hurt hit, but jis' tu disapint hit. Ur say, a littil calf, a-buttin fas' under the cow's fore-laigs, an' then the hine, wif the pint ove hits tung stuck out, makin suckin moshuns, not yet old enuf tu know the bag aind ove hits mam frum the hookin aind, don't yu want tu kick hit on the snout, hard enough to send hit backwards, say fifteen foot, jis' tu show hit that buttin won't allers fetch milk? Ur a baby even, rubbin hits heels apas' each uther, a-rootin an' a-snifflin arter the breas', an' the mam duin her bes' tu git hit out, over the hem ove her clothes, don't yu feel hungry tu gin hit jis' one 'cussion cap slap, rite ontu the place what sum day'll fit a saddil, ur a sowin cheer, tu show hit what's atwixt hit an' the grave; that hit stans a pow'ful chance not tu be fed every time hits hungry, ur in a hurry? An' agin: ain't thar sum grown up babys what yu meets, that the moment yer eyes takes em in, yer toes itch tu tetch thar starns, jis' 'bout es saftly es a muel kicks in playin; a histin kine ove a tetch, fur the way they wares thar har, hat, ur watch-chain, the shape ove thar nose, the cut ove thar eye, ur sumthin ove a like littil natur. (pp. 245-247)

To be sure, nearly everybody has noticed these superbly articulated passages. But no one, to my knowledge, has seen them as the most direct statements of themes which in fact darkly underlie all of the exuberant comedy of the *Yarns*, and which give thematic and structural unity to the collection. Though my comments could and should be extended to the fugitive pieces collected by Inge in *High Times and Hard Times*, I am limiting my discussion in this paper to the twenty-four sketches which Harris himself brought together in the *Yarns*, for the reason that the *Yarns* is a deliberate book — not a random selection of things already published, but a collection of new material, apparently written specifically for this volume (only seven of the twenty-four had received prior publication). I do not, however, intend to make this a brief for the structural integrity of the *Yarns*, for that would take a much longer essay. What I would like to do is discuss a few of the numerous patterns of recurring images and themes which give philosophical weight and complexity to the comedy, to try to come to terms with Sut Lovingood as a human being, and, finally, to suggest that the *Yarns* is not merely a minor masterpiece but a major work of American fiction.

## II. Bulls

Perhaps the best entrance into the whole subject is by way of disagreement once again with Milton Rickels, whose ideas about Sut as Fool have, as I've suggested, led him into a misreading of the *Yarns*. Sut, he says, is a Fool. Sut, he says, is mindless. He is "outside the law, outside social morality, outside religion, even outside rational life."[18] He even suggests that the major theme of "Dad's Dog School," the final story in the collection, is Sut's "Rejection of reason and of order,"[19] and he has already been quoted as suggesting that "For Sut, every practical joke is a delight because it is a conspiracy against all order."[20] But here, as elsewhere, Rickels overlooks some basic facts: in the first place, no more than six of the twenty-four stories in the *Yarns* can even remotely be considered as having to do with "practical jokes" ("A Razor Grinder in a Thunder-Storm," "Sut Assists at a Negro Night-Meeting," "Frustrating a Funeral," "Parson John Bullen's Lizards," "A Snake-bit Irishman," and "Mrs. Yardley's Quilting"). In the second place, Sut causes the chaos in only ten out of the twenty-four sketches; and of those ten, four depict Sut's righteous (perhaps self-righteous) revenge against persons

18.   Ibid., p. 102.
19.   Ibid., p. 80.
20.   Ibid., p. 84.

Figure 1. "Sut Lovingood's Daddy Acting Horse," the original illustration from the 1867 Dick & Fitzgerald first edition of *Yarns*.

who have done him or others injustice ("Parson John Bullen's Lizards," "Sicily Burns's Wedding," "A Snake-bit Irishman," and "The Widow McCloud's Mare"). Two are rather vicious jokes at the expense of Negroes ("Sut Assists at a Negro Night-Meeting" and "Frustrating a Funeral"); given the post-war social and political context in which these two were published, Sut's attitude toward the Negroes here is perhaps understandable: but even at that, Harris is at pains to depict the Negroes as damn fools, with the same vices as their white owners. One story ("Old Burns's Bull Ride") is simply a happy but unlooked-for extension of Sut's actions in "Sicily Burns's Wedding." One ("Mrs. Yardley's Quilting") is a genuinely innocent practical joke. One ("Old Skissum's Middle Boy"), as I have suggested, is Sut's earnest, if metaphorical, attempt to do a good deed, to wake up the world. And only one, "Sut Lovingood's Dog," represents Sut's angry and irrational and totally unjustified attack upon a fellow human being – and this is told with a definite pedagogical purpose, a purpose to be discussed later in this essay.

One also has to remind oneself, as Rickels does not, that the actual violence depicted in the *Yarns* is largely the product of Sut's imagination. We are not actually expected to believe – are we? – that the mole in "Hen Bailey's Reformation" actually, literally, crawls up Hen's pantsleg and through his anus, chasing that lizard out of Hen's stomach, into his esophagus, and then out his mouth? Or, for that matter, that the soda powders Sicily Burns administers to Sut actually, literally, produce all the foam that Sut describes:

> Thar wer a road ove foam frum the hous' tu the hoss two foot wide, an' shoe mouf deep – looked like hit hed been snowin – a-poppin, an' a-hissin, an' a-bilin like a tub ove soap-suds wif a red hot mole-board in hit. (pp. 81-82)

This is not at all to say that violence is not a large part of Sut's world, or that he is unaware of it – indeed, he is all too aware of it, and I would suggest that the constant recurrence of the imagery of violence, even the most revolting images, are a conscious part of Sut's story-telling methods, a deliberate aspect of his attempt to teach something, through the *Yarns*, to his auditors and to his readers. But this is quite different from saying that he is an anarchist, a conspirator against all order, for he simply is not. It might be an oversimplification to say that Sut classifies people into at least two classes — the wicked and the fools — but it is a useful oversimplification to consider for a moment. There's plenty of overlapping, of course, but in general the wicked are those people who take advantage of other people, use them unfairly — economically, socially, legally, or sexually (e.g., Parson Bullen, Sheriff Doltin, Mary Mastin and her mother, Lawyer Stilyards, and Sicily Burns). The fools, on the other hand, are characterized by a tendency to excess in whatever they do (Hen Bailey's drunkenness, Mrs. Yardley's quilting, Skissum's boy's sleeping, and, of course, Dad's acting horse): that is, the fools tend to lose rational control of themselves. Sut is more often than not disgusted by the results of these excesses; he is certainly disgusted, even outraged, by Hen Bailey's habitual drunkenness, as he is disgusted and shamed by Dad's excesses.

If it is possible to argue that Sut is opposed to excesses in any form, and I think it is, it is then necessary to observe that he himself is not the Compleat Hedonist that he has been assumed to be. He is, for example, generally described as a heavily excessive drinker, and certainly he is seldom without his flask. But we see him drunk only twice, in "Sut Lovingood's Dog" and "Contempt of Court — Almost," and in both cases he uses his probable drunkenness as reasons, but not excuses, for his own violent behavior. He drinks regularly throughout the sketches, but seldom enough to lose control of himself.[21] Nor

---

21. Sut definitely likes his whiskey, but he is not an indiscriminate drinker, like Hen Bailey, and in "Sut Lovingood's Love-Feast Ove Varmints," one of the fugitive sketches collected in *High Times and Hard Times*, Sut advises George not to take unnecessary risks when he drinks, giving sound advice:

"Why, durn yer little fool picter, are you gwine tu take yer warter

does he exclude himself from the category of Fools — *vide* the discussions later of "Sut Lovingood's Dog" and "Contempt of Court — Almost." He knows only too well that he must maintain a constant and sober virgil over the irrational part of himself, else he too cause the chaos he abhors.

In general, then, he is a civilising force and not a destructive one in the Tennessee backwoods. He is committed to taming, bringing under control, the chaos in which he lives, and the need for order is the burden of his tales. Sheriffs, lawyers, and preachers are so frequently his victims precisely because they are violators of the order Sut knows is essential if civilisation is to survive, and which they are specifically sworn to uphold.

Harris announces this as a theme immediately, in the first two pages of the book. In "Sut Lovingood's Daddy, Acting Horse," Sut is introduced in a vortex, astride the wildly bucking Tearpoke, who has apparently been "redpeppered" by some of Sut's friends as a practical joke:

> "Hole that ar hoss down tu the yeath." "He's a fixin fur the heavings." "He's a spreadin his tail feathers tu fly. Look out, Laigs, if you aint ready tu go up'ards." "Wo, Shavetail." "Git a fiddil; he's tryin a jig." "Say, Long Laigs, rais'd a power ove co'n didn't yu?" "Taint co'n, hits redpepper." (p. 19)

Before he can proceed with his tale about Tickeytail and Dad, however, Sut must, and does, bring Tearpoke under control, restore order:

> "Sut's tongue or his spurs brought Tearpoke into something like passable quietude while he continued." (p. 20)

The first paragraph, emphasizing the chaos, appears virtually unchanged in the story's first publication, in the *Spirit of the Times*.[22] The second, however, Harris added to the book version

> afore you licker? Dont ye no that licker's the lightest an ef ye take hit fust, hit cums up thru the warter an makes a ekel mixtry an spiles all chance ove bein pisened by hit? Allers take yer whisky fust, fur you don't allers know what mout be in hit. I'se monsus keerful about everything fur all natur's agin me . . . ." *High Times and Hard Times*, p. 243.

22. 4 November 1854.

in order to indicate that Sut is to be throughout the book an agent of order and not of chaos, and to anticipate the situation in "Taurus in Lynchburg Market," one of the most thematically significant stories in the collection, in which Sut actually risks his life in order to bring a raging bull under control. So the basic conflict in the *Yarns* is not at all that between Sut and the hypocrites of the world, or even that between right and wrong, but that between Chaos and Order, with Sut strongly on the side of Order.

At the metaphorical center of that conflict is the image of the bull, which is traditionally, and in the *Yarns* specifically, a symbol of masculine power and virility: not just sexuality, though the connection between masculine sexuality and chaos is very significant in terms of the number of sexual sins committed in the *Yarns*, and especially in terms of the characterization of Sut's Dad. The bull is much more than sexual, moving beyond sexual aggressiveness to symbolise a larger aggressiveness which is the pursuit of power, of whatever kind — sexual, legal, religious, financial — over the rest of the world. This seems to me the meaning of "Sicily Burns's Wedding" and "Old Burns's Bull Ride." In the first, Sut gets his revenge for the sexual mistreatment he has gotten from Sicily Burns. The blinded bull Ole Sock backs through the house during Sicily's wedding dinner, his very phallic tail very erect, obviously displaying his genitals prominently, and frightening the entire wedding party with his brute sexuality: he passes through the bedroom first and destroys the bed (p. 92), and moves on, wreaking havoc, through the house to the dining room, where Mrs. Clapshaw, the mother of the bridegroom, is hoisted by Ole Sock onto the dinner table. She so fears what she sees that she can only shout "rape, fire, an' murder" (p. 93). Sut, then, uses the bull to de-sex,[23] at least metaphorically, Sicily's marriage. Sicily's femi-

23. Sut's initial intention was to "shave ole Clapshaw's hoss's tail, go tu the stabil an' shave Sicily's mare's tail, an' ketch ole Burns out, an' shave his tail too" (p. 90). Ormond Plater, p. 148, remarks that Sut intends to "de-sex" the marriage by symbolically defoliating Sicily's and

nine sexuality, which has so deceived, humiliated, and unmanned Sut, is simply overwhelmed by this unleashed masculine
sexuality, which she cannot control as she can Sut's. In the fol-
low-up story, however, the conflict moves beyond sexuality
when Ole Sock, with Burns riding quite accidentally and un-
willingly, moves out into the world and encounters not women
and effeminate men, but one of his own kind, Old Mills, another bull. With tails hoisted very high they proceed to thrash
each other, the relatively innocent Burns, a victim of the capricious circumstance which put him on top of Ole Sock, dangling
helplessly from a tree, upside down, while the bulls, violent,
anarchic forces, rage all around him.

So the bull well symbolizes the chaotic forces set loose in
the Tennessee backwoods, not to mention in the whole nation,
during the Civil War, to destroy civilisation. But it is more
complex than that, for the bull is not just a destructive force;
properly harnessed and controlled he is a tame and useful creature. Ole Sock is in fact generally a very domesticated beast
who is regularly saddled and ridden (p. 90). It is only when they
are allowed to get away from the confines of their own pastures
(e.g., the bull in "Taurus") or are challenged on their own turf
(e.g., Ole Mills), or are otherwise provoked, that bulls lose control of themselves and go on destructive rampages. Thus bulls
symbolise in the *Yarns* not just the abstract forces of chaos, but
the very concrete cause of much of it: onregenerit human nater.
Harris is specific: "Now, George," Sut says, "ef yu knows the
nater ove a cow brute, they is the durndes' fools amung all the
beastes, ('scept the Lovingoods;)" (p. 90), and as epigraph to
"Taurus," Sut sings of the "blind bull, Human nater" (p. 123):
and so it is structurally and thematically no accident that Sut

Clapshaw's "pubes." But in light of what happens and in light of the tremendous metaphorical importance of tails throughout the *Yarns*, his comment seems a bit short of the mark. Plater's dissertation is useful and in-
telligent, and definitely worth consulting, even though its insights are frequently limited by its approach from sources and by its strained over-read-
ing of certain symbols and passages.

provokes Ole Sock by covering his head with a feeding basket, blinding him. Ole Sock totally disrupts Sicily's Wedding celebration with a blind, malevolent, and backwards rush through the house.

### III. Dad

Of course what Sut sings is that "Daddy *kill'd* the blind bull, Human nater" (my emphasis), and in doing so suggests a relationship between "Hoss" Lovingood and the image of the blind bull which is to be more fully and more meaningfully developed in the book's final story. So "dod-dratted mean, an' lazy, an' ugly, an' savidge, an' durn fool tu kill" (p. 22), as Sut says, Dad quickly becomes the touchstone in the *Yarns* for all the foolish and irrational behavior, the onregenerit human nater, that Sut continually animadverts against. Dad appears in only two of the sketches, "Sut Lovingood's Daddy, Acting Horse," and "Dad's Dog School," but their placement at the beginning and the end of the collection provides an important frame for the other twenty-two yarns: if the bull is the book's central metaphor, Dad is its figurative and literal frame of reference. He is the human exemplum of all the things the bull comes to symbolise, the *reductio ad absurdum* of all the irrational behavior in the book. By placing him at both the beginning and the end of the collection, Harris casts his shadow over everything that Sut says and does, and emphasizes how important Dad is to an understanding of the *Yarns*.

The two stories in which Dad appears are very much alike. In both he acts damn fool, and gets himself severely punished for it. In both he reduces himself quite deliberately to an animal level, and in both he is stripped naked. In both Mam offers her unasked-for running commentary on the proceedings, caustic commentary which centers around Dad's ability to play "hoss better nur yu dus husban" (p. 23). In both Sut "assists," and in both an outsider intrudes.

As Sut tells the first story, their plow-horse Tickeytail dies, leaving the Lovingoods without a way to plant their crops. "Well we waited, an' wished, an' rested, an' plan'd, an' wished, an' waited agin, ontil ni ontu strawberry time, hopin sum stray hoss mout cum along" (p. 22), Sut says, characterising Dad: that is, the lazy Dad, instead of trying to buy or even borrow or steal another horse, uses the lack of one as his excuse to do nothing at all. When he does decide that no "stray hoss" is going to come along and save the day, he determines that he will himself pull the plow, and Sut will drive. But Dad is not content just to pull the plow, he must *become* a horse; Sut sees him "a-studyin how tu play the kar-acter ove a hoss puffectly" (p. 22). Dad demands a bridle and bit, and then whinnies and kicks when he drops to his all fours. The order/disorder theme is sounded clearly when Dad insists that he wants the bridle bit made "kurb, es he hedn't work'd fur a good while, an' said he mout sorter feel his keepin, an' go tu ravin an' cavortin" (p. 23). Rave and cavort, of course, he does. Dad keeps up his "kar-acter" as a horse throughout, and we watch him gradually though deliberately slough his humanity, a sloughing which is total when he finally divests himself of Reason: instead of going around a "sassafrack" bush, as a sensible person would, he "buljed squar intu an' thru hit" like a horse (p. 24), and inflicts upon himself a severe hornet attack. Chaos and destruction ensue; Dad goes completely out of control, pulls out of Sut's hands the geers, which symbolise the restraints, the laws which keep men from behaving like animals, and which therefore make civilisation possible. As he runs through a fence, his one garment snags and is pulled off of him, leaving him naked, stripped of all vestige of civilisation and exposed, as it were, for the fool he is. Sut watches him run over the bluff and into the creek, then taunts him cruelly as he keeps ducking to get away from the pestiferous hornets, his just recompense for not acting like a rational human being.

    "Sut Lovingood's Daddy, Acting Horse," then, is an essentially comic fable about man's propensity to divest himself of his humanity; but it is not difficult to see, especially from the point of view of "Dad's Dog School," the seriousness underlying the comic action, the tragic potential in the characters of Dad and of Sut. This potential is realised in "Dad's Dog School," the book's masterful finale, in which all of the *Yarns'* important themes and images converge. It is, then, the book's thematic climax.

The plot of "Dad's Dog School" is, like all of the *Yarns*, basically very simple. It opens with Dad's determination to teach Sugar, the pup, to "hold fast." School begins when Dad strips himself naked. In "Acting Horse," his clothes were pulled from him accidently when they snagged on a rail of the fence; here, however, in an unmistakably symbolic act, he deliberately and consciously strips himself – of his clothes and, as we shall see, of his humanity. He forces Sall to sew him up into the hide of a yearling bull. As when he acts horse, however, he foolishly sets out to *become* the bull, and begins snorting and pawing the ground. He orders Sut to sick Sugar on, and unwisely threatens punitive action if Sut should restrain the dog before he is "made." Of course the plan backfires. Sugar manages to get a death hold, through the mouth of the hide, onto Dad's nose, to Dad's infinite displeasure. Sut perversely refuses to pull Sugar off, and Dad comes very close to being killed – he does lose part of his nose and a finger – when Sall separates him and Sugar with a swing of the axe.

But it is much more complicated than this simple plot would suggest. Sugar is a "bull pup," Sut tells us, as "Ugly as a she ho'net" (p. 278), both of which images remind us of the other bulls and hornets in the book, and which augur ill, very early in the story, for Dad. In the earlier story Dad "acted horse"; here he is just as intent on "acting bull." The hide, that of "a-tarin big black an' white yearlin bull beastes" (p. 278) that they have killed some time before, suggests a specific association of Dad with the bull in "Taurus in Lynchburg Market," which is also black and white. Daddy thus symbolically and literally becomes the bull which he has killed. Later in the story the "snout ove the hide what wer tied back on the naik, worked sorter loose, an' the fold hung down on dad's an' Sugar's snouts"; Dad's eyes are covered and, as Sut puts it, "my onregenerit dad wer blinefolded" (p. 293). Dad's transmogrifi-

cation is complete: he has literally, at this point, *become* the
blind bull — "the blind bull, Human nater."

It is a wonderfully complex image, for Dad has been
"acting bull" all of his life; he is a bestial, destructive man
whose rampant sexuality (he has apparently fathered eighteen
children on Mam [p. 21]) is almost a parody of the bull as symbol of masculine virility. But it is precisely to the extent that he
has "acted bull" all of his life that he has "killed" his own human nature; that is, he has abandoned his rational self. Harris
shows this in "Dad's Dog School" with a series of details which
depict the diminishment of Dad's sexual virility and his humanity: it is, in the first place, a "yearling" bull that Dad becomes,
an adolescent, as it were, in contrast to the fully grown Ole
Sock and Ole Mills and the bull in "Taurus." Further, while the
obviously phallic tails of the other rampant bulls remain very
erect throughout the sketches in which they appear, the tail
Dad assumes as part of his animal nature is very flaccid indeed:
it "trail'd arter him *sorter dead like*" (p. 282, my emphasis), Sut
tells us; it "trail'd limber an' lazy, an' tangled sumtimes amung
dad's hine laigs" (p. 283), making it difficult for him to walk,
much less, in his state, to function as a human being. After
Sugar bites him on the nose, the tail becomes "stiff strait out,
way high up, an' sweepin the air clar ove insex, all roun the
yard" (p. 284), but this is centrifugal force, Dad being twirled
around the yard by the uninvitiated strength and vitality of the
dog.

The story becomes even more explicit: whenever the tail
points toward Mam, in what can only be a grotesque parody of
Dad's sexual excesses with her, Mam hits him with a bean-pole
(pp. 294-295), repulsing his advances, and punishing him for his
bestiality and for the lifetime of misery and poverty he has
made for them all. Dad's debilitation, his dehumanisation, is almost complete: he tries "tu rise tu the human way ove standin"
(p. 294) at one point, but isn't able to, with Sugar still clamped
to his nose. Later he does manage to stand momentarily, but it
is by this time an unbearable burden to "act human"; Sut notes
that Dad "begun to totter on his hine laigs" (p. 296), and that

"his tail [wer] a-trimblin, a mons'ous bad sign in ho'ned cattil" (p. 297).

The tail, however, is only one of two phallic symbols in the story; the other, obviously, is Dad's nose, which receives the brunt of the punishment. And when Sister Sall "tuck a chunk ofen dad's snout" (p. 297), the implications are pretty clear: Dad is, finally, completely, if symbolically, unmanned. That is, to borrow from Eliot, the "polyphiloprogenitive" Dad has become "enervate Origen" — the self-castrated man. Dad, then, emasculates himself by the excessive exercise of that very virility which makes, or made, a "man" of him. He becomes a beast because he refuses to act rationally; he kills his own human nature by refusing to control his bestial impulses. Whereas in "Acting Horse" he is merely punished for his foolishness, slapped on the wrist, so to speak, and then more or less restored to human status, here he is shown in his ultimate degradation. He loses all of what is left of his tenuous hold upon humanness; his descent to animality is total and, with his symbolic castration, so is his dehumanisation; there is no suggestion of a chance that he will, this time, be restored.

Thus Dad receives his just deserts, for his actions here as well as in "Acting Horse." But Dad is essentially unchanged from one story to the other, his behavior basically no different, and so his punishment here is merely the logical extension, a thematic intensification, of his punishment in the earlier story. The different element here is Sut himself, or perhaps it is more accurate to say that the different element is Sut's changed relationship to the action. His reactions here reveal a different aspect of his character, and help explain his view of himself, of Dad, and of human nature in general.

The essential difference is that Sut here has *control* of the situation. In "Acting Horse" he is, after Dad wrenches the reins loose from his hands, primarily a bystander. There is nothing he can do to help Dad out of his predicament; he cannot, as it were, save Dad from himself. Perhaps he would not have even if he could have — certainly he takes a dim view of "acting horse" — but he cannot, and so contents himself with taunting Dad from the top of the bluff, and entreating him a moral: "Better say yu wish yu may never see anuther ball ho'net, ef yu ever play hoss agin" (p. 27). But in "Dad's Dog School" he is in complete control, he *is* in a position to save Dad from himself, and refuses to, even though he clearly knows how much pain Dad is undergoing: "The childer all yell'd, an' sed 'Sick 'im;' they tho't hit wer all gwine jis' es dad wanted, the durn'd littil fools" (p. 285), he tells us, implying that *he* understands exactly what is happening. And so he not only allows but encourages the episode to proceed, painful page after painful page, and Mam joins him in humiliating Dad.

Part of the reason Sut refuses to stop it is, apparently, the years of stored-up resentment which he understandably feels. But the immediate cause is the intrusion into the "famerly devarshun" (p. 286), as Sut calls this Sunday morning activity, of Squire Haney,[24] an outsider. This too is set up for us in "Acting Horse." In that story, a stranger appears after all the excitement, and sees only the aftermath of Dad's foolishness. He asks Sut to tell him "what ails" the man he has just seen back down the road, a "pow'ful curious, vishus, skeery lookin cuss. . . . His head am as big es a wash pot, an' he hasent the fust durned sign ove an eye — jist two black slits" (p. 28). Sut explains that the man is just "gittin over a vilent attack ove dam fool" (p. 28), and the stranger asks, "Well, who is he eny how?" Sut bridles, expecting the man to say something derogatory about Dad or the rest of his family, "ris tu [his] feet, an' straiched out [his] arm" (p. 28), preparatory to defending his family's honor, and says, defying him to criticise, "Strainger, that man is my dad" (p. 28). But Sut has either misjudged or scared off his man; trouble is averted when the stranger looks at Sut's "laigs an' pussonel feeters" (p. 28), recognizes the physical likenesses, especially the long legs, between Sut and Dad, and simply admits, "Yas, dam ef he aint" (p. 28).

In "Dad's Dog School," however, the intruder is not a

---

24. Also called Squire Hanley the first two times his name is mentioned, pp. 285-86.

stranger, but a man well known to Sut and Mam for his hypo-critical piousness. Sut sees him approach, "a regular two hun-dred an' twenty-five poun retribushun, arter us, an' our famerly devarshun sure enuf, armed wif a hyme book, an' loaded tu the muzzil wif brimstone, bilin pitch, forkid flames, an' sich uther nicitys es makes up the devil's brekfus' " (pp. 285-86). So far, this story is a pretty typical one, not that much different from the others in the *Yarns*. But with the entry of Squire Haney the tone changes considerably; Sut begins to feel shame:

> A appertite tu run began tu gnaw my stumick, an' I felt my face a-swellin wif shame. I wer shamed ove dad, shamed ove mam's bar laigs an' open collar, shamed ove mysef, an' dam, ef I minds right, ef I warn't a mossel shamed ove the pup. (p. 286)

This is a convincing passage; Sut's shame at having an outsider witness the degradation of his family, even though the outsider be a hypocrite easily dealt with, is very real, and it is not, there-fore, difficult to understand why Sut then sadistically allows Sugar to keep tormenting Dad, long after his point has been made. Harris' psychology is perfect: Sut turns from Squire Haney, the purveyor of his shame, to Dad, the cause of it; he lashes out, angrily and bitterly, with the only means he has at hand, by perversely following his orders not to pull Sugar off until he is "made." "Stan hit dad," he taunts, "stan hit like a man; hit may be a littil hurtin tu yu, but dam ef hit ain't the makin ove the pup" (p. 296). Suddenly the story is not funny any more; or, if it is, it is the painful black humor of an *As I Lay Dying*, funny only in the telling. It is Sut's way of flogging Dad, striking out at the one who is responsible for all of the misery in his life; it is revenge against Dad and, by extension, perhaps against all the forces which make the world a difficult place to live in.

It is not a pretty picture, much less a funny one, that we are left with: the worthless Dad, completely degenerated, his wife cursing and beating him with her every breath, and Sut, at this, the darkest point in an often dark book, unleashing all of his own stored-up hatred and venom. And even though the story is told with the ironic rhetoric of the detached story teller, it is clear that the episode, and his relations with Dad generally, have a profound effect upon Sut. Dad is for Sut a sort of foolish Everyman, in whose character are crystallised all of the faults of the human race, and his memory is a dark and troubling one which casts a shadow over Sut's entire life: "I blames him fur all ove hit," he tells George earlier in the book, "allers a-tryin tu be king fool. He hes a heap tu count fur, George – a heap" (p. 107).

## IV. Sut

Profound as that effect is, though, Dad is not the only influence on Sut's vision. He is, of course, the dominant one, the one foremost in Sut's mind at all times, the standard of foolishness against which he measures all human behavior. And he has seen nothing to make him alter the basic vision he has gleaned from his observations of his father; nearly everything has in fact tended to confirm it. In the world he knows, the Tennessee backwoods – and in the fugitive sketches collected in *High Times and Hard Times* the range is even further – people are vain and selfish and mean, and do not understand that their disregard of the laws of decency and kindness is as debilitating to themselves personally as their flouting of the laws of society is to civilisation as a whole. Sut knows it, though, and it is, as I've suggested, part of the burden of the *Yarns* to preach that particular gospel.

This is not a lesson Sut has learned easily, however, even with Dad's pristine example before him; and at least part of what the other stories in the *Yarns* do is to help us trace Sut's education in the ways of the world. Consider the possibility, for example, that "Sut's New-Fangled Shirt," the second story in the book, is among other things an allegorization of Sut's "birth" into the real world. In that story, Betts Carr, Sut's land-lady, forces him to wear a heavily over-starched shirt, even though it is, to Sut, an "everlastin, infunel, new fangled sheet iron cuss ove a shut" (p. 32) which makes him feel as though he's "crowded intu a ole bee-gum, an' hit all full ove pissants" (p. 32). As he works and sweats, however, the shirt "quit hits hurtin, an' tuck tu feelin slippery'" (p. 33). Hot and tired, Sut

**Figure 2. "Old Burn's Bull Ride," the original illustration from the 1867 Dick & Fitzgerald first edition of *Yarns*.**

climbs into his quarters in the loft and takes a nap. When he wakes, the shirt has dried again, this time cemented to his body, and is quite painful:

> "I now thort I wer ded, an' hed died ove rhumaticks ove the hurtines' kind. All the jints I cud muve wer my ankils, knees, an' wrists; cudn't even move my hed, an' scarsely wink my eyes; the cussed shut wer pasted fas' ontu me all over, frum the ainds ove the tails tu the pints ove the broad-axe collar over my years." (p.33)

He manages to get his pants off, so that he is naked save for the shirt. Removing a plank from the ceiling of the house, he nails the front and back tails of the shirt to the floor, and jumps through the opening; the shirt tears off, turning inside out as it does, and Sut hits the floor stark naked. It seems clearly a birth image, even to the shirt hanging there, to push the image as far as possible, as a grotesque parody of a placenta; it looks, Sut says, "adzactly like the skin ove sum wile beas' tore off alive, ur a bag what hed toted a laig ove fresh beef frum a shootin match" (p.35). It is, then, if birth it is, a violent, painful, and humiliating entrance into the world for Sut, who begins to learn about the world the moment he is born.

It is perhaps too much to say that Sut learns about life, in the course of the *Yarns*, in any systematic manner: that is, I'm not sure it is either possible or necessary to think that in each story he learns something different, or that from each person he encounters he learns a specific thing — that would be a bit too neat for a book as rough-hewn as the *Yarns*. It is clear, however, that Sut is a keen observer of mankind, and that over the years his initial observations, gleaned mostly from Dad, have been both confirmed and expanded. What Sut learns, and how he learns it, are very nicely summed up, condensed, into a superb story, "Taurus in Lynchburg Market," which stands directly, and significantly, at the center of the book, the twelfth of twenty-four stories.[25]

"Taurus" is introduced by Sut's singing of the important quatrain referred to earlier, which suggests the allegorical significance of the story Sut is to tell:

> "Daddy kill'd the blind bull,
> Human nater, human nater!
> "Mammy fried a pan full,
> Sop an' tater, sop an' tater." (p. 123)

Sut sings this in reaction against George's reading, and obviously approving, Henry Wadsworth Longfellow's very sentimental poem, "Excelsior," which is about, as Sut describes it, a "feller . . . what starts up a mountin, kiver'd wif snow an' ise, arter sundown, wif nuffin but a flag, an' no whisky, arter a purty gal hed offer'd her bussum fur a pillar, in a rume wif a big hath, kiver'd wif hot coals, an' vittils" (p. 124) — flouting, it seems to

25. And, had "Sut Lovengood's Chest Story" been published in the *Yarns* following "Old Burns's Bull-Ride," as the fourth story in the Sicily Burns tetralogy, as apparently the original plan had been, "Taurus" would have been squarely in the middle, the thirteenth story of twenty-five.

Sut, the laws of reason and common sense. He is not, however, merely teasing George; indeed, he is considerably upset that George could be so duped by a view of human nature as sentimental and naive as that of the Longfellow poem. In order to make his point, Sut rises "to his tip-toes, and elevated his clenched fists high above his head" (p. 124); such a fellow, he says, "am a dod durn'd, complikated, full-blooded, plum nat'ral born durn'd fool" (p. 124). This is apparently one of a series of heroes whom George has admired and spoken of, for Sut then alludes to "Lum Jack . . . darin the litenin" (p.124). George responds, obviously irritated at Sut's attack, "Ajax, I suppose you mean" (p. 124), and Sut speaks contemptuously of Ajax's heroic dare by pointing out a couple of facts which George has overlooked:

An' he wer a jack, ove the longes' year'd kine, fus', because eny fool mout know the litenin wudn't mine him no more nur a locomotum wud mine a tumble-bug. An' then, spose hit hed met [his] dar, why durn me ef thar'd been a scrimshun ove 'im lef big enuf tu bait a minner hook wif. (pp. 124-125)

Sut knows what George doesn't know, that no individual has any control over the real world, and so his contempt is both for the hollowness and stupidity of Ajax's meaningless gesture and for George's willingness to be impressed by it. Sut relates his experience in Lynchburg, then, as a fabliau, to teach George a lesson about human nature and about the meaning of "heroism" and "sacrifice" in the real world.

"Taurus" is, again, a simple story. Sut, in the mountain city of Lynchburg, Virginia — and significantly it is a town, a center of civilisation, and not just the usual backwoods settlement, where the episode takes place — sees a "thuteen hunder' poun' black an' white bull" (p. 126) rampaging violently through the town, causing destruction everywhere. His tail is "es strait up in the air as a telegraf pole" (p. 126). Here represented, then, is the conflict between chaos and order, between civilisation and anarchy. Sut takes sides in the conflict "agin the critter" (p. 129), that is, against chaos. He sees his chance, grabs the bull's tail and wraps it around a light pole — which if not a symbol of civilisation is at least one of its products, one of the things which help make civilisation possible. Sut describes them as "mity good things . . . fur a feller tu straiten up on, fur a fresh start" (pp. 128-129), foreshadowing Dad's inability, finally, to stand up straight like a human being in "Dad's Dog School"; and he underscores the point that civilisation is the instrument whereby brute natural chaotic forces can be tamed when he declares that the poles "can't be beat at stoppin bulls frum actin durn'd fool" (p. 129). Sut, then, steps in, puts himself into a very dangerous situation, in an attempt to halt the destruction of Lynchburg — heroically taking sides "agin the critter."

What does he get for his trouble? The bull defecates on him, for one thing, and he is abandoned by the very people whose civilisation he is trying to save; one of the townspeople finds Sut's predicament funny, and even begins to taunt him from behind the safety of a door. Sut tells George, "Ef hit hadn't been fur the cramp, skeer, an' that feller's bettin agin me, I'd been thar yet, a monument ove enjurance, parsavarance, an' dam fool, still holdin a dry bull's hide by the tail" (p. 131). That is, he says, if he had had some help or even some moral support from anybody else, the fight would have been worth it, worth keeping up even indefinitely; but he gets none. All he gets, literally and metaphorically, is shat upon. All he can do alone is to put a couple of kinks in the tail of chaos (p. 132).

This is not at all to suggest that Sut is right to undervalue heroism, or that two kinks in that metaphorical tail is not a magnificent gesture in itself, perhaps the best that man can ultimately do. But it is no wonder that Sut is so bitter and disillusioned about mankind, or that he is so exercised about George's sentimentality.

What, then, does Sut learn? He learns about wickedness and foolishness, of course, that it is human nature to be unregenerate, to court violence and self-destruction. But the implications of "Taurus" suggest that he learns even more: not just that man is capable of and delights in doing Evil in all of

its manifest forms; not just that he is capable of destroying himself and his civilisation through his wickedness and folly; — not
just that he is capable of these things and more, but that like
Dad he does them deliberately, consciously, and will not lift a
hand either to save himself or to help somebody else save him.
It is a profoundly pessimistic vision.

It is, of course, a vision which he shares with many others.
But Sut does not make the self-righteous mistake that many of
his "victims" do, of separating himself from the rest of mankind
in this regard; he does not believe he is different. Indeed, he
knows himself too well to deny, and is too honest to avoid con-
fessing, his own tendencies to lose control, to act irrationally.
As early as "Sut's New-Fangled Shirt," for example, he specifically associates himself with his Dad. The stiffened, starched
shirt stands up against Betts Carr's cabin "like a dry hoss hide"
(p. 32), and Sut sweats "like a hoss" (p. 32) when he wears it to
work. Even more pointedly, Sut sleeping dreams that he has
been "sowed up in a raw hide," and wakes to find the shirt
pasted to him "es clost es a poor cow [is] tu her hide in March"
(p. 33).

Like all of his victims he is capable of meanness and violence, and two important episodes in the *Yarns* are in fact
stories which Sut tells on himself. The lesser of the two is "Sut
Lovingood's Dog," a story in which Sut's dog is mistreated by
someone, we are not told who, while Sut is inside a doggery,
"gittin on a hed ove steam" (p. 151). Incensed and, significantly, probably drunk, Sut "got mad an' looked roun fur sum wun
tu vent rath on, an' seed a long-legged cuss, sorter ove the
Lovingood stripe" (p. 152) riding down the street on his horse.
Without knowing whether the man is guilty or innocent, Sut
decides "yu'll do, ef yu *didn't* start my dog on that hellward
experdition" (p. 152). Sut tries unsuccessfully to provoke a
quarrel, and so in a caveman-like rage hits the man with a rock:
"I jist lent him a slatharin calamity, rite whar his nose commenced a sproutin from atween his eyes, wif a ruff rock about the
size ove a goose aig. Hit fotch 'im!" (p. 152). During the en-
suing fight, Sut puts a blazing box of matches into one of the

man's coat pockets — but this is before he knows that in the other pocket the man is carrying two pounds of gunpowder. Telling it, Sut recognizes that he could easily have gotten himself killed or seriously injured. If he had known, he says, "durn me, ef I hedn't let him beat me inter a poultis, afore I'd a-sot him on fire" (p. 153).

"Sut Lovingood's Dog" is primarily comic, and its moral is lightly stated. The other episode is deadly serious, however, and much more sobering in its effect. It appears in "Contempt of Court — Almost," in the wake of Sut's frank admission that he "hates ole Onsightly Peter" and of his long monologue on "univarsal onregenerit human nater" (pp. 245-247), quoted earlier. The anecdote is intended, Sut says, "Jis' tu show the idear" of "univarsal onregenerit human nater," and he himself is the onregenerit human.

A foppish fellow enters a doggery where Sut is, again significantly, busy drinking; he looks at Sut "like [he] mout smell bad" (p. 247), and Sut is perhaps understandably irritated by the man's arrogance and general manner. "Baw-keepaw, ole Champaigne Brandy," the fop orders, "vintage over thuty-eight, ef yu please, aw" (p. 247). Sut's toes, he says, begin to tingle. He speaks to the stranger, again apparently trying to provoke a quarrel, but the man ignores him, and turns to leave. Enraged and for no rational reason, Sut kicks the stranger as hard as he can. As the man flies out the door he turns, pulls a derringer, and fires twice. "I wer sorter fooled in the nater ove that feller," Sut confesses: "that's a fac'. The idear ove Derringers, an' the melt to use em, bein mix't up wif es much durned finekey fool es he show'd, never struck me at all . . ." (pp. 248-249). Sut of course "outruns" the bullets, but the point is lost on neither Sut nor the reader; like nearly everybody else in the book, Sut here loses control of his rational, basically decent self, and nearly destroys himself in the process. He knows, then, that he is no different from the rest of mankind, that he no less than anybody else will, upon the slightest provocation, act horse or bull or damned fool, and so create the very chaos and destruction he abhors.

But the central episode of "Contempt of Court – Almost,' of which Sut's brush with the fop is introductory, entails a situation which seems to contradict the case for Sut as a proponent of Order, and which provides an essential insight into Sut's character. The one person in the *Yarns* whom Sut admires is Wirt Staples, who assists in righting the wrongs done by Sheriff Doltin to his rather slow-witted and cuckolded cousin Wat Mastin. Sut introduces Wirt in terms with which we have been describing his typical villains: Wirt is drunken and violent; coming out of a doggery he "histed his tail" (p. 249), stepped out into the street "short an' high, like ontu a bline hoss" (p. 250), and looked up and down the street "like a bull looks fur tuther one, when he thinks he hearn a beller" (p. 250). "Wirt wer bilin hot; nobody tu gainsay him [that is, nobody to control him], hed made him piedied all over; he wer plum pizen" (p. 252). Bragging loudly and looking for a fight, he throws a little Negro boy up in the air and kicks him as he comes down so that he flies like a football through a watch-tinker's window, wrecking the business, and causing destruction generally. That is, even allowing for Sut's obvious exaggeration, clearly Wirt under the influence is very much like the bull of "Taurus in Lynchburg Market." And yet Sut sees him as the epitome of manhood:

> His britches wer buttoned tite roun his loins, an' stuffed 'bout half intu his boots, his shut bagg'd out abuv, an' wer es white es milk, his sleeves wer rolled up tu his arm-pits, an' his collar wer es wide open es a gate, the mussils on his arms moved about like rabbits onder the skin, an' ontu his hips an' thighs they play'd like the swell on the river, his skin wer clear red an' white, an' his eyes a deep, sparklin, wickid blue, while a smile fluttered like a hummin bird roun his mouf all the while. When the State-fair offers a premin fur *men* like they now dus fur jackasses, I means tu enter Wirt Staples, an' I'll git hit, ef thar's five thousand entrys. (p. 253)

Why this apparent contradiction? It is only apparent, I think, and can be resolved. In the first place, Sut insists that Wirt's drunkenness, and therefore his "acting bull," is a freak chance, unusual for Wirt: he "hed changed his grocery range, an' the sperrits at the new lick-log hed more scrimmage seed an' raise-devil intu hit than the old biled drink he wer used tu" (p. 249). In the second place, Sut understands the world, of course, but understanding it is not quite the same thing as having to live in it. For the fact that he understands it as capricious and violent doesn't necessarily make living in it any easier – it can in fact make it more difficult. He is constantly on the run, Sut keeps saying, from one person or another, trying to escape whatever doom is about to overtake him. He is a man with many fears and anxieties, weary of constantly contending with this world, and yet afraid of confronting the next: "I feels like I'd be glad *tu be* dead, only I'se feard ove the dyin" (pp. 106-107), he tells George. Sut has a great deal of courage, and a lot of spiritual toughness, but in the end he realises that the preachers and lawyers and sheriffs have the upper hand, and that to get on in the world he must either avoid them entirely, outsmart them, or outrun them: he runs. What Sut admires about Wirt Staples, then, is not at all his capacity for violence, but his competence, his ability to deal with the world on its own terms, in a way that Sut is not able to. Wirt is big enough and strong enough not to have to be afraid of anything – not even the sheriff or the judge.

Finally, and this is perhaps more important, there is nothing mean or vicious or selfish about Wirt; he is not out to use or misuse anyone, and his marriage is the only healthy, harmonious relationship in the book. So he and his wife stand in vivid contrast to the other characters, even, to a certain extent, to Sut himself. They are fine examples of what human beings can be if they want to be, and are willing to make the effort to be. Wirt, and not Dad, is obviously what Sut would like to be, what he would like mankind to be.

## V. Yarns

A final perspective on the meaning of the *Yarns* can be gained by a brief look, here, at the book's magnificent Preface. No book was ever so introduced, and no preface I know of functions so brilliantly as a structural component of the book it prefaces. For the Preface to the *Yarns* does much more than merely introduce the book: it establishes character, conflict, and theme; and it states, clearly but indirectly, the serious moral tone and purpose of the entire book.

Sut initially objects, though not very strenuously, to the inclusion of a preface in "his" book, arguing that because most prefaces preachily try to sum up the moral content of the book, readers usually ignore them:

> Smells tu me sorter like a durned humbug, the hole ove hit — a littil like cuttin ove the Ten Cummandmints intu the rine ove a warter-million; hits jist slashed open an' the inside et outen hit, the rine an' the cummandmints broke all tu pieces an' flung tu the hogs, an' never tho't ove onst — them, nur the 'tarnil fool what cut em thar. (p. ix)

His association of prefaces generally and of his own specifically with the Ten Commandments clearly suggests the high moral intent of the *Yarns*, and Sut agrees to the preface, however reluctantly, with a highly ironical and even slightly cynical disdain of the whole business: "Buf ef a orthur *mus'* take off his shoes afore he goes intu the publick's parlor," he continues, metaphorically describing the moral disorder in the world as dirt, "I reckon I kin du hit wifout durtyin my feet, fur I hes socks on" (p. ix).

He proceeds to discuss his book, then, indirectly by discussing not the book itself but his readers, whom he divides into two large and perhaps all-encompassing classes, the Lucky and the Unlucky. The latter he describes in a highly moving passage which almost certainly wells up out of Harris' own experiences during his years of wandering:

> Ef eny poor misfortinit devil hu's heart is onder a mill-stone, hu's raggid children am hungry, an' no bread in the dresser, hu is down in the mud, an' the lucky ones a-trippin him every time he struggils tu his all fours, hu hes fed the famishin an' is now hungry hissef, hu misfortins foller fas' an' foller faster, hu is so foot-sore an' weak that he wishes he wer at the ferry — ef sich a one kin fine a laugh, jis' one, sich a laugh as is remembered wif his keerless boyhood, atwixt these yere kivers — then, I'll thank God that I *hes* made a book, an' feel that I hev got my pay in full. (p. xi)

This is directly related in many and obvious ways to "Sut Lovingood's Sermon" and "Tripetown: Twenty Minutes for Breakfast" and the diatribe in those sketches against the many unscrupulous "Perpryiters" who out of simple mean greed make Rest, surcease from wandering, prohibitively expensive for those "poor misfortinit devils" who need it most. Sut's sympathies are clearly for these "Unlucky" ones, and his compassion is all the more heartbreaking for the implicit recognition in the passage of the fact that any comfort he can offer, any laughter, any relief, can be only a momentary stay, and that they must eventually face the struggle again. This melancholy note is gently but firmly sounded even as early as the book's title page, in the legend, which states with Shakespearean simplicity that the laughter in the *Yarns* is inextricably commingled with the portent, the actual foreknowledge, of doom:

> "A little nonsense, now and then,
> Is relished by the wisest men."

> "Suppose I am to hang the morrow, and
> *Can* laugh to-night, shall I not? " — OLD PLAY

The only comfort that Sut can offer the Unlucky is the catharsis of laughter — the satisfaction of seeing their oppressors brought humiliatingly low by one of the Unlucky. The *Yarns* are full of the Lucky ones, the "perpryiters" and sheriffs and preachers who take advantage of or mistreat other people out of greed or simply because they have the power to. It is generally the Lucky ones who become Sut's victims, and it is these that he advises to stay away from his book:

> "I dusn't 'speck this yere perduckshun will sit purfeckly quiet ontu the stumicks ove sum pussons — them hu hes a holesum fear ove the devil, an' orter hev hit, by geminey. Now, fur thar speshul well-bein herearter, I hes jis' this tu say: Ef yu ain't fond ove the smell ove cracklins, stay outen the kitchin; ef yu is fear'd ove smut, yu needn't climb the chimbley; an' ef the moon hurts yer eyes, don't yu ever look at a Dutch cheese. That's jis' all ove hit.
>
> "Then thar's sum hu haint much faith in thar repertashun standin much ove a strain; they'll be powerful keerful how an' whar they reads my words. Now, tu them I haint wun word tu say: they hes been preached to, an' prayed fur, now ni ontu two thousand

years an' I won't dart weeds whar thuty-two poun shot bounces back." (pp. ix-x)

Finally, Sut tells George that he wants "tu put sumwhar atween the eyebrows ove our book, in big winnin-lookin letters, the sarchin, meanin words, what sum pusson writ ontu a 'oman's garter onst, long ago —" and George supplies the words: "*Evil be to him that evil thinks*" (p. xi). These words are indeed writ large throughout the book, for most of Sut's victims do in fact *think evil*, if we can understand "evil" to mean not just wickedness but foolishness too — any of the things which cause misery and chaos and destruction. And Sut's "tremenjus gif . . . fur breedin skeers amung durned fools" (p. xi) is his genius for producing for his victims the very retribution which they most fear. Time and time again in the *Yarns* the evil that men do simply turns around, sometimes with and sometimes without Sut's help, and consumes the evil-doer in the very deed: Sut's Dad, of course, and Parson Bullen. The Irishman who most fears snakes is run out of camp by what he thinks is a snake. Hen Bailey is nearly destroyed by his love of liquor. Sheriff Doltin is frightened by a man he believes to be Wat Mastin, a man he has deliberately wronged. And in "Frustrating a Funeral" Sut arranges for the sins of the past to come back and haunt all the main characters. That is, Sut's victims know they are doing evil at the time they are doing it, and so walk in fear of the retribution they know they deserve. In producing that retribution, or a figment of it, Sut breeds his "skeers."

There is not, of course, in the *Yarns* or in life, a simple division of Mankind into the Lucky and the Unlucky. It is rather Harris' metaphor for describing relationships among men: all men are capable of rapacity and meanness, and given the chance all men are capable of using their fortuitously (to keep Harris' metaphor) gained power over others for their own aggrandisement. At the whim of fate common people become elders and elders become bishops, the worm becomes the chicken and the chicken becomes the possum (cf. p. 228); any may become, for the moment, a "lucky" one. And so it is with complete seriousness that Sut is able, finally, to dedicate his book *"tu the durndest fool* in the United States, an' Massachusets too, he or she". . . .

DEDERCATED

WIF THE SYMPERTHYS OVE THE ORTHUR,

TU THE MAN UR 'OMAN, HUEVER THEY BE,

WHAT *DON'T* READ THIS YERE BOOK.

Obviously, the *durndest fool* is the man who persists in his own self-destruction, and Sut hopes that man will learn from his book not just how not, but *why* not, to destroy himself and his civilisation.

But there is no indication that hope will be realised. Sut knows nobody pays any attention to the Ten Commandments anyway, and Harris, in his warping and weaving of Sut's yarns, structures the book deliberately in such a way as to confirm the bleak world view that Sut has been giving voice to: the *Yarns* ends not with the bright ameliorating picture of Wirt Staples and his wife and their happy healthy relationship, but with the much darker portrait of Dad and Mam and *their* relationship. And in that contrast, I think, lies much of the ultimate meaning of the *Yarns*: Man must learn to control his animal nature if the institutions of civilisation, and therefore civilisitation itself, are to survive, and he is capable of doing so. But he simply will not do it.


Perhaps it is too early in the study of Harris to start making claims for him as an important American author; but it is difficult to escape the conclusion that the *Yarns* is among the most ambitious and complex achievements in nineteenth century American fiction. I am convinced that it is a major work of art, and that it both deserves and will repay a serious and sustained effort to come to grips with it. Its artistry is highly sophisticated and original; its philosophical and intellectual scope is broad; and its articulation of the old truths and verities, the problems of the human heart, is among the most profound and moving that I know of. It is a dark, pessimistic book, among the darkest in nineteenth century American literature, precisely because it does not end on a hopeful note; there is no Life-in-the-midst-of-Death coffin buoying up from the dark depths to sustain life or give hope to those with the courage or the luck to survive. It is a darkness punctuated and illuminated all the way through by Harris' unmatched sense of humor; but it is ultimately unrelieved by any suggestion that Man will ever be saved. Here in Harris' vision man is not being destroyed by forces beyond himself, though of course those forces do exist in Harris' world. He is rather hell-bent on destroying himself; and that is dark indeed.

# William Tappan Thompson as Playwright

*by*

HERBERT P. SHIPPEY

William Tappan Thompson is best known as the author of *Major Jones's Courtship*, the *Chronicles of Pineville*, and *Major Jones's Sketches of Travel.* The first and last of these works are written in a form in which he excelled, the fictitious dialect letter to the editor. But Thompson wrote other works which are now not so well known. Among these are three plays composed while he was living in Baltimore between 1846 and 1849. Only one of the plays, *Major Jones' Courtship; or Adventures of a Christmas Eve*, is now known to be extant.[1] The other two, "The Live

---

1. [William Tappan Thompson], *Major Jones' Courtship; or Adventures of a Christmas Eve, A Domestic Comedy, in Two Acts*, by Major Joseph Jones (Savannah: Edward J. Purse, 1850). Copies of this edition can be found at the Library of Congress; the Clements Library, University of Michigan, Ann Arbor; the Perkins Library, Duke University, Durham, North Carolina; the North Carolina State Library, Raleigh, North Carolina; the University of Georgia Library, Athens, Georgia; and the Uncle Remus Regional Library, Madison, Georgia.

I would like to take this opportunity to thank the following people: Mr. and Mrs. Walter B. Williams, Jr., of Milledgeville, Georgia, generously allowed me to use and quote from materials in the Thompson collection which they have placed in the Georgia College Library. The two manuscript versions of *Major Jones's Courtship; or Adventures of a Christmas Eve* are part of this collection. Dr. Henry Prentice Miller of Emory University, Atlanta, has given much kind assistance which I deeply appreciate. I would like to thank him for granting me permission to see his notes as well as to quote from them and from other materials. My thanks also go to

Indian" and a dramatized version of Oliver Goldsmith's *The Vicar of Wakefield*, have dropped from sight.[2] Thompson as a dramatist has been practically forgotten. Although the three plays he wrote are not especially significant in the history of American drama, they are worth consideration as part of his literary career. Apart from brief mention in newspaper eulogies and biographical sketches written shortly after his death in 1882, they have received little attention.[3]

his secretary, Katharine Dunlap, for copying helpful notes so patiently and efficiently. Mr. Charles E. Beard, Librarian of the Georgia College Library, Milledgeville, and Mr. Gerald C. Becham, Assistant Librarian, gave generous help by providing access to the Thompson collection and by making arrangements for me to obtain copies and photographs of needed items. The Reverend Frank McElroy of Quitman, Georgia, and LeAnne McLendon, a student at Georgia College, also rendered kind assistance. Finally, I wish to thank Dr. James B. Meriwether of the University of South Carolina for encouraging and helping me in many ways.

2.    *The Savannah Morning News* for 19 March 1881 carried this announcement: "The *Southern Dramatic Critic,* of Atlanta, for this week will contain a lengthy and interesting sketch of 'The Live Indian,' the 'screaming farce' which Mr. John E. Owens, the great comedian, has made famous for more than a quarter of a century. The author, Colonel Wm. T. Thompson, of Savannah, is well known as the writer of 'Major Jones' Courtship,' and other humorous works. The sketch in the *Critic* will be illustrated with an elegant picture of the original 'Live Indian,' which will be a great addition to the attractiveness of the publication. Copies will be for sale at Estill's News Depot as soon as received." Henry Prentice Miller (see note 4) cites this announcement on p. 100 of his dissertation, although he does not quote from it. I have not yet been able to find any issue of the *Southern Dramatic Critic.* For information on Thompson's dramatic version of *The Vicar of Wakefield,* see H. W. G. [probably Henry W. Grady], "Throttled Talent: Col. Thompson's Venture in the Literary World," *Atlanta Daily Constitution,* 9 June 1878, p. 1. This article is based on a conversation with Thompson, but it should be used with caution. Also see the fourth chapter of Miller's dissertation (note 4).

3.    A collection of newspaper clippings on Thompson that were published shortly after his death can be found in the scrapbook kept by his daughter, Mary Augusta Thompson Wade. This scrapbook and a collection of other Thompson materials have recently been placed in the Georgia College Library, Milledgeville, Georgia, through the generosity of Mr. and

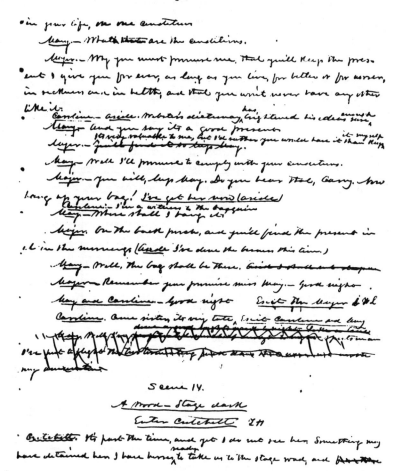

Figure 1. Leaf 38 from the holograph fragment of the play. Reproduced by permission of Mr. and Mrs. W. B. Williams, Jr., and Georgia College Library.

Mrs. Walter B. Williams, Jr., of Milledgeville. This collection also includes editions of Thompson's works, letters, photographs, and two holograph versions of the play *Major Jones's Courtship; or Adventures of a Christmas Eve.* Mr. Williams is one of Thompson's great-grandsons.

There has been only one scholarly discussion of them: Henry Prentice Miller's chapter on Thompson as a playwright in his unpublished 1942 dissertation, "The Life and Works of William Tappan Thompson."[4] Since his dissertation is not easily available, a brief summary of this chapter might be appropriate here. Miller states that Thompson was compelled to write plays during 1848 and 1849 because of the financial failure of *The Western Continent*, the Baltimore weekly newspaper which he edited.[5] *Major Jones' Courtship; or Adventures of a Christmas Eve* was first staged at the Baltimore Museum on 7 July 1848, with Tom Kemble as Major Jones and Mrs. D. P. Bowers as Mary Stallings.[6] Miller summarizes the action of the play and notes that its events are arranged in a different order from those in the book. He shows that the play was popular at one time, citing a *Savannah Morning News* article which claimed that Kemble had given over two hundred performances of the comedy by 1857.[7] In the appendices of the dissertation there is a partial list of performances in cities in the North and South during the period 1848-1866.[8]

According to Miller, the play is almost certainly the first sympathetic treatment of Georgia backwoods dialect and characters in American drama; in the last analysis it is "another play humorously glorifying the common man. . . ."[9] Though the

4. Henry Prentice Miller, "The Life and Works of William Tappan Thompson," Ph. D. dissertation, University of Chicago, 1942, pp. 95-107. Hereafter cited as Miller. This dissertation was thoroughly researched. It provides basic information necessary to any subsequent scholarly work on Thompson and is the most significant study of him to date. Portions of the dissertation were published in two articles. See Henry Prentice Miller, "The Background and Significance of *Major Jones's Courtship*," *The Georgia Historical Quarterly*, 30 (December 1946), 267-96; Miller, "The Authorship of *The Slaveholder Abroad*," *The Journal of Southern History*, 10 (February 1944), 93-95.

5. Miller, p. 95.

6. Ibid.

7. Ibid., p. 97.

8. Ibid., p. 145.

9. Ibid., p. 98.

play has no claims to literary merit, it was popular, "especially in the South, chiefly because it offered a humorous contrast between the North and the South in terms of the man from the city and the man from the country, in assumed effete education against genuine rustic common sense."[10]

Miller also discusses Thompson's "The Live Indian" and his dramatic version of *The Vicar of Wakefield*, giving more attention to the former drama since there is more information available about it. The dissertation includes a partial list of performances of "The Live Indian," which was successfully staged for many years by the actor John Edmond Owens.[11] At the conclusion of the dissertation chapter, Miller observes that Thompson was not an especially important American dramatist, but that he did write two plays which remained popular for a long time. Thompson's dramatic efforts "have value primarily in understanding some phases of the tastes of the play-going audiences in America for the third quarter of the nineteenth century."[12]

There is no reason to disagree with Miller's assessment of the literary merit of *Major Jones' Courtship; or Adventures of a Christmas Eve*, or with his estimate of Thompson's rank as a dramatist; but a further study of this aspect of Thompson's career is still worthwhile, since some additional manuscript material, unknown to Miller in 1942, has recently come to light. This material consists of a complete holograph draft of the play *Major Jones's Courtship*, as well as a holograph fragment which appears to be from an earlier draft of the play.[13] A comparison of these holographs with the two printed versions of the play provides some interesting insights on Thompson's writing techniques. The holographs and the printed versions also deserve

10. Ibid.
11. Ibid., pp. 146 and 106.
12. Ibid., p. 107.
13. See note 3. In a conversation with me on 30 June 1975, Miller said that he had not seen these holographs of the play while he was writing his dissertation.

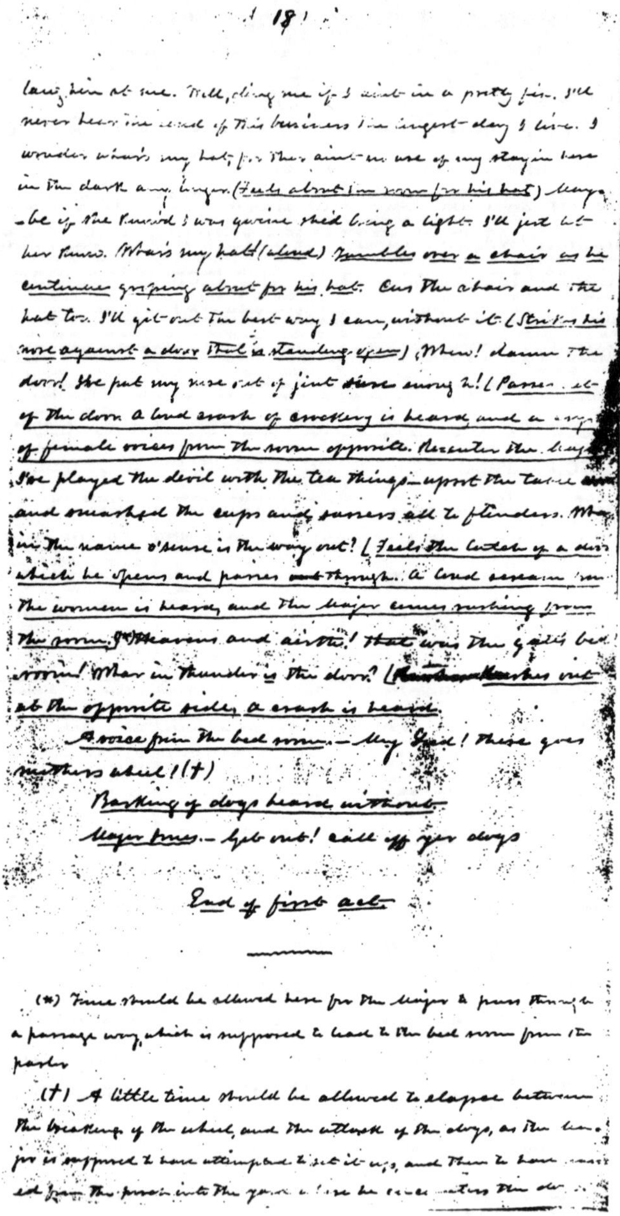

Figure 2. The final leaf of the first act of the complete holograph manuscript of the play. Notes at the bottom of the leaf indicate how portions of the scene are to be played. Reproduced by permission of Mr. and Mrs. W. B. Williams, Jr., and Georgia College Library.

attention in themselves as unique works in the humorous literature of the antebellum South.

I

Before proceeding into a discussion of the play, we should
give some attention to the background of its writing and performance. During February of 1844, Cornelius R. Hanleiter, the
proprietor of the Madison, Georgia, *Southern Miscellany*, released Thompson as the editor of the paper, since he could no
longer afford to pay him.[14] *Major Jones' Courtship* had first
been published in 1843 while Thompson was editor of the
*Miscellany*.[15] He had in fact written the Major Jones letters
for this paper.[16] Toward the beginning of 1844, however,

14.    Editorial notice by C. R. Hanleiter in the Madison, Georgia,
*Southern Miscellany*, 2 (16 February 1844), 3. For information on
Thompson's association with the *Miscellany*, as well as a bibliography of
his contributions to the paper, see George R. Ellison, "William Tappan
Thompson and the *Southern Miscellany*, 1842-1844," *The Mississippi
Quarterly*, 23 (Spring 1970), 155-68. For an overall survey and discussion
of the *Southern Miscellany*, consult Bertram Holland Flanders, *Early
Georgia Magazines: Literary Periodicals to 1865* (Athens: University of
Georgia Press, 1944). The University of Georgia Library has microfilm of
the *Southern Miscellany* for 5 April 1842-22 March 1844. Missing are the
15 October 1842 issue and the first sheet of the 4 March 1843 issue. This
microfilm was made from originals in the Washington Memorial Library,
Macon, Georgia, but at the present time these originals cannot be located.

15.    There is a copy of this first edition in the Perkins Library, Duke
University.

16.    The first Major Jones letter originally appeared in *The Family
Companion and Ladies' Mirror*, 2 (June 1842), 191-92. Thompson was at
the time an associate editor of this magazine published in Macon, Georgia,
by Benjamin F. Griffin. (The Wesleyan College Library, Macon, Georgia,
has volumes one and two of this magazine, including the issue in which the
first Major Jones letter was published.) This initial letter was reprinted in
the Madison *Southern Miscellany* on 20 August 1842, p. 2, and the remainder of the courtship letters in the book, through letter twenty-six,
were published subsequently in this paper. Letters twenty-seven and
twenty-eight, as they are numbered in the book, initially appeared in print
elsewhere (see the bibliography of Thompson's works in Miller's disserta-

Hanleiter was in financial straits and reluctantly had to let his able editor go. Thompson returned for a time to Augusta and then in the spring of 1845 went to New York, where he remained until the beginning of the new year.[17] There he met the poet Park Benjamin, and the two men made plans to establish a Southern family newspaper in Baltimore.[18]

*The Western Continent* was the fruit of this planning.[19] It was established as a weekly newspaper; the first number ap-

tion). Letter twenty-eight was published in the *Spirit of the Times*, 14 (13 April 1844), 73. Miller notes in his dissertation (p. 155) that he did not discover where the twenty-seventh letter first appeared in print. I have not yet determined the original publication either.

17. Notes used by Miller in preparing his dissertation contain transcripts which he made from original materials formerly in the possession of Mrs. Lewis E. McIntosh of Quitman, Georgia. Among these materials there is the fragment of a letter written by Thompson. The date and address are missing, but a letter dated 17 October 1866 reveals that this fragmentary letter containing autobiographical information was probably written to Salem Dutcher on 16 October 1866. In the letter Thompson states that he went to New York in 1845 and that while there he conceived the plan of starting a weekly Southern family newspaper in Baltimore. Miller also possesses the transcript of a biographical sketch (probably in the hand of Thompson's daughter, Mary Augusta Wade), which states that Thompson went to New York in the spring of 1845. I have used Miller's transcripts of the two letters to Dutcher and the biographical sketch since I have not yet been able to trace the present location of the originals.

18. For background information on Park Benjamin see Merle M. Hoover, *Park Benjamin: Poet and Editor* (New York: Columbia University Press, 1948); and Lillian B. Gilkes, "Park Benjamin: Literary Agent, *Et Cetera,*" *Proof,* 1 (1971), 35-89. Benjamin wrote letters to Brantz Mayer of Baltimore setting forth plans to establish a newspaper in Baltimore. This proposed paper became *The Western Continent.* He also wrote two letters to Mayer expressing his sentiments about the paper after he had left it. Originals of these letters are in the Maryland Historical Society, Baltimore, Maryland. Their dates are 23 June, 22 July, 6 September 1844; 17 January, 27 September, 6 October, 10 October, 4 November 1845; 8 August [1846]; 19 February 1847.

19. The most nearly complete file of this newspaper is at the Enoch Pratt Free Library, Baltimore.

# MAJOR JONES' COURTSHIP;

OR

# Adventures of a Christmas Eve,

# A DOMESTIC COMEDY,

## IN TWO ACTS.

BY MAJOR JOSEPH JONES.

SAVANNAH:
EDWARD J. PURSE, BOOK & JOB PRINTER,
No. 102 Bryan-Street—Up Stairs
1850.

Figure 3. The title page of the 1850 pamphlet edition. Reproduced from the copy at the University of Georgia Library, Athens.

peared on 3 January 1846. In this issue Thompson was listed as the associate editor. The two men co-edited the paper only a short time, though, for on 11 July 1846 Benjamin relinquished editorial charge.[20] Benjamin and Thompson apparently differed in temperament and editorial policy. Thompson remained with the paper as editor until the first of July 1848, when he was apparently forced to give it up as a result of financial difficulties. On 8 July of that year, a new series of *The Western Continent* began under new proprietorship and editorship.[21] During 1849 Thompson worked for a time on the *Baltimore American* and contributed articles to the *Baltimore Clipper*,[22] but he finally returned to Georgia and became the founding editor of the Savannah *Daily Morning News,* the first issue of which appeared on 15 January 1850.[23]

Between the first of 1848 and his commencement of the *Morning News*, Thompson wrote three plays. One can only speculate why he decided to write *Major Jones' Courtship; or*

20. Park Benjamin, "To the Readers of The Western Continent," *The Western Continent*, 1 (11 July 1846), 2.

21. By 22 July 1848 *The Western Continent* was owned and edited by H. M. Garland, Jr., and John Donaldson. The first number of this new series, published on 8 July 1848, is missing from the files of the Maryland Historical Society and the Enoch Pratt Free Library, but a prospectus for the paper in the 22 July issue reveals that the first number was issued on 8 July. See *The Western Continent*, N.S. 1 (22 July 1848), 3. The Maryland Historical Society has a file of this paper with issues from 22 July 1848 through 10 February 1849 (30 September and 7 October 1848 are missing).

22. The biographical sketch (probably made by Mary Augusta Wade), which Miller transcribed, states that Thompson served as associate editor of the *Baltimore American* during the summer of 1849. For evidence that Thompson was associated with the *Baltimore Clipper*, see John H. Hewitt, *Shadows on the Wall Or Glimpses of the Past* (Baltimore: Turnbull Brothers, 1877), pp. 30-31.

23. The *Daily Morning News* was the original title of *The Savannah Morning News*. Thompson was the founding editor, and John M. Cooper was the founding publisher. The Georgia Historical Society in Savannah has a fairly complete file of original issues of this paper.

*Adventures of a Christmas Eve*, but financial troubles and a growing family were most likely his chief motivations. He may also have decided to capitalize on the widespread popularity of his book *Major Jones's Courtship*, published by Carey and Hart of Philadelphia in 1844[24] and issued in a new edition in 1847.[25] Thompson, in fact, had good reason to try to benefit from a dramatic adaptation of his book. During the first year of its publication, he had received $750, at five cents per copy from its sales. Thinking after this sale of some 15,000 copies that the book had had its run, he accepted $250 for the copyright.[26] He must have been unpleasantly surprised to see how well the book continued to sell over the years. Carey and Hart kept *Major Jones's Courtship* in print up through the time that Thompson wrote the play.[27] The copyright did not return to Thompson until 1872.[28] He stated that 80,000 copies of the

24. [William Tappan Thompson], *Major Jones's Courtship: Detailed, with Other Scenes, Incidents, and Adventures, in a Series of Letters, by Himself*. Second Edition, Greatly Enlarged, With Illustrations by Darley (Philadelphia: Carey & Hart, 1844). This was the first nationwide editon of the book, since the 1843 edition was published in Madison by C. R. Hanleiter.

25. See Miller, p. 162.

26. Letter by Thompson probably to Salem Dutcher, [16 October 1866]. Transcript in Miller's notes. Also, for a published excerpt from this letter, see Miller, "The Background and Significance of *Major Jones's Courtship*," op. cit., 287. Hereafter I will cite this article as Miller, "Background and Significance," but I will continue to cite Miller's dissertation as "Miller."

27. Miller, "Background and Significance," 287-89.

28. See Thompson's 1872 preface "To the Reader" in [William Tappan Thompson], *Major Jones's Courtship: Detailed, with Other Scenes, Incidents, and Adventures, in a Series of Letters by Himself*. Revised and Enlarged. To Which Are Added Thirteen Humorous Sketches. With Illustrations by Cary (New York: D. Appleton & Company, 1872). A copy of the 1872 edition, signed by Thompson and presented to his daughter, Mrs. Millie A. Wade, is among the Thompson materials recently given to the Georgia College Library, Milledgeville, Georgia. The inscription is dated 14 November 1872, Savannah.

book had been sold by 1852.[29] The popularity of the work may have prompted him to try to capitalize on a dramatic version of it, since he was receiving nothing from sales of the book. Thompson began to dramatize the book before he left *The Western Continent*. In an 1866 letter to Salem Dutcher of Augusta, Georgia, he mentioned that he had dramatized the story of *Major Jones's Courtship* in 1848 while he was living in Baltimore and editing *The Western Continent*.[30] Also, in a note to the readers included in a pamphlet version of the play (Savannah, 1850), he wrote:

> This farce was written at the suggestion of the Managers of the BALTIMORE MUSEUM. It was hastily prepared for representation, without a thought of its ever appearing in printed form. It was produced by the Dramatic Corps at the Saloon of the Museum in the Spring of 1848, and succeeded far beyond the author's expectations. It was repeated several nights in succession, and has since been frequently performed in that establishment, which alone has the right to use it. – Having been frequently solicited to put it in print by friends who valued it more for its domestic character than for any literary merit, the author has consented that it should assume its present form.[31]

The managers of the Baltimore Museum at this time were Albert N. Hann and Josh Silsbee.[32] After Silsbee formed a partnership with Hann in the spring of 1847, the Museum was remodeled. The third story was removed "to admit three tiers of boxes and a neat parquet, giving the saloon a much greater capacity, enabling the management then to engage a larger number of actors and to produce a better class of entertain-

29. Miller, "Background and Significance," 289.

30. Letter by Thompson to Salem Dutcher, 17 October 1866. Transcript in Miller's notes.

31. See note "To the Readers" at the conclusion of the pamphlet edition.

32. J. Thomas Scharf, *History of Baltimore City and County*. With a new introduction by Edward G. Howard, reprinted in two parts (1881, rpt. Baltimore: Regional Publishing Company, 1971), II, 693. Hereafter cited as Scharf.

ments."[33] In 1849 Silsbee sold his interest to the actor John Edmond Owens, who in turn became Hann's partner.[34] Thompson's farce "The Live Indian" was produced under this management, having its first performance on 19 November 1849.[35]

Owens' wife, in a book of reminiscences about his theatrical career, also described how the Museum appeared after the remodeling in 1847:

> The Baltimore Museum had been much improved during the summer, the Lecture room having been altered and enlarged into a cosey theatre, with cushioned seats, private boxes, parquette, and gallery. New scenery, and decorations were designed and executed by that well known artist, Charles S. Getz. When completed, the theatre was as pretty a little place as one could wish to see.[36]

*Major Jones' Courtship; or Adventures of a Christmas Eve* was first performed in this theatre on the evening of 7 July 1848, following a comedy entitled *The Wolf and Lamb.*[37] The price of admission was twenty-five cents. The play was billed at the Museum by *The Baltimore Sun* for July 7, 8, 10, 11, and 15.[38] It remained popular for several years in both the North and the South and was sometimes offered as a holiday piece around Christmas time. Miller notes that it played in Baltimore; New York; Philadelphia; Savannah; Columbus, Georgia; and Wilmington, North Carolina, through 1866.[39] According to Thompson,

33. Scharf, II, 693.

34. Ibid.

35. [Mary C. Owens], *Memories of the Professional and Social Life of John E. Owens, by His Wife* (Baltimore: John Murphy and Company, 1892), p. 48. Hereafter cited as *John E. Owens.*

36. *John E. Owens*, p. 33.

37. *The Baltimore Sun*, 23 (7 July 1848), 3.

38. *The Baltimore Sun*, 23 (7, 8, 10, 11, and 15 July 1848), 3 (all issues).

39. Miller, p. 145. Most of the information on performances which I present in this paragraph and in the following paragraphs is derived from Miller's dissertation and from material in his notes which was not incorporated into the dissertation. "Appendix B," on p. 145 of his dissertation, provides a representative list of dates and places of performance for the play. I have found this list and citations of books on theatre history in his

the play was also performed from time to time in Northern cities, in Georgia theatres, and at many country school exhibitions.[40]

It played at Barnum's Museum in Philadelphia for nine nights during December of 1851.[41] In the same city, it appeared at the City Museum for seven days in December of 1854 and continued for six performances into January 1855.[42] The play was produced at Barnum's Museum in New York in 1851, 1857, and 1866.[43] In the latter year it was staged under the title *Major Jones's Christmas Present* during the Christmas season.[44] It was also offered as a holiday piece by this museum in 1851. The play was produced in Savannah in 1850, 1857, 1859, and 1863.[45] The first Savannah performance, in May 1850, came at

notes and bibliography especially useful in tracing performances of *Major Jones' Courtship* and "The Live Indian." By referring to sources cited by Miller, and by examining newspapers for some of the dates and places listed in "Appendix B," I have elaborated material on the performances and have also provided some information which he chose not to include within the dissertation. I have also listed a few additional newspaper sources where further accounts of specific stage productions enumerated by Miller can be found. Miller, however, deserves full credit for providing dates and places of performance and for citing books and papers which give facts on the stage history of *Major Jones' Courtship*. Even though some of this information is not contained in the dissertation, most of it is available in his notes.

40.    Letter by Thompson to Salem Dutcher, 17 October 1866. Transcript in Miller's notes.

41.    Arthur Herman Wilson, *A History of the Philadelphia Theatre 1835 to 1855* (Philadelphia: University of Pennsylvania Press, 1935), p. 611.

42.    Ibid.

43.    George C. D. Odell, *Annals of the New York Stage* (New York: Columbia University Press, 1931), VI, 168, 566-567; and Odell (1936), VIII, 179. Hereafter cited as Odell. See also: *The New York Herald*, 16 (23 December 1851), 3; *The New York Herald*, 22 (31 January 1857), 7; and *Wilkes' Spirit of the Times*, 15 (5 January 1867), 304.

44.    Odell, VIII, 179.

45.    See the following issues of the Savannah *Daily Morning News*: vol. 1 (9 May 1850), 3; vol. 8 (27 March 1857), 2; vol. 10 (7 February 1859), 2; and vol. 14 (25 December 1863), 2.

approximately the same date that the play was printed as a paperback volume. A theatrical group called the "Histrionics" staged *Major Jones' Courtship* at the concert hall in Columbus, Georgia, on 6 February 1852.[46] It was presented as an after-piece to *The Golden Farmer, or Jemmy Twitcher in England.* The editor of *The Columbus Enquirer* had some remarks about the performance. He commended the behavior of the audience and suggested:

> . . . if played again, that some words "less grating to ears polite" be substituted for those oaths of Major Jones. They may be in keeping with the character of a "Georgia hoosier," but considering the diversity of taste existing in such an audience as was present, they can be easily dispensed with for others equally common in their use, and much less objectionable.[47]

Part of the popular appeal of *Major Jones' Courtship* no doubt depended upon the actors who were portraying the principal characters. A talented actor, by exaggerated gestures, language, costumes, and makeup, could make even a dull piece come to life. During the mid-nineteenth century, actors did not feel bound to adhere too closely to the script. A prominent actor sometimes revised a play to suit his own taste, since the playwright's text was not considered sacrosanct. John E. Owens altered "The Live Indian" after he had purchased it from Thompson by changing the dialogue and introducing a new character called "Miss Crinoline."[48] Through his personal style he made the play popular for many years.[49] Mrs. Owens gives this account of the manner in which her husband performed "The Live Indian":

> *Miss Crinoline* made the farce a success. The quick change (three minutes), from the dress of a gay young man to that of a fashionably costumed lady, was startling; and (at that time) a novelty. With blonde wig, and stylish dress of handsome material, he came on the stage so soon after *Corporal Tim's* exit, that the audience were

46. *The Columbus Enquirer*, 25 (3 February 1852), 3.
47. *The Columbus Enquirer*, 25 (10 February 1852), 2.
48. *John E. Owens*, pp. 48-49.
49. See Miller, p. 146, for a partial record of performances.

dazed; and, until they became familiar with the piece, doubted the identity of the two. The dress-maker's scene, with old Brown and his niece, was full of telling points, which evoked roars of laughter. From this to the Indian made another striking contrast, enlivened by Owens' inimitable acting.[50]

There is evidence that *Major Jones' Courtship* was also staged in this free manner. It was originally written for the actor Thomas Kemble at the Baltimore Museum.[51] After a performance of the drama by Kemble at the Athenaeum in Savannah on 27 March 1857, the following review, perhaps written by Thompson himself, appeared in the *Daily Morning News*:

> The petite comedy of *Major Jones' Courtship* went off very well. We would have been gratified if the principal character of the piece had followed more closely the text. But this defect was more than compensated for by the spirit and earnestness with which the other characters in the piece, especially the ladies, entered into the performance.[52]

Such alterations, though dismaying to playwrights, may sometimes have enhanced the popular appeal of dramas.

The play was performed in the South during the Civil War. It was offered as a Christmas piece in Savannah on 25 December 1863, following the performance of *Christmas Eve; or, A Duel in the Snow.*[53] The theatre in Wilmington, North Carolina, staged the play on 7 February 1865, with Major Jones being played by a soldier "home on a visit from Lee's Army in Virginia."[54]

*Major Jones' Courtship* was frequently presented with other dramas (also with operas and spectacles), since it was not

50. *John E. Owens*, p. 49. For another description of Owens' personal style in "The Live Indian," see *Wilkes' Spirit of the Times*, 11 (7 January 1865), 304, under the notice for the Broadway Theatre.

51. Savannah *Daily Morning News*, 8 (27 March 1857), 2.

52. Savannah *Daily Morning News*, 8 (28 March 1857), 2.

53. Savannah *Daily Morning News*, 14 (25 December 1863), 2.

54. Playbill for the Wilmington Theatre, advertising *Major Jones' Courtship* and *Sketches in India*. Clifton Waller Barrett Collection, Alderman Library, University of Virginia, Charlottesville.

lengthy enough to fill an evening. Some of the titles of pieces with which it was staged include *The Wolf and Lamb, Love in All Corners, Maid of Artois, Right Way Is the Best, The Boston Tea Party, Boots at the Swan, Alma Mater, Charles II, The Honey Moon, Palace of Peacocks, The Golden Farmer, Therese, Forty Thieves, Lucretia Borgia, Rich and Poor of New York, The Hunchback, Christmas Eve; or, A Duel in the Snow, Sketches in India,* and *Away with Melancholy.*[55] Often other entertainment was offered as well, including singing and dancing. At the Baltimore Museum, pictures and curiosities of various sorts were on display.[56] Barnum's Museum in New York offered the play as part of a grand array of amusements. During the Christmas season of 1866 the visitor to Barnum's could see, in addition to the play, a performing elephant, educated mules, a leopard child, a mammoth fat man weighing 615 pounds, two dwarfs, a learned seal, wax figures, and 200,000 other curiosities[57] Obviously, attending such a play as *Major Jones' Courtship* was not a high cultural experience. Plays of this nature were a part of middle-class recreation during the mid-nineteenth century and were intended chiefly to amuse, and sometimes in addition to supply moral instruction. It is significant that dramatic performances at Barnum's establishment on Broadway

55. For citations of these pieces in consecutive order see *The Baltimore Sun*, issues for 7, 8, 10, 11, 15 July; 22 September 1848 and 4 December 1849; the Savannah *Daily Morning News*, issues for 10, 15 May 1850; *The New York Herald*, 22 December 1851; *The Columbus Enquirer*, 3 February 1852; Wilson, p. 611; Wilson, p. 611; Wilson, p. 611; the Savannah *Daily Morning News*, 7, 8 February 1859, 25 December 1863; playbill in Clifton Waller Barrett Collection, Alderman Library, University of Virginia, Charlottesville; and *Wilkes' Spirit of the Times*, 29 December 1866. I have been unable to determine the authors for all of these works. For lists of several of the authors see: "Catalogue of the Becks Collection of Prompt Books in the New York Public Library," *Bulletin of the New York Public Library*, 10 (February 1906), 100-48. Also, Reginald Clarence, compiler, *The Stage Cyclopaedia: A Bibliography of Plays* (1909, rpt. New York: Burt Franklin, 1970).

56. Scharf, II, 693.

57. *Wilkes' Spirit of the Times*, 15 (29 December 1866), 285.

and Ann Street in New York were given in a "Moral Lecture Room."[58]

## II

*Major Jones' Courtship; or Adventures of a Christmas Eve* was first published after Thompson had moved to Savannah in 1850. The year before, Edward J. Purse, one of Thompson's old acquaintances from Augusta, had founded a weekly literary paper in Savannah called *The Friend of the Family*.[59] This paper carried the play serially from 23 March through 20 April 1850. A headnote printed with the first installment indicated that the play had already been copyrighted.[60] On 11 May Purse informed his readers that he had published an edition of the play in pamphlet form.[61] The pamphlet contained Thompson's note, dated April 1850, which explained the background of the play. This text was basically the same as *The Friend of the Family* version, though there were differences, since Thompson revised the text before it appeared as a separate edition.

These printed texts of the drama are two of four known versions which survive. The holograph of the entire play, and

---

58. T. Allston Brown, *A History of the New York Stage from the First Performance in 1732 to 1901*. Reissue (New York: Benjamin Blom, Inc., 1964), I, 71.

59. The first issue appeared as *A Friend of the Family*, 1 (1 March 1849). The title of the paper changed to *The Friend of the Family* in the 9 March 1850 issue. Purse and Thompson both served in Augusta, Georgia, units during the Florida Seminole War of 1836. In a document dated 23 May 1854, Chatham County, Georgia, Purse confirms that Thompson served in the Florida Seminole War (Thompson's application papers for bounty land warrant in the National Archives, Washington, D. C.). These papers reveal that Purse served in the "Richmond Hussars" from Augusta, Georgia, while Thompson served in the "Richmond Blues."

60. The play was carried in the following issues for 1850 (vol. 2): 23 March, pp. 1-2; 30 March, p. 2; 6 April, p. 1; 13 April, p. 1; 20 April, p. 2. (Microfilm, University of Georgia Library.)

61. *The Friend of the Family*, 2 (11 May 1850), 3.

the holograph of a fragment of the play, both mentioned above, are now located at the Ina Dillard Russell Library at Georgia College in Milledgeville, Georgia. The holograph versions differ from each other and from the two printed texts as well. A thorough comparison of variants among these four different versions would be tedious and confusing without accompanying textual tables, but a general description of each text and a brief analysis of the most salient differences between and among them is worthwhile. Such a comparison shows how Thompson revised and reworked the play.

The manuscript fragment appears to be earlier than the complete draft, and so for convenience of discussion, this fragment will be referred to as the first holograph, and the complete manuscript will be referred to as the second holograph. Likewise, *The Friend of the Family* version will be called the first printed text, and the pamphlet version will be called the second printed text.[62] All three of the complete texts have two acts, with a total of nine scenes, four in the first act and five in the second.

The two manuscripts are written in Thompson's own hand. Neither is signed, but the idiosyncrasies of the handwriting correspond to those in letters to which he affixed his signature.[63] The entire text, and all revisions and insertions in both versions, show no evidence of non-authorial intervention in the compositional process.[64] In both holographs the text is written on the rectos only; the versos are blank except for occasional

62. The following abbreviations will be used: "*MJC* 1Ms." for the first holograph, "*MJC* 2Ms." for the second holograph, "*FOF*" for *The Friend of the Family* text, and "*MJC* pamp." for the pamphlet version of the text. Page and line numbers (as well as column numbers where appropriate) will be given in the text of the discussions.

63. For comparison, three letters signed by Thompson and addressed to Mary E. Moragné can be found in the South Caroliniana Library at the University of South Carolina, Columbia. One of the letters, addressed from Augusta, is dated 21 May 1841. The other two letters, both written from Macon, Georgia, are dated 4 February and 21 March 1842.

64. On the verso of p. 25 in the second holograph there is writing in a

stage directions and dialogue insertions. There are abbreviations indicating points of entrance and exit for characters in the two texts. These stage directions are not present in either of the printed versions.

The first holograph, or incomplete manuscript, is inscribed on short white paper in brown ink. It has a total of twenty-six sheets numbered 20-41 [unnumbered leaf] 42-44. The unnumbered sheet is actually two torn half-pages pasted together by two drops of wax. This unnumbered page contains passages of dialogue to be inserted on pages 41 and 42. The fragment begins on page 20 with the final lines of Major Jones' soliloquy at the opening of the second act. The fragment ends in the fifth scene at the point where the Major and Mary Stallings step forward to address the audience after Mrs. Stallings has given them permission to marry. The first page of the fragment is scorched and soiled, but the other pages are undamaged and legible. The pages were originally bound with thread, which has recently been removed so that the manuscript may be read more easily. It appears that the pages were sewed together after Thompson had inscribed them, since the writing occasionally extends into the left margin beyond the point where the pages were bound. There is writing on the versos of three of the sheets; this writing includes the stage directions "Voice without" and *"Dark Stage"* and the name of one of Mary Stallings' sisters, "Miss Carrie."[6][5]

Evidence indicates that the fragment is probably an earlier draft of the drama than the complete manuscript. The fragment is more heavily revised than the complete holograph and is not so finished in details. It contains deleted lines which appear neither in the full holograph nor in the printed texts. "Prissy" occurs on the first page of the fragment as the name of one of the servants, but it is marked out, and "Ned" is written above.

---

hand different from the handwriting in the rest of the manuscript, but this writing does not appear to have any relation to the text of the play. It reads as follows: "Home dary hom to our own native home."

65. *MJC* 1Ms. verso of p. 26, verso of p. 37, and verso of unnumbered sheet between pp. 41 and 42.

"Ned" is the name of the servant at this point (Act II.1) in the other three texts. "Caesar" is the name for an old servant in the fragment,[66] but the corresponding character in the other versions is "Brutus." Neither "Prissy" nor "Caesar" appears in the other texts.

The second holograph, or complete manuscript, is written on long blue paper in brown ink. The sheets are folded in folio and were apparently at one time bound into a volume. The first and last pages of this draft are badly frayed and stained, but most of the text can be read without difficulty. There are forty-five pages of text plus a title page. The title and "Dramatis Personae" appear on the initial page, which is unnumbered. The title differs from the title in the printed versions. The pamphlet is titled *Major Jones' Courtship; or Adventures of a Christmas Eve, A Domestic Comedy, in Two Acts.* The title had been the same in *The Friend of the Family*, except for differences in punctuation. In the complete manuscript, however, the title appears as *Major Jones's Courtship; or Adventures of a Christmas Eve, A Farce in Two Acts.* The next recto page with writing on it is numbered as page 1. The opening scene of Act I begins on this page, and the succeeding pages are numbered in sequence through page 44, which concludes the play. Act II begins on page 19. There are some deleted words and lines throughout the manuscript, but on the whole, that part of the second holograph which corresponds to the fragment has fewer crossed out words, phrases, and lines. The variants between the two manuscripts are most numerous in the final scene of the play, in which Major Jones presents himself in a bag as a Christmas present to Mary.[67] Some stage directions occur on the versos of the sheets

66. *MJC* 1Ms. unnumbered sheet between pp. 41 and 42.

67. At this point Thompson's revisions in the fragment are more complicated and more interesting than they are elsewhere. Between pages 41 and 42 occurs the unnumbered page which consists of two torn half-sheets attached by wax. In pasting the two halves together, Thompson covered six lines which read as follows (angle brackets enclose deleted words):

*<Enter Ned cautiously, the other negroes close behind him>

opposite the lines to which they apply on the facing page. These directions include such phrases as "Laugh without R.H," "Knock at D.L.1.E.," *"Voice off L.1.E.,"* and *"Stage dark."*[6][8] At the end of the first act in this manuscript there are also two footnotes directing how the scene should be played. No other version of the play contains these notes.[6][9]

Occasionally the printed texts have small details about sets and staging which are missing in the complete manuscript, but overall this manuscript provides more detail about how sets are arranged and how scenes should be played than either of the printed versions. For example, a significant variant occurs in the scene portraying a dance at the Christmas Eve party at the Stallings home. The lines in the following passage which are not

> Reenter Caesar Dinah and the other negroes, armed with a gun pitchfork broomsticks &c.
> 
> Maj Jones. – Dont shoot Caesar
> 
> *Caesar – Dropping his gun.* Gosh a mighty um massa Joe (*MJC* 1Ms. unnumbered page between pp. 41 and 42, 6 lines covered by paste over)

68. *MJC* 2Ms. page facing p. 1, verso of p. 5, verso of p. 8, and verso of p. 16.

69. The notes are marked in the second holograph by an asterisk and a dagger. The asterisked footnote applies to the following action description in the scene in which the Major is trying to find his way out of the Stallings house. He has accidentally extinguished the fire with tobacco juice while mustering courage to propose to Mary: *"Feels the latch of a door which he opens and passes <out> through. A loud scream from the women is heard, and the Major comes rushing from the room."* (*MJC* 2 Ms. 18.15-18). The footnote reads: "Time should be allowed here for the Major to pass through a passage way, which is supposed to lead to the bed room from the parlor" (*MJC* 2Ms. 18.26-28). The dagger appears at the end of the following passage beginning three lines below the asterisked stage description: *"A voice from the bed room.* – My Lord! there goes mothers wheel! (†)" (*MJC* 2Ms. 18.21-22). The footnote gives instructions on how this part of the scene should be played:

> (†) A little time should be allowed to elapse between the breaking of the wheel, and the attack of the dogs, as the Major is supposed to have attempted to set it up, and then to have passed from the porch into the yard where he encounters the dogs. (*MJC* 2Ms. 18.29-32)

italicized are an asterisked insert from the verso of page 26 in the complete manuscript:

> *Dr. Peter leads Miss Kesiah to the floor. Crotchett talks aside with Mary while the other characters take their places.* *Negro musicians, with the instruments common on the southern plantations, viz: the violin tamborine and bone castanets, may be introduced on the stage in lieu of the orchestra. During the dance and the games the negro house-ser*v*ants &c &c, should be discovered at the doors and windows laughing at the fun; dancing, &c *Country dance, directed by Dr. Jones. After the dance Crotchett remains in conversation with Mary. (MJC 2Ms. 27.24-27, six lines from verso of 26)

The descriptions in the two printed texts are identical with each other but much less detailed than the manuscript description:

> *(Dr. Jones leads Miss Kesaih to the floor, Crotchett talks aside with Mary while the other characters take their places. Country dance. After the dance Crotchett engages Mary in conversation.) (MJC pamp. 40.25-28)*

The corresponding passage in the fragment is also less detailed than the passage in the complete manuscript. The fragment differs in wording and does not have the unitalicized insert which the other manuscript contains.[70] It varies from the printed texts as well.

There are numerous variants of wording, spelling, and punctuation between the complete manuscript and the final printed text. Overall, the printed play has also been simplified and contains less dialogue and scene description. In this final text, Thompson also exaggerated the traits of his characters. He made Crotchett's speech more affected by having him frequently pronounce *r*'s as *w*'s, and he sharpened the rural dialect of Major Jones and Mrs. Stallings. He placed slightly more emphasis on the differences between the North and South as repre-

---

70. The passage appears as follows in the fragment:
    *Caroline takes the Majors arm. Dr Peter leads Miss Kesiah to the floor. Crotchett talks aside with Mary while the other characters take their places. Country dance or cotillion. Dr Jones calls out the figures. At the conclusion of the dance the company retire up. < Crotchett and Mary advance >. (MJC 1Ms. 28.10-14)*

sented by Crotchett and the Major. For example, in the manuscript the Major tells Crotchett that he does not believe in phrenology and then thrusts out his head for Crotchett to attempt to mesmerize him. The major speaks these words: "Go ahead. You needn't be afraid. You won't find nothing that'll bite [three illegible words marked out] in my head" (*MJC* 2Ms. 10. 21-22). But in the pamphlet text, the Major declares that he does not believe in "freenology" and then tells Crotchett: "Go ahead. You needn't be afraid, you won't find no Free-Soilers in my head" (*MJC* pamp. 18.26-27). Thompson also emphasized Major Jones' masculinity in the printed texts by deleting lines in which the Major remembers romping in the fields with Mary "after wild flowers to put in her butiful hair" (*MJC* 2Ms. 3.29).

At one point Thompson was somewhat careless in revising for print. It is clear in the two holographs that he wanted to portray Crotchett as a bigamist. The holographs contain lines which reveal that he has a wife and five children in New York and possibly another family in New Jersey, but the printed versions have no reference to a New Jersey family. Crotchett is given only one family, in New York. Yet Major Jones, in the final scene of the printed text of the play, seeing Dr. Peter Jones disguised in women's clothes, remarks that he must be one of Crotchett's wives come after him. Later in the scene the Major says to Dr. Jones, "I thought you was Crotchett's first wife come after him" (*MJC* pamp. 59.2-3). These lines are not clear within the context of the printed versions of the play, since there is no mention of a New Jersey family. The manuscripts, however, clarify the obscurity.

The text of *Major Jones' Courtship; or Adventures of a Christmas Eve* which Purse published in *The Friend of the Family* is basically the same text which he published in pamphlet format. But there are a number of minor differences, particularly in punctuation, spelling, and capitalization. The second printed text, for instance, is more heavily punctuated than the first. And Thompson seems to have made other more substantial revisions in preparing the play for pamphlet publication. He increased the dialect characteristics of Major Jones' and Mrs. Stallings' speech. Such words as *clear, politeness, there, vagabonds, sure,* and *metropolitans* were changed to *clare, perliteness, thar, vagabones, shore,* and *Mettypolitans.* He also made Crotchett's speech more affected by inserting additional *w*'s for *r*'s in such words as *Doctor, country,* and *phrenology,* which became *Doctaw, countwy,* and *phwenology.* Such affectations were present in *The Friend of the Family* text, but were increased in the pamphlet.

A few of the differences involve even greater revision. For example, in the first printed text the Major greets Mary by saying, "I hope you're very well, Miss Mary" (*MJC FOF* 23 March 1850, 1.5.89-90). In the second printed text, he simply says, "Howdy, Miss Mary" (*MJC* pamp. 16.29). At another point, Thompson perhaps changed a line to make it less open to improper interpretation. When Mary gives the Major a doll baby as a Christmas present, he responds in the periodical installment, "How I would love to have the care of her dear little babies" (*MJC FOF* 13 April 1850, 1.5.77-78). In the pamphlet, however, the Major's words become "How I would love her dear little babies" (*MJC* pamp. 51.8-9). Standards of the time necessitated another revision between manuscript and printed text. When Dr. Peter Jones, disguised as a woman, rushes into the arms of Crotchett, thinking that he is meeting Mary, he exclaims (in the pamphlet version), "Mr. Crotchett, your conduct is d —— d rascally, sir" (*MJC* pamp. 54.19-20). *Damned* is also given this way in the periodical (*MJC FOF* 20 April 1850, 2.1. 82-83), but it is written in completely in the two manuscripts and was evidently intended to be spoken on stage (*MJC* 1Ms. 40.1-2; *MJC* 2Ms. 38.17-18).

At the conclusion of the complete manuscript of the play the names "Caroline," "Major," "Mary," "Mrs. Stallings," and "Kesiah" appear just above the final words "Curtain Drops" (*MJS* 2Ms. 44.5). These names are written in a semicircular line with "RH" and "LH" ("Right Hand" and "Left Hand") above either end, from the stage point of view, as if the actors portraying these characters were to stand in this order facing the audience as the curtain drops. This arrangement does not appear at the conclusion of the printed versions.

There is no further evidence now available to reveal why the two manuscript copies of the play were prepared. They were apparently intended either as prompt copies or stage copies rather than as printer's copies. Both manuscripts were probably written earlier than the printed versions: if Thompson had revised the play after publication of *The Friend of the Family* and pamphlet versions, he would likely have made his revisions on printed copy. In the complete manuscript, nevertheless, there are a few marked-out lines which appear in the final printed text of the play. Thompson either restored these lines as he revised the second holograph in preparing another manuscript, now lost, for printer's copy; or he already possessed such a manuscript, written at an earlier time, which he submitted to the printer instead of the second holograph which survives. At any rate, the second holograph was evidently not the copy from which Purse published the play in *The Friend of the Family* and the pamphlet edition. The fragment (or first holograph), which was undoubtedly complete at one time, is apparently an earlier draft than the complete manuscript, for the reasons already given. It resembles the complete manuscript more than it does the printed texts and could not, therefore, have been used as printer's copy.

The two manuscripts and the printed texts reveal that Thompson revised the play rather extensively. It was not written so hastily as one might think from Thompson's remarks in his note in the pamphlet edition. The manuscripts show that Thompson had some skill in preparing a play for the stage. The play was written to be performed rather than simply to be read, and its long record of performances over a period of many years demonstrates that it did entertain audiences.

## III

The book *Major Jones's Courtship* lends itself to dramatization as many other works of antebellum Southern humor do not. The best-known volumes in this genre are often simply collections of sketches, with some unity in subject matter and character but no single narrative shaped and sustained throughout. Thompson's book, by contrast, develops a continuous story with the same central characters over a considerable period of time. This continuity results in part from the letter form in which the material appeared in the *Southern Miscellany*. Although Thompson claimed that originally he had no plot or plan for the letters,[71] he no doubt soon realized that a gradually unfolding narrative centered around a courtship and marriage would increase sales of the paper. Such a serialized story would also permit him to include many different humorous episodes.

When he dramatized the book, however, Thompson saw that he could not use all, or even most, of these episodes. The play had to be more compressed. Accordingly, he selected events from only the first fifteen letters of *Major Jones's Courtship*. The first edition of the book published in 1843 would have served his purpose, since it contains the complete courtship of Major Jones and Mary Stallings in sixteen letters. Thompson had by 1847 written all the letters that the book was ever to contain; Carey and Hart of Philadelphia published the full complement of twenty-eight in that year.[72] He could, therefore, have drawn events for the play from all of the letters, but he preferred not to carry the action beyond Mary's acceptance of the Major's proposal. The fifteenth letter of the book contains the game "Brother Bob," which is included in altered form in the play. The sixteenth letter is the Major's narrative of the wedding, but the play ends with the Major and Mary about to be married on Christmas Day.

The book and the play differ in many respects. Thompson completely rearranged and changed most of the book's events. He deleted many of the episodes contained in the first fifteen letters and added some new material. Events such as the Major's

71. Letter by Thompson probably to Salem Dutcher, [16 October 1866]. Transcript in Miller's notes.
72. Miller, p. 162.

trips to Macon and Madison were not used in the play, nor were the militia muster, the incident where the Major falls into the creek trying to skin the cat, the coon hunt, the candy pulling, and the account of the earthquake, along with Mrs. Stallings' reaction to it. Thompson made the rivalry between Crotchett and the Major for the hand of Mary Stallings the chief source of conflict, but in the book the rivalry is only one of many events. He added the scene in which Crotchett tries to mesmerize the Major, a trick rendezvous between Dr. Jones and Crotchett, and a scene depicting the capture of Crotchett by Bill Simpson.

Many of the small details and descriptive passages in the letters could not be included, since Thompson had to make the action compact. As a result, the play is not nearly so valuable a record of the customs and culture of Middle Georgia during the 1840s as is the book.[73]

The demands of genre produced a more significant change. Since Thompson could not retain the Major as narrator on stage he lost one of the most effective aspects of the book. In the play, he had to omit most of the Major's wry commentary and homespun wisdom. Many of the Major's rustic figures of speech and mispronunciations, which give the book much of its humor, could not be retained. Major Jones is supposedly the author of the play, but even so, Thompson could not present the action from the Major's point of view. The letter format provided more occasions for humor arising from striking figures of speech and inaccurate orthography.

The dialect speech, though reduced and less vivacious than in the book, is still one of the most interesting features of the play. The Major's figures of speech, mispronunciations, and malapropisms save the play from being a dull comedy of farcical situations and threadbare stage devices. The Major pronounces *impudence* as *imperence, going* as *gwine, insolence* as *insurance,*

---

73. For an account of how accurately the book *Major Jones's Court-ship* mirrors antebellum Georgia life, see: Laura Doster Holbrook, "Georgia Scenes and Life in the Works of William Tappan Thompson." M.A. thesis, University of Georgia, 1967.

*earth* as *airth, vagabonds* as *vagabones,* and *by-and-by* as *bimeby.*
As in the book, he mistakes the names of the subjects which
Mary studies at the Female College in Macon as the names of
rival suitors. He uses rustic figures of speech when he expresses
fear of a rejection of his proposal: "I've been kicked by a mule
afore now, and got over it; but if Mary Stallings was to kick me,
all the Sands' Sarsaparilly in Georgia would'nt save my life"
(*MJC* pamp. 6.13-17). He also pronounces a bit of homespun
philosophy: "We're all a runnin after the butterfly of happiness,
and jest as like as not the very moment we think we've got it by
the legs, we pitch head over heels into the mud-puddle of disap-
pintment" (*MJC* pamp. 30.12-16). "The gig's up, and my cake
are dough" (*MJC* pamp. 30.18-19) is his way of saying that he
fumbled his attempt to propose to Mary by putting the fire out
with tobacco juice. The language of the play has its bright spots,
but overall it is less pungent than the language of the book.
Thompson was more at home in the prose epistle written in
dialect than he was in dramatic dialogue.

The play suffers in comparison with the book, but it demonstrates some skill of organization for staging. Thompson incorporated material into the drama to make it more appealing
as a theatrical piece. He constructed the play around a few farcical scenes such as the Major's putting out the fire by spitting
on it, the games of "Brother Bob" and Introduction to Court,"
and the Major's giving himself in a bag as a Christmas
present to Mary. Thompson also decided to include a dance on
stage, even though in the book there is no dance. Another innovation is the trick rendenzvous between Dr. Peter Jones and Crotchett. Mary deceives the two dandies into thinking that she will
elope with them and arranges for them to meet and embrace
one another before discovering the ruse. Thompson also saw
that it would be effective on stage for the Major to obtain a
clear victory over his rival by realizing that Crotchett is the run-
away barber for whom a reward is offered.

In the play, Bill Simpson, the constable for Pineville, ap-
prehends Crotchett, but in the book Crotchett is not taken

prisoner. He simply leaves town when notice of the reward for him is posted, and the Major then learns his true identity.

In the complete manuscript Thompson called the play a farce. It was designed to entertain by humorous situations, and by the countrified dialect of the Major and Mrs. Stallings and the dandified speech of Crotchett and Dr. Jones. Undoubtedly, though, part of the entertainment value of the play for many of the playgoers must have come from their recognition of scenes and characters already familiar from the book.

Overall the play is less significant than the book as a literary work or a social and cultural record of antebellum Georgia life. It is noteworthy not so much for its content as for its format. As a play it is unique, one of the few humorously realistic dialect plays by a writer of the Old South. It may in fact be the only drama which depicts rural middle-class life in Georgia before the Civil War. That Thompson wrote it attests to his versatility as a writer. The play at one time possessed some merit as a light piece of entertainment, and it is still interesting because of its relation to *Major Jones's Courtship* and because of its value, in itself, as an artifact of our Southern cultural heritage.

# Porter's Edition of
# *Instructions to Young Sportsmen*

*by*

## LELAND H. COX, JR.

> It is one thing to speak of things plausibly, another to state them correctly.
> Peter Hawker, *Instructions to Young Sportsmen*

> A man fully possessed of his subject and confident of his cause, may always write with vigor and effect, if he can get over the temptation of writing finely, and really confine himself to the strong and clear exposition of the matter he has to bring forward.
> William Porter, quoted from Brinley's *Life of William T. Porter*

In 1846 the Philadelphia firm of Lea and Blanchard published the American edition of Peter Hawker's *Instructions to Young Sportsmen*. The title page of the volume transcribes as follows:

INSTRUCTIONS | TO | YOUNG SPORTSMEN, | IN ALL THAT RELATES TO | GUNS AND SHOOTING. | BY | LIEUT. COL. P. HAWKER. | FIRST AMERICAN, FROM

THE NINTH LONDON EDITION. |T O W H I C H I S A D D E D T H E | HUNTING AND SHOOTING OF NORTH AMERICA, | WITH | DESCRIPTIONS OF THE ANIMALS AND BIRDS. | CAREFULLY COLLATED FROM AUTHENTIC SOURCES. | BY WM. T. PORTER, ESQ., | EDITOR OF THE NEW YORK "SPIRIT OF THE TIMES," ETC., ETC., ETC. | WITH ILLUSTRATIONS. | [rule] | PHILADELPHIA: | LEA AND BLANCHARD. | 1846.

The front matter of the book includes a frontispiece (a copper-cut engraving of the wild turkey – donated by Audubon[1]), Hawker's dedications to Prince Albert and King William the Fourth, Porter's dedication to Col. Wade Hampton, Jr., and Hawker's preface to the English edition.

The complex and comprehensive nature of the American edition, and the various needs it was designed to fulfill, make it one of the most ambitious and successful efforts of Porter's editorial career. Of course, by 1846 William T. Porter had already established himself as the editor of America's leading sporting periodical, the *Spirit of the Times*; and his editing of two collections of humorous material – *The Big Bear of Arkansas* (1845) and *A Quarter Race in Kentucky* (1846) – had brought him further acclaim. Even today, twentieth-century commentators on Porter's career tend to emphasize his energetic promotion of a lively, humorous, and realistic vein of writing in American literature during the ante-bellum period.[2] But such

---

1.  The cost account books of Lea and Blanchard credit Audubon with the donation of the wild turkey engraving (see Figure 1). The entry also shows that Porter was paid $250.00 for his editorial labors, and that the total production cost was $1,129.23. For an initial printing of 1,500 copies, for which it seems 2,000 bindings were prepared, the cost per volume was rated at $1.04. A later entry in the cost account books (see Figure 2) indicates that a second printing, numbering 750 copies, was issued in 1853. (I wish to thank Mr. John F. Spahr of the firm of Lea and Febiger for making these records available to me.)

2.  This is the basic assumption behind Norris Yates' study, *William*

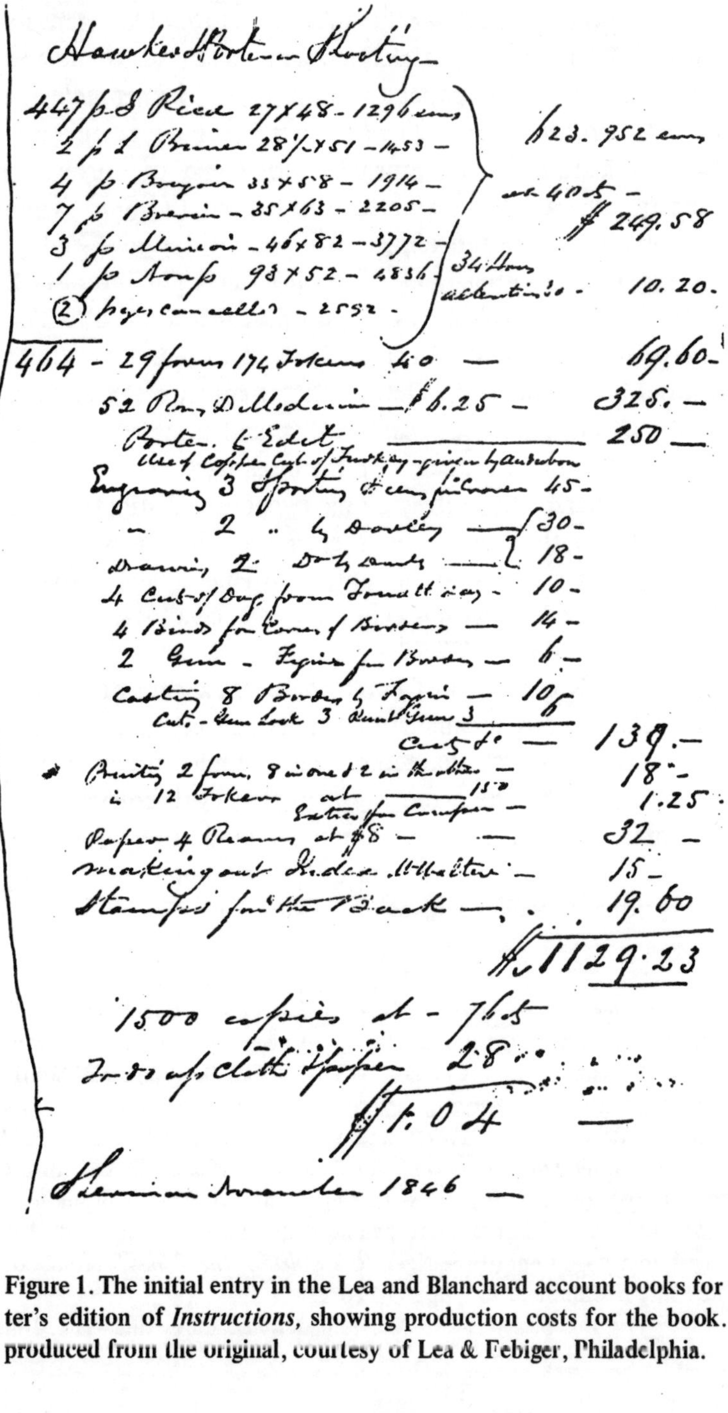

Figure 1. The initial entry in the Lea and Blanchard account books for Porter's edition of *Instructions,* showing production costs for the book. Reproduced from the original, courtesy of Lea & Febiger, Philadelphia.

plaudits, though well deserved, often obscure the full range and depth of Porter's editorial labors. The masthead of the *Spirit*, which proclaimed the paper to be, in part, "*A Chronicle of the Turf, Agriculture,* [and] *Field Sports,*" should be taken as a literal indication of the journal's scope and of Porter's own interests. One of the major factors behind the *Spirit's* popularity was its technical dealings with the world of men and dogs, of guns 'and shooting, and these are the chief interests that Porter sought to exploit in his edition of *Instructions to Young Sportsmen*. The intent of this essay is to examine in detail the editorial intentions and practices that went into the making of the American edition of *Instructions*, and to assess the significance of the final product. For the most part, Porter's editorial policies disperse themselves along two fairly distinct lines, the technical and the literary, in such a way that he was able to blend elements of entertainment, amusement, and instruction into a unified whole with maximum audience appeal.

In his editing of *The Big Bear* and *A Quarter Race*, Porter had stated his intention of exploring a "new vein of literature, as original as it is inexhaustible in its source," and of dealing with "extraordinary characters" and "their strange language and habitudes."[3] The claim is apt in that both collections deal with material that is truly American in nature. The general thrust of each is in the direction of native humor with realistic descriptions of scenes and events. Considering its close proxim-

*Trotter Porter and the Spirit of the Times: A Study in the Big Bear School of Humor* (Baton Rouge: Louisiana State University Press, 1957). Articles, such as Eugene Current Garcia's " 'York's Tall Son' and His Southern Correspondents," *American Quarterly*, 7 (1955), 371-384, reveal a similar emphasis. References to Porter and the *Spirit* in Jay B. Hubbell's *The South in American Literature: 1607-1900* (Durham: Duke University Press, 1954), pp. 659-60, stress the importance of Porter's promotion of humorous writing. For a more balanced discussion see Richard Hauck, "The Literary Content of the New York *Spirit of the Times*," unpub. diss., University of Illinois, 1965, pp. 69-110.

3. *The Big Bear of Arkansas* (Philadelphia: Carey and Hart, 1845), pp. vii-viii.

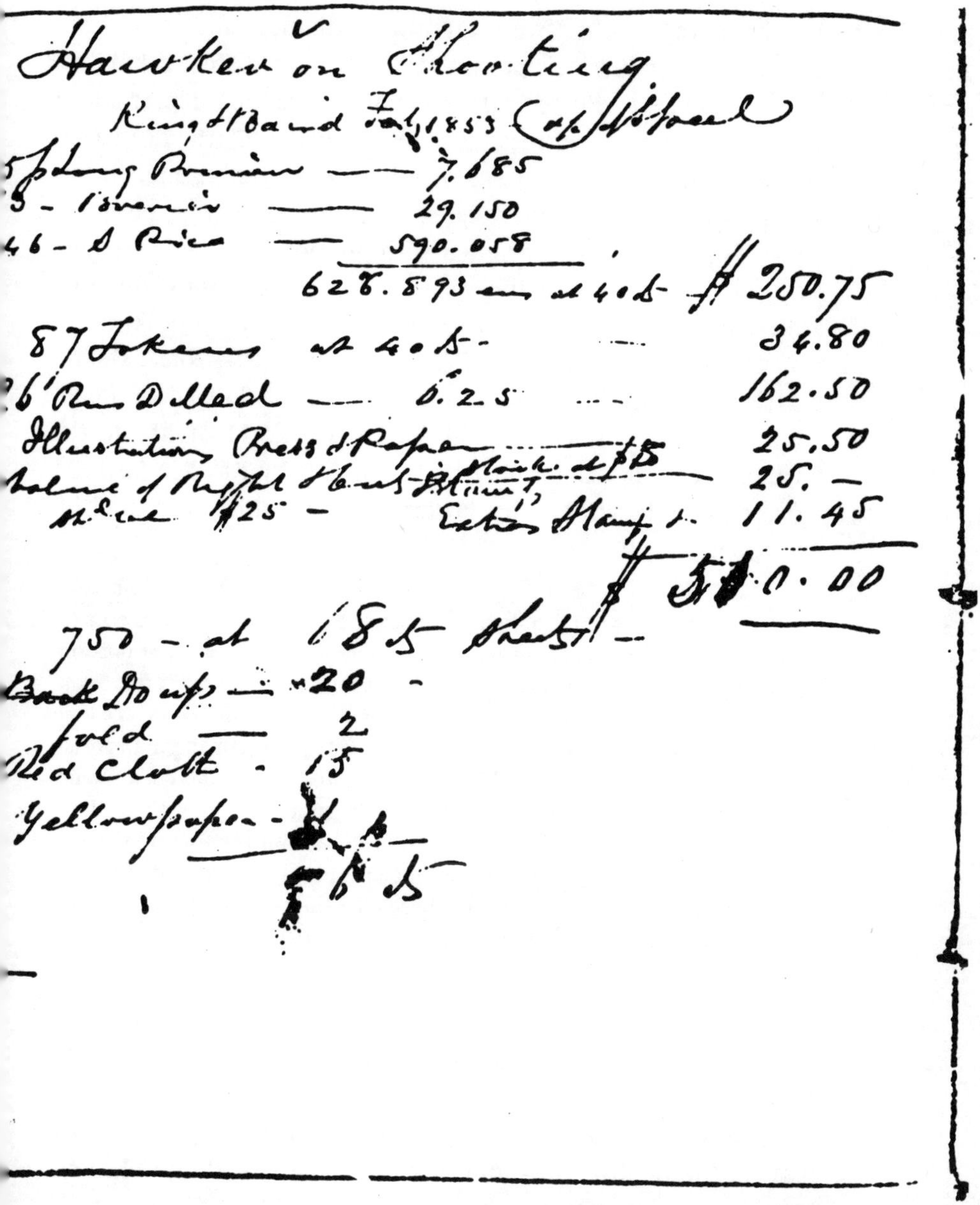
Hawker on Shooting
Knight & Band Feb/1853
5 ... Premium — 7.685
3 - Bourgeois — 29.150
46 - S Pica — 590.058
628.893 ems at 40 cts — $250.75
87 Tokens at 40 cts — 34.80
26 Rms ... 6.25 — 162.50
Illustration Press & Paper — 25.50
Balance of ... — 25. —
McC... $25 — Extra Stamp ... 11.45
$510.00
750 — at 18 cts Sheets —
Book Doing ups — 20 -
fold — 2
Red Cloth - 15
Yellow paper - ...
... cts

Figure 2. The entry in the Lea and Blanchard account books for the 1853 reprinting of *Instructions*. Reproduced from the original, courtesy of Lea & Febiger, Philadelphia.

ity in time to the two humorous volumes, the American edition of *Instructions* appears to be a totally different kind of book. However, Porter's *Instructions* does not represent a departure from the editorial principles which underlie both *The Big Bear* and *A Quarter Race* so much as it signifies a return to the roots of Porter's interests — the world of manly, outdoor sport. Porter was still concerned with promoting the importance of realistic writing and the worth of native materials. But the American edition of *Instructions* was for him a far more serious undertaking than either *The Big Bear* or *A Quarter Race*. Deliberately, I think, Porter selected a work that belonged as much to the realm of science as it did to the world of literature. Evidence for this claim may be found in a "puff" for *Instructions* (probably written by Porter himself) which appeared in the *Spirit*:

> Here is a book, a hand book, or rather a text book — one that contains the whole routine of the science. It is the Primer, the Lexicon, and the Homer. Every thing is here, from the minutest portion of a gun lock, to a dead buffalo. The sportsman who reads this book understandingly, may pass an examination. He will know the science, and may give advice to others. Every sportsman, and sportsmen are plentiful, should own this book. It should be a "vade mecum." He should be examined on its contents, and estimated by his abilities to answer. We have not been without treatises on the art, but hitherto they have not descended into all the minutae of equipments and qualifications to proceed to the completion. This work supplies deficiencies, and completes the sportsman's library.[4]

Porter never applied such high terms of professional praise to *The Big Bear* or *A Quarter Race*. In fact, the general tone of Porter's editorial approach to *Instructions* clearly indicates its eminence in his mind.

More evidence of Porter's high regard for *Instructions* may be found by comparing some elements of the publishing history of *Instructions* to that of *The Big Bear* and *A Quarter Race*. In a letter dated 18 January 1845, Porter

4.   *Spirit*, 16 (19 December 1846), 516.

wrote to the Philadelphia publishing firm of Carey and Hart in response to their praise of a story by Thomas Kirkman entitled "Jones's Fight," which had been published in a recent issue of the *Spirit*. Porter writes that "'Jones's fight,' though a capital thing, is not comparable with another story . . . by the same writer. There is material for half a dozen volumes of the size of 'Maj. Jones's Courtship,' and I make no doubt the volume *you propose* will be immediately succeeded by others of a similar character."[5] The letter suggests that the original idea for *The Big Bear* probably came from Carey and Hart.[6] Further, the reference to "half a dozen volumes" seems almost prophetic, for in 1846 Carey and Hart began publishing their Library of Humorous American Works. *A Quarter Race* was the fifth volume of the series, and *The Big Bear* was reprinted in 1847 as volume ten. These books, like the others in the series, were bound in cheap paper wrappers and were obviously designed to yield the greatest possible profit at the least possible expense. These data are important with relation to Porter's own methods in preparing his edition of *Instructions*.

In the first place, the idea behind the American edition of *Instructions* was Porter's own, not a publisher's. The editor therefore had to consider carefully who he was going to take his proposal to. Carey and Hart? They would hardly be deemed likely candidates, especially in view of the need for absolute printing accuracy in the kind of volume that Porter had in mind. If Porter were going to take responsibility for "the minutest portion of a gun lock" or for the exact amount of powder to be used in a given load, he was also going to make certain that the information he was supplying was correct. The alternative of finding himself in very low esteem with a large number of unhappy (and perhaps disfigured) sportsmen would not have appealed to him. So instead he went to another Philadelphia firm − Lea and Blanchard − which had extensive experience in the

5.   The letter is quoted in Yates, *William Trotter Porter*, p. 45.
6.   This point is also made by Yates. See p. 45 of *William Trotter Porter*.

publication of technical and scientific works,[7] as is indicated by this statement from his "puff" for *Instructions*:

> All praise is due to the publishers, for the very handsome manner in which they have brought out the work. It may now claim a place at the side of the *sportsman's* souvenir, as the grey hound takes up his rest with the lap dog, and the true sportsman will feel the compliment which the clear type, white paper, beautiful engravings, and richly bedighted covers, pay to his gentle craft.[8]

This is singular praise, quite unlike any compliment ever accorded by Porter to Carey and Hart. It should also be noted that the editor is not simply praising the cosmetic appearance of his book. Rather he is indicating that the physical makeup of the volume is itself warranted by the quality of its contents.

In addition to Porter's own statements about *Instructions*,

7.  There is a rather complex relationship between the firm of Lea and Blanchard and the firm of Carey and Hart. The history of Lea and Blanchard can actually be traced back to the old Philadelphia firm of Henry Carey. The partnership of H.C. Carey and I. Lea was formed on 1 January 1822 as the result of the marriage between Isaac Lea and Frances Anne Carey (Henry Carey's sister) in 1822. Within five years he had become a full partner and the name of the firm was changed once more — this time to Carey, Lea & Carey. Edward remained with the firm until 1829 when, on 1 November, he entered into partnership with Abraham Hart. This union represents the birth of Carey and Hart, the firm that was to publish *The Big Bear* and *A Quarter Race*, and which was to originate the Library of Humorous American Works. In 1838 Henry Carey sold his interests in the firm of Carey & Lea to Isaac Lea and William A. Blanchard, who had been with the firm since 1812. On 1 October 1838, the firm started publishing its books under the rubric of Lea and Blanchard. See David Kaser, *Messrs. Carey & Lea of Philadelphia: A Study in the History of the Book Trade* (Philadelphia: University of Pennsylvania Press, 1957), pp. 21, 35, 41, 47-48, 63. It should also be noted that Isaac Lea was himself a prominent naturalist (he was one of the earliest members of the Academy of Natural Sciences), and while associated with Henry Carey, one of his chief duties was that of ruling on scientific works that were submitted to the firm. See Newton Pratt Scudder, *Bibliographies of American Naturalists: The Published Writings of Isaac Lea, LL.D.* (Washington: Government Printing Office, 1885), II, viii.

8.  *Spirit*, 16 (19 December 1846), 516.

THE WILD TURKEY.

Figure 3. The frontispiece to Porter's edition of *Instructions* – an engraving of the wild turkey by Audubon.

one may gather further information about the volume by considering its conceptual relationship to *The Big Bear* and *A Quarter Race*. Scarcely a year's time separates the publication of all three volumes, and so it is difficult to know just when the idea for an American edition of *Instructions* began taking shape in Porter's mind. Viewed purely from the standpoint of chronology, it would appear that the non-fictional work was roughly contemporaneous with *A Quarter Race*. This does not mean, however, that the courses from conception to birth for the two volumes were parallel in any sense. In fact, the available evidence casts *A Quarter Race* more in the role of an editorial stumbling block. Some useful information on this point can be gained by touching briefly upon a misconception over the relationship between *The Big Bear* and *A Quarter Race*. Norris Yates (ignoring altogether the American edition of *Instructions*) argues that even though "*A Quarter Race in Kentucky* was probably issued in the last days of 1846 . . . it obviously grew in Porter's mind and in the external world almost simultaneously with *The Big Bear of Arkansas.*"[9] Whatever the surface logic of this argument might be, it is not supported by the available evidence; for Porter, in his March 1845 review of *The Big Bear*, makes it quite clear that his mind was occupied with another, more ambitious plan. After giving an initial description of *The Big Bear* as "a volume of humorous sketches," Porter goes on to state that " 'One of these days,' we intend giving the world, in a handsome volume, a taste of the quality of our correspondents of American *Sporting* Topics, in which we expect to beat 'Nimrod, on Sporting,' fairly out of sight!"[10] Obviously, the idea for an American edition of *Instructions*, or something very much like it, had planted itself in Porter's mind by March of 1845 and was germinating at a rapid rate. To what extent the idea for *Instructions* antedates the March review of *The Big Bear* cannot be determined. In this context, however, Porter's letter of 18 January to Carey and Hart (quoted above) indicates that the

9. Yates, *William Trotter Porter*, p. 49.
10. *Spirit*, 16 (19 December 1846), 516.

# INSTRUCTIONS

TO

# YOUNG SPORTSMEN,

IN ALL THAT RELATES TO

# GUNS AND SHOOTING.

BY

## LIEUT. COL. P. HAWKER.

FIRST AMERICAN, FROM THE NINTH LONDON EDITION.

TO WHICH IS ADDED THE

## HUNTING AND SHOOTING OF NORTH AMERICA,

WITH

## DESCRIPTIONS OF THE ANIMALS AND BIRDS.

CAREFULLY COLLATED FROM AUTHENTIC SOURCES.

By WM. T. PORTER, Esq.,

EDITOR OF THE NEW YORK "SPIRIT OF THE TIMES," ETC., ETC., ETC.

WITH ILLUSTRATIONS.

--------------

PHILADELPHIA:

## LEA AND BLANCHARD.

1846.

Figure 4. The title page of the 1846 first impression of *Instructions*.

idea for a volume dealing with American sport might have taken root in Porter's mind some time during the late days of 1844 or early in 1845. *The Big Bear* and *A Quarter Race*, then, considered strictly in a conceptual framework, impeded (perhaps for financial reasons) the realization of Porter's vision.

There is a fine irony in the fact that Porter, attempting to produce a book that would not only rival but beat Nimrod, should go to an English book and an English author for his ammunition. It is, moreover, an irony which Porter was surely aware of, and one that he played to the hilt. As early as 1839, writing in his capacity as editor of the *American Turf Register,* Porter had boasted the superiority of America as the most fruitful field for sporting literature:

> In the purely literary magazines the English beat us a long way. In England, which for more than a century has boasted the most respectable Sporting Magazines, the Great Race meetings are necessarily monotonous. To give spirit and the interest of adventure to their sketches, the greater number of sporting writers lay the scenes of their articles in foreign lands. British India and our own country are most often selected; and it is rare that you open either of the Sporting Magazines without finding a bear, a buffalo, or a panther hunt in the United States. It is to the exhaustless supply of material of this nature . . . [that] is to be attributed the greater freshness and raciness of American sketches.[11]

Such a statement in no way invalidates Hawker's authority or his abilities as a sportsman. Instead, what Porter seems to have been aiming at was the transmuting of an English book into an American one, a task made easier for him by the universality of Hawker's *Instructions*. It is, in fact, the high professional quality of the English book that Porter emphasized in his dedication to the American edition:

> The high character of the book, its great reputation, both in this country and in England, and the number of editions through

11. Quoted from Francis Brinley, *Life of William T. Porter* (New York: D. Appleton and Company, 1860), p. 69. According to Brinley this quote appeared in the April 1841 issue of the *American Turf Register*; however, I have been unable to locate it there.

which it has passed, having attracted the attention of the American publishers, they confided to my care the task of adapting it to the wants of the American sporting world.[12]

Here, concisely phrased, is Porter's broad statement of purpose. Stressing the essential "Americanness" of the work, Porter next explains that he has deleted all material that applies only to English sporting matters. This cutting, however, does not make for a skimpy volume:

> The space thus obtained I have filled up with a series of articles upon THE HUNTING AND SHOOTING OF NORTH AMERICA, from the pens of our most practical and scientific sportsmen . . . . [*Instructions*] is the first [volume], of a purely sporting character, ever published in the United States; and should it be deemed worthy of those for whose instruction and amusement I have compiled it, I shall feel amply repaid for the labour expended upon it. (pp. vii-viii)

Again Porter emphasizes the scientific nature and the ambitiousness of his book, identifying the work as primarily a source of information and instruction.

Before considering further the American edition of *Instructions*, we should first examine the book that Porter used for his base text and the author of that book as well. Lieutenant Colonel Peter Hawker was a professional hunter. A severe leg wound, suffered during the peninsular campaign against Napoleon, brought his career in the regular army to an early close. Consequently he dedicated himself in civilian life to guns and shooting – an activity which he chose not because it was easy for him, but because he was challenged by it. In this profession Hawker insisted upon and lived up to the highest of standards. A man who recognized the need for precision, whether in hunting, publishing, or in tuning a piano forte, he insisted upon accuracy in all things. For these and other reasons Hawker's *Instructions* provided Porter with the ideal source for an American sporting book. The volume itself was well known,

---

12. *Instructions to Young Sportsmen* (Philadelphia: Lea and Blanchard, 1846), p. vii. Subsequent references to this edition will be cited in the text.

and its accuracy was sworn to on both sides of the Atlantic. First published in 1814 by Longmans, Green, and Company, the English *Instructions* went through eleven editions in the nineteenth century — nine of them published during Hawker's lifetime. In 1893, forty years after Hawker's death, Sir Ralph Payne-Gallewey pointed out that the great "common sense with which [*Instructions*] was written" makes its "contents . . . just as useful to the present generation as they were to the last."[13] Hawker was also a talented writer. In this connection Eric Parker, editor of the single twentieth-century edition of *Instructions*, has noted:

> He was a writer of English as vigorous as his own heart and thews. His words go straight as his shot. He knows what he wants to say, and he says it, and whether he is writing of his shooting, his travels, his health [which was frequently bad], the weather, or the men whom he meets shooting, his language is as terse, as vivid, and as varied as you would expect a soldier and a naturalist to make it. He seldom repeats an epithet; he explodes like his guns.[14]

Porter would have seen in Hawker a highly attractive combination of the hunter, writer, and scientist. Yet still the problem remained as to how Porter was to convert the work into the kind of American field manual he had in mind — an objective which could not be achieved by simply reissuing an English book, no matter how eminent it might be.

Appropriately, Porter began by insuring that his book would be as accurate as possible. This was done by selecting the ninth revised English edition (1844) as his base text. Not only was this the most recent edition of *Instructions*, but it was also the last to be published during Hawker's lifetime. Thus it stands both as the author's final word on a subject he knew thoroughly, and as the last edition in which authorial revisions were made. As would be expected in what was essentially a technical manual, substantive revisions were made throughout its printing history

13. See *The Diary of Colonel Peter Hawker* (London: Longmans, Green and Co., 1839), I, v-vi.
14. *Instructions to Young Sportsmen* (London: Herbert Jenkins Limited, 1922), p. xiii.

whenever innovations (especially mechanical ones) changed the techniques of English sport. Hawker himself stated in his preface to the ninth edition that much of the information contained in earlier volumes "has . . . been in many parts materially altered and enlarged. The improvements here added have been the result of still further experience and therefore may be considered, in some degree, as finishing lessons to those young sportsmen, who have before done him the honour to attend to his earlier instructions."[15] Hawker then goes on to state that, aside from those areas in which no significant changes had occurred, "every thing, that can be improved, up to the present year, is introduced on a different, and, he trusts, a more perfect system."[16] In keeping with these objectives, Hawker's opening chapter, entitled "Guns and Gunmakers," reads much like a history of English gunlore in the nineteenth century. Hawker's discussion of proper armaments not only contains a lengthy disquisition on flint and percussion weapons, but also includes comments upon the evolution of military service weapons. The ninth English edition was further updated by the inclusion of a listing of London gunmakers for the year 1845.

Porter's editorial method in dealing with his base text was conservative. He deleted only those materials which dealt primarily with the English sporting scene. Though these excisions were sizeable, they did not alter the essential instructional nature of the book. Hawker's discussion of English game laws, originally added as an appendix to the sixth edition of 1830, was removed, along with various other chapters dealing with game listings, water craft, fowling methods, and angling. Almost all of the material having to do with guns and dogs, however, was retained. Next, in order to put the desired American stamp on his work, Porter added a collection of articles under the heading of "American Hunting and Shooting." This section was composed of thirty-eight separate articles and oc-

15.  Quoted from the preface to the ninth edition, reprinted in the American edition of 1846, p. x.

16.  Ibid.

cupied 275 pages of text – more than sufficient bulk to give the volume a distinct American flavor. The articles themselves provided information on a broad variety of game, both airborne and earthbound, and were dramatized in several instances by descriptions of specific hunts.

Like Hawker, William T. Porter was a man who knew exactly what he wanted to say. Porter's editorial methods in handling the section on American sport show clearly the various ways in which he was trying to shape that portion of his book. The initial chapter on "The Game of North America," by Frank Forrester (Henry William Herbert), is actually a collage taken from a series of articles first published in *The Democratic Review* and later reprinted in the *Spirit*. Porter used as printer's copy the first two articles of the *Spirit* series.[17] From the first he reproduced the nine initial paragraphs just as they had appeared in the *Spirit*, but the last two paragraphs were cut, probably because they were repetitive. Porter also exercised considerable editorial license in restructuring parts of Herbert's first article which, when it appeared in the *Spirit*, was composed of general introductory remarks, followed by a lengthy and detailed description of the woodcock. Porter took this single article and made it serve as the first two chapters (or articles) in the American section of *Instructions*. Then, in the second of these articles, Porter cut the length of the *Spirit* version drastically. There are also numerous changes in punctuation here, nearly all of which indicate editorial intent rather than slipshod work by the printers. The general effect is to make the article smoother and to quicken its pace.

After following the *Spirit* text fairly closely through the

17. See *Spirit*, 15 (14 February, 21 February 1846), 604-605, 612. The series of articles entitled "The Game of North America" first appeared in *The United States Magazine and Democratic Review*, 17 (December 1845), 461-66; 18 (January-April 1846), 17-23, 130-35, 187-92. The two pieces that appear in *Instructions* had been reprinted in the *Spirit*. Of course, the entire series ran well beyond the publication date of *Instructions*.

first three and most of the fourth paragraphs, this second article skips eight full paragraphs and picks up, quite smoothly, with Herbert's description of the woodcock's nesting habits in the northern sections of the country. Three more paragraphs continue the discussion and the remaining nineteen are abruptly cut. That is not the end of Porter's structuring of the second article, however, for he then turns to a continuation of Herbert's series, using the second number (see n. 17) for the remainder of his material. A few words (not Herbert's) are added here in order to effect an easy transition. The net result is that Porter makes Herbert look very good by taking two sprawling, directionless, and repetitive articles and working them into a single, concise, and thoroughly interesting essay on the habits of a popular game bird.

Porter's handling of the Herbert material is in no way indicative of a general editorial pattern. Rather, he seems to have approached each contribution individually, assessing the specific merits of each, and wielding the blue pencil only in the case of badly or "finely" written pieces, or where some adjustment was necessary to shape the American section of the book. In the case of articles written by Thomas Bangs Thorpe, for example, Porter, obviously recognizing the sound and forceful character of Thorpe's prose, did very little editing. The only variants to be found all involve minor punctuation changes.

Porter's handling of material by John James Audubon shows another interesting feature of his editorial policy – a sort of middle-of-the-road approach between Hawker and Thorpe. While Porter did not appreciably alter Audubon's writing, he did not hesitate to intermix the writings of other naturalists with it. Out of the total of nine articles attributed to Audubon in the table of contents, six are credited to Audubon alone; but according to Porter, the other three were co-authored with J.P. Giraud and H.D. Chapin.[18] There is no evidence to show that

18. Jacob Post Giraud was the author of *The Birds of Long Island* (New York: Wiley and Putnam, 1844). Very little information is to be had concerning Henry Dwight Chapin. It is fairly certain that he practiced law

Audubon ever entered into active collaboration with either of these men, and Porter does not say outright that Audubon did. The fact that their names appear together in the table of contents is therefore a source of potential confusion. This is merely surface confusion, however, easily resolved by a look at the original appearances of Audubon's ornithological essays. Of the nine essays with which Audubon's name is connected, eight were taken from the naturalist's *Ornithological Biography*.[19] In the three essays not credited to Audubon alone, Porter simply supplemented Audubon's writing with writing by the two other men. His reasons are not difficult to deduce. Many of the essays in the *Ornithological Biography* are highly scientific and hence not always useful to the sportsman. While Porter could delete these purely scientific portions, he could not, with any pretense of authority, substitute passages for continuity as he could for Herbert. Chapin and Giraud were therefore used, in effect, as stopgaps.

"The Rice Bird" is a good example of this practice. First of all, Porter cuts the first three paragraphs from the original text, and then emends the wording in order to smooth out some of the rough edges of the *Ornithological Biography* text. With the exception of a few more cut paragraphs and an added final paragraph, presumably by Giraud, the article is as Audu-

in Baltimore and New York and that he was living in New York during the period of 1845-1849, which means that it would have been possible for him to have known Porter. (This information is based on a private communication from the New York Historical Society dated 1 August 1972.)

19.   This was a five-volume work meant to provide an accompanying text for *The Birds of America*. The first volume was published by the Edinburgh firm of Adam Black in 1831. The remaining four volumes (1834, 1835, 1838, 1839) were published in Edinburgh by Charles and Adam Black. There were two American reprintings of the first volume: one by the American Philosophical Society (1831), the other by E.L. Carey and A. Hart (1835). The full title of the work is *Ornithological Biography, or an Account of the Habits of the Birds of the United States of America; Accompanied by Descriptions of the Objects Represented in the Work Entitled The Birds of America, and Interspersed with Delineations of American Scenery and Manners.*

bon wrote it. An essay entitled "Wild Geese" (Audubon and Giraud) quotes extensively from Audubon's work; and the last of the twin-authored articles is almost completely Audubon's. Porter simply adds a note at the conclusion, saying that Henry Chapin of Baltimore is responsible for the essay's concluding remarks on duck shooting.

These, then, are examples of some of Porter's specific editorial practices. But his broader application of editorial method is even more interesting because it shows just what he was trying to accomplish in the ordering of the separate essays on "American Hunting and Shooting."

One of the subtle ironies of the American section of *Instructions* is that Porter should have turned to Henry William Herbert, an English expatriate, in what amounts to the introduction for the American section of the book. In the opening essay Herbert writes:

> There is, perhaps, no country in the world which presents to the sportsman so long a catalogue of the choicest game, whether of fur, fin, or feather, as the United States of North America; there is none, probably, which counts more numerous or more ardent devotees; there is none, certainly, in which the widespread passion for the chase can be indulged under so few restrictions, and at so trifling an expense. (p. 181)

In addition to praising the quality of native American sport, Herbert gives high marks to American sporting writers. He observes that they have chosen " 'rather to depict scenes and incidents to the life, than to draw from those scenes a moral and a theory,' " with the result that their writing forms " 'perhaps the most original branch of our national literature' " (p. 183).

Of the thirty-eight essays which make up the section on "American Hunting and Shooting," thirteen deal with the hunting of birds, nineteen with quadrupeds, and six are more general in nature. Out of the thirteen articles on bird hunting, there are two each on the woodcock and the grouse, while the quail, snipe, rice bird, rail, plover, duck, wild goose, wild turkey, and curlew merit one apiece. Among four-legged game, the deer and the bear rate three articles each, the moose and the squirrel get two, and there are single essays on the wild cat, buffalo, wolf, 'possum, caraboo, panther, and elk. Of the more general essays, there are two on hunting dogs (the setter and the pointer), and three entitled "Hunting and Shooting in Canada West" (Sir J.E. Alexander); "Hunting in the Western Prairies" (H.H. Sibley); and "English and American Game" (Henry William Herbert).[20] A general subject index to the entire volume makes for easy reference.

Though the titles of the various articles indicate that they are addressed, for the most part, to specific subjects, they are in no way "compartmentalized." A few of the more important interconnections may be noted here. Herbert's strictures upon the wanton killing of game, and his insistence upon observing sensible conservation practices (not hunting game birds during the nesting season, for example) are echoed generally in most of the essays. Further, it is not unusual to find references to more than one kind of game in an individual article. Audubon's essay on the wild turkey also contains an incident of wolf hunting, and articles on the setter and the pointer are enlivened by accounts of actual bird hunts. Finally the different essays are perhaps most strongly interrelated through their combined, comprehensive nature. For example, the three articles on bear hunting, far from being redundant, describe hunts that are distinctively different, that take place in different parts of the country, and that involve different species of bears. Geographically, the essays are as American as they could possibly be. Every section of the country is covered — north, south, east, and west — including Canada as well as the United States.

Herbert's article on "English and American Game" provides an apt conclusion to the American section. The scene is set in the Hudson River Valley of New York, and the action concerns a visit made by an English sportsman to the home of

20. For comments by Herbert, who considered Sibley's contributions to *Instructions* to be the best of the entire volume, see Stephen Earl Meats, ed., "The Letters of Henry William Herbert," unpub. diss., University of South Carolina, 1972, p. 279.

a friend — also an Englishman, but one who has been living in America for some time. Throughout almost the entire narrative, the different nature of American sport is stressed. Commenting on his friend's dogs, the host claims that " 'Pointers are no use here . . . . English-broke pointers, I would say — they range too high, and cannot face our coverts' " (p. 442). Later the host becomes even more explicit, remarking to his guest that " 'You'll find game here one thing, and game in England quite another . . . and covert shooting here in these wild swamps and wooded hills a very different sort of matter from a Norfolk battu' " (p. 447). Finally, the physical difficulties of bird hunting in the region are so many as to make the sport an almost hopeless enterprise for the stranger:

> The unstable bottom, the fallen trunks, the mossy tussucks under foot, the tangled vines and thorny briers, woven in strange inextricable mazes about your knees and thighs, and even up to your breast and face, the dense impenetrable foliage over head, the impossibility of seeing your dog half the time, although he may be on a dead point ten feet from you — the necessity of firing nine shots out of ten, even when pointed, as if they were chance shots. . . all these things, and the farther fact that two at least of the winged game of these regions — the quail, namely, and the ruffed grouse — are the quickest and strongest on the wing, the hardest to hit at all, and the most difficult to stop, by hitting, of any birds that fly, — make the odds so very great that the best English shot will bungle it cruelly the first season; and if he shoot well on a second, I call him a right apt disciple. (pp. 448-49)

In his introductory essay Herbert had been speaking, in part, of the superiority of the American scene as the source for a lively sporting literature; here he centers on the thing in itself: the greater difficulties and more rewarding challenges that are presented to the American sportsman. Porter shows himself to be a very shrewd editor indeed. By framing his "American Hunting and Shooting" section with the essays by Herbert, he makes strong claims for both the American sporting writer and the American sportsman. And the intervening thirty-six articles, written for the most part by Americans and featuring almost every variety of popular field sport, support his claims that much more.

The structural organization of Porter's edition of *Instructions to Young Sportsmen* is a fair index to the nature of his achievement, for it is not just the content of the book that gives it its American character. The interrelationships among the sketches themselves, as well as the connections between them and the English portion of the book, give Porter's *Instructions* its particular distinction. In a sense, Porter uses Hawker's English section to set up his own American one. In the first 180 pages of the text, there is much general information to be had on guns and dogs, items of dress for the field, and methods and equipment used for hunting salt and freshwater wildfowl. All of this information, though useful, is primarily general. The reader must turn to the American section for descriptions and advice concerning specific game. And nowhere in Hawker will the reader find references to the hunting of the deer, bear, buffalo, panther, or any other four-legged animal. It is almost as though Porter were saying, "Here in Hawker we get an excellent notion of how one ought to prepare and conduct oneself in the field. But to get a proper idea of what real hunting is about, the true sportsman must look to this side of the Atlantic."

# Mark Twain Reads
# Longstreet's *Georgia Scenes*

*by*

## ALAN GRIBBEN

Mark Twain's indebtedness to ante-bellum Southern humorists is well accepted, but little can be established about his familiarity with specific stories. Origin, overlapping, and borrowing among tales are, in fact, virtually impossible to identify in this genre. Publications were generally issued in ephemeral format, and even the facilities of the best research libraries do not provide the comprehensive collections and adequate indexes necessary to recognize the true nature of the humorists' interchanges. Yet the work of such writers as A. B. Longstreet, George W. Harris, Joseph M. Field, William Tappan Thompson, Johnson J. Hooper, Joseph G. Baldwin, Thomas B. Thorpe, and Richard Malcolm Johnston was unquestionably present in Mark Twain's fund of memories. One may read the conjectures of Bernard DeVoto[1] and Walter Blair[2] with profit, but even these authorities remain cautious about assigning "influence." Blair simply concludes that "whether his indebtedness was specific in any particular instance or not, there is no denying that in many passages of his works the subject matter and the attitudes of Mark Twain are definitely in the tradition of Southwestern Humor" (*Native American Humor*, pp. 155-156).

1. *Mark Twain's America* (Boston: Little, Brown, and Co., 1932), pp. 252-257.
2. *Native American Humor, 1800-1900* (New York: American Publishing Co., 1937; San Francisco: Chandler Publishing Co., 1960), pp. 147-162.

The problem of gauging Mark Twain's knowledge of these humorists is further complicated by the lack of documentary materials. Many of the tales originally appeared in newspapers and magazines; even if Mark Twain read and remembered these pieces, he would not have retained perishable clippings. He might have acquired books that reprinted these sketches, but during his early adulthood Clemens' nomadic existence precluded his owning much of a personal library.[3] Consequently we have no books that record his interest in this influential group of authors during the first four decades of his life. But after Clemens and his wife moved into their new home in Hartford late in 1874, they had the income and leisure to stock their new library shelves; a large proportion of their extant books bear inscriptions dated 1875, 1876, and 1877. Among these is a copy of A. B. Longstreet's *Georgia Scenes.*

During the 1880's this Longstreet volume and others by Southern humorists figured in a program of systematic reading that surely had ramifications for Mark Twain's subsequent writings. The immediate purpose of his reading was the compilation of a large one-volume collection of sketches representing the foremost native humorists in American literary history. Under the arrangement agreed upon early in 1882, Mark Twain read selections submitted to him by Charles H. Clark and William Dean Howells. Though Mark Twain's notebooks register his industry on the project as early as 1880, the volume would not be issued until 1888, when it appeared as *Mark Twain's Library of Humor* without credit to the co-editors. In the early 1880's, however, Mark Twain read avidly in hopes of bringing out the book straightaway. "I am at work upon Bret Harte," he informed Howells on 23 March 1882, "but am not enjoying it. . . . The things which you and Clark have marked, are plenty good enough in their way, but to my jaundiced eye, they do seem to

---

3.   See my article, "The Formation of Samuel L. Clemens' Library," *Studies in American Humor*, 2 (January 1976), 171-182.

Figure 1. Illustration opposite p. 24 in Clemens' copy of *Georgia Scenes*. Clemens jotted an instruction to his printer at the top of the page. Henry W. and Albert A. Berg Collection. The New York Public Library, Astor, Lenox and Tilden Foundations.

be lamentably barren of humor."[4] Two Bret Harte volumes that he was reading are now in the Mark Twain Papers at Berkeley, replete with caustic marginalia which detail his reasons for rejecting Harte's stories.

Mark Twain intended to complete his share of the editing during his summer sojourn in Elmira; on 27 March 1882 he insisted to Howells that he could evaluate additional material while simultaneously writing the manuscript that would become *Life on the Mississippi*: "I think there is no reasonable doubt that I can read all summer without any inconvenience. I can read all the Saturdays and Sundays and also an hour each evening" (*MTHL*, p. 398). And though the anthology soon fell behind his optimistic schedule, Mark Twain's notebooks between 1880 and 1888 record his enthusiastic search for suitable material.

The volumes used for this editorial stint would likely contain clues to what Mark Twain valued in Southern humor — that is, if they survived. But apparently they did not. The very preference Mark Twain showed in choosing from their contents also doomed them as documents of literary history. At Mark Twain's behest, the printers of his anthology tore apart the volumes he selected and used the loose pages as typesetting copy. Originally Mark Twain also planned to employ engravings from these volumes as illustrations for his book; however, E. W. Kemble was commissioned to draw most of the pictures that ultimately decorated the text. Presumably this explains why no copies of George W. Harris' *Sut Lovingood. Yarns*, Johnson J. Hooper's *Adventures of Captain Simon Suggs*, Richard Malcolm Johnston's *Dukesborough Tales*, or William Tappan Thompson's *Major Jones's Courtship* are included in the auction lists of Mark Twain's library.[5] Selections from all of these books ap-

4. *Mark Twain-Howells Letters*, ed. Henry Nash Smith and William M. Gibson (Cambridge: Harvard University Press, 1960), p. 396; hereafter cited as *MTHL*.
5. "The Library and Manuscripts of Samuel L. Clemens," Anderson Auction Company, Catalogue No. 892. To be sold 7-8 February 1911.

peared in Mark Twain's anthology of American humor. Like his first copy of Malory's *Le Morte d'Arthur*, which he seems to have cannibalized for the convenience of his typist when he quoted from it extensively in *A Connecticut Yankee* (1889), these books apparently were mutilated and discarded. His copies of the Bret Harte volumes in the Mark Twain Papers at Berkeley only exist today because he found them insufficiently amusing (aside from the pages containing "A Jersey Centenarian," which he tore out of *Tales of the Argonauts, and Other Sketches*), and chose instead several pieces from Harte's other books.

One surviving exception to this policy of "perish to publish" illustrates the types of annotation that Mark Twain very likely made in the margins of the vanished books. The Henry W. and Albert A. Berg Collection in the New York Public Library contains Clemens' copy of *Georgia Scenes, Characters, Incidents, &c., in the First Half Century of the Republic. By a Native Georgian*, second edition, illustrated (New York: Harper & Brothers, 1845), a reimpression from the 1840 second-edition plates. Augustus Baldwin Longstreet (1790-1870) first published these collected sketches in 1835. The volume was listed in the catalog of books sold from Clemens' library in 1911.[6] The recto of its front free endpaper is signed "James W. Hunt"; below this signature Clemens added his own in pencil: "S. L. Clemens | Hartford, 1876." A 1911 auction label and the bookplate of W. T. H. Howe are on the inside front cover. A note dated 26 August 1938 to Howe from Isabel V. Lyon, Clemens' one-time secretary, authenticates Clemens' ownership of the volume; Lyon's note is laid in the book.

Clemens' marginalia mainly transform two passages into

(Items #1-500 are mostly books from Clemens' library.) An additional 310 books are listed in a catalog titled "Mark Twain Library Auction," 10 April 1951, Hollywood, California.

6. "Library and Manuscripts," item #298. This catalog quotes Clemens' marginalia, which I have corrected against the book in the Berg Collection.

and hip bones had not disclosed the fact, *he* never would have done it; for he was in all respects as cheerful and happy as if he commanded all the corn-cribs and fodder-stacks in Georgia. His height was about twelve hands; but as his shape partook somewhat of that of the giraffe, his haunches stood much lower. They were short, strait, peaked, and concave. Bullet's tail, however, made amends for all his defects. All that the artist could do to beautify it had been done; and all that horse could do to compliment the artist, Bullet did. His tail was nicked in superior style, and exhibited the line of beauty in so many directions, that it could not fail to hit the most fastidious taste in some of them. From the root it dropped into a graceful festoon; then rose in a handsome curve; then resumed its first direction; and then mounted suddenly upward like a cypress knee to a perpendicular of about two and a half inches. The whole had a careless and bewitching inclination to the right. Bullet obviously knew where his beauty lay, and took all occasions to display it to the best advantage. If a stick cracked, or if any one moved suddenly about him, or coughed, or hawked, or spoke a little louder than common, up went Bullet's tail like lightning; and if the *going up* did not please, the *coming down* must of necessity, for it was as different from the other movement as was its direction. The first was a bold and rapid flight upward, usually to an angle of forty-five degrees. In this position he kept his interesting appendage until he satisfied himself that nothing in particular was to be done; when he commenced dropping it by half inches, in second beats, then in triple time, then faster and shorter, and faster and shorter still, until it finally died away imperceptibly into its natural position. If I might compare sights to sounds, I should say its *settling* was more like the note of a locust than anything else in nature.

Either from native sprightliness of disposition, from uncontrollable activity, or from an unconquerable habit of removing flies by the stamping of the feet, Bullet

C

Figure 2. Page 25 of Clemens' copy of *Georgia Scenes*, on which he removed an indelicate expression. Henry W. and Albert A. Berg Collection, The New York Public Library, Astor, Lenox and Tilden Foundations.

printer's copy. He made blue ink marks on pages 9 and 11 of "Georgia Theatrics" and on pages 23 and 31 of the story titled "The Horse-Swap." In the same ink he also jotted a few instructions: concerning the illustration that depicts a youth's imaginary fight (opposite page 10) he wrote, "Reproduce & use this picture. SLC"; on pages 23 and 24 of "The Horse-Swap" he changed several italicized words to "Rom." (i.e., roman type) in the margins; near the illustration of a horseback rider opposite page 24 he directed, "Make fac-simile of this picture & use it. SLC"; and on page 25 he deleted the words "or hawked" in the sentence reading "If a stick cracked, or if any one moved suddenly about him, or coughed, or hawked, or spoke a little louder than common, up went Bullet's tail like lightning." Evidently Clemens felt that the latter emendation was necessary for a subscription book directed toward a family audience.

A notebook that Clemens kept during 1880 and 1881 confirms that he intended to employ portions of *Georgia Scenes* in his projected anthology of humor. The title of Longstreet's book appears in a list of humorists and their works which Mark Twain began in 1880.[7] Shortly thereafter he wrote the words "Hall (Georgia Scenes [)]" (Notebook 19, TS p. 6), alluding to one of the pseudonyms Longstreet assigned to his sketches in *Georgia Scenes*. The title page of Longstreet's book does not name the author, and Longstreet alternates between "Hall" and "Baldwin" in crediting most of his tales. In 1881 Mark Twain reminded himself of "Georgia Sketches" (Notebook 19, TS p. 68), more likely a reference to Longstreet's work than to Richard Malcolm Johnston's *Georgia Sketches* (1864), which Johnston republished in 1871 as *Dukesborough Tales*.

The two stories Mark Twain annotated in his copy of *Georgia Scenes* were both ascribed by Longstreet to "Hall." One of them, "Georgia Theatrics," is the first sketch in Longstreet's collection (pp. 9-11); it describes a ploughboy's pretended thrashing of an absent but detested opponent. Walter Blair has remarked on the similarities between this bloodless battle and Tom Sawyer's struggle with an imaginary foe in chapter 18 of *The Adventures of Tom Sawyer*.[8] The other tale, "The Horse-Swap" (pp. 23-31), relates how a boastful fellow nicknamed Yellow Blossom ("I'm a *leetle*, jist a *leetle*, of the best man at a horse-swap that ever trod shoe-leather") trades an ornery swayback called Bullet for the gentle sorrel, Kit, owned by a farmer named Peter Ketch. "I'm for short talk in a horse-swap," declares the seemingly gullible Ketch, so the inequitable exchange takes place hurriedly. Afterward the wily Blossom assures Ketch, "I'm for no rues and after-claps," and Ketch agrees: "I never goes to law to mend my bargains" (p. 29). In addition to Bullet's obvious flaws, Ketch soon discovers that the horse has a huge sore on his back — Blossom hid the infirmity under a blanket and saddle. The townspeople laugh at Ketch's disappointment, but moments later Blossom learns that he has acquired an animal both blind and deaf. "Come, Neddy, my son," Ketch says to his boy, "let's be moving; the stranger seems to be getting snappish" (p. 31).

Longstreet's stories are worthy of inclusion in Mark Twain's anthology, and Mark Twain's marginal notes signal his desire to use the illustrations as well; yet for some reason Longstreet's work was omitted from the final version of *Mark Twain's Library of Humor*. Possibly Charles L. Webster & Company, Mark Twain's publishing firm, encountered difficulties in copyright and royalty negotiations with Harper & Brothers, which had reprinted *Georgia Scenes* as recently as 1884. In fact, not a single author on the house list of Harper & Brothers is represented in *Mark Twain's Library of Humor*. Whatever the obstacle, it preserved for us the only volume of ante-bellum

---

8. *Native American Humor*, pp. 153, 287-289; also discussed in Blair's *Mark Twain & Huck Finn* (Berkeley and Los Angeles: University of California Press, 1960), p. 62.

Southern humor known to have belonged to Mark Twain. His reading program of humorous works during the 1880's — along with the probable destruction without replacement of nearly all his copies of works by these Southern humorists — should be taken into account by those studying the sources and traditions of Mark Twain's comic devices.

# Edited
# Source Materials

# T. B. Thorpe's
# Far West Letters

In the 26 August 1843 issue of the *Spirit of the Times*, William T. Porter printed the first of Thomas Bangs Thorpe's "Letters from the Far West." In succeeding issues, between 9 September 1843 and 16 March 1844, eleven more of these letters would appear, each one having been extracted from the corresponden-ce of the Concordia, Louisiana, *Intelligencer* – a newspaper edited by Thorpe – and each purporting to be an actual report by a correspondent traveling with Sir William Stewart's western expedition.[1]

Of course, the entire series of twelve letters that appear in the *Spirit* are nothing less than an elaborate and masterfully executed spoof. They are all based upon an actual series of let-ters and sketches written by Matthew C. Field, an erstwhile actor who did in fact travel as a correspondent with Sir William Drummond Stewart on his expedition from St. Louis, along the Oregon trail (which paralleled the Platte River for a consider-able distance), to the Wind River mountain range in what is to-

---

1. According to Milton Rickels, in the bibliography of his *Thomas Bangs Thorpe: Humorist of the Old Southwest* (Baton Rouge: Louisiana State University Press, 1962), "The 'Letters from the Far West,' [*sic*] originally appeared [in the *Intelligencer*] between the fall of 1843 and the spring of 1844. Among the extant copies are two of the letters, one in the issue for Nov. 25, 1843, and the other in the issue for Dec. 30, 1843" (pp. 266-67). There are in fact a total of nine of the original "Letters" (which probably did not number more than twelve) to be found in extant copies of the *Intelligencer*. In addition to the issues cited above, the issues for 12 August, 23 September, 30 September, 14 October, 4 November, and 16 December 1843, and the issue for 10 February 1844 each contain one of Thorpe's "Letters."

day the state of Wyoming.[2] The expedition was launched on 22 May 1843 and ended approximately five months later on the 24th of October.[3] While traveling with the expedition, Field sent at least eight letters back to the New Orleans *Picayune*; then, following his return to civilization, Field began publishing a series of sketches under the general heading of "Prairie and Mountain Life." From mid-November of 1843 until his death on 15 November 1844, some thirty-eight of these pieces appeared in the New Orleans *Picayune*, while seven others were published in the St. Louis *Reveille* – a newspaper founded by Field, his brother Joe, and Charles Keemle in 1844 just a few months prior to the author's death.[4]

In his own sequence of letters Thorpe scored a number of nicely conceived "hits" on Field. When in his *Spirit* letter of 26 August 1843 he speaks of Field "walking like a robber on a theatrical stage," he is obviously referring to Field's association with the theatrical company managed by his father-in-law, Noah Ludlow. A further comparison between sporting travel and melodramatic stage productions is made in the letter for 9 September, where Thorpe writes that the Indian Tar-pot-wan-ja, in his dramatic posturings, is reminiscent of "Forrest the actor, in Metamora." The actor referred to is Edwin Forrest, who gained wide notoriety for his role as the Indian chief in the play.[5] However, Thorpe's own parody of Field's corpus of journalistic material was directed, I think, not so much at Field himself but rather at the particular journalistic genre represented by Field's writings. Thorpe was especially interested in exploding some of the romantic notions in the travel literature of the day, especially the idea that "travel" and "sport" (in the sense of "fun")

2.    These writings have been collected in *Prairie and Mountain Sketches by Matthew C. Field*, comp. Clyde and Mae Reed Porter, ed. Kate L. Gregg and John Francis McDermott (Norman: University of Oklahoma Press, 1957).

3.    Ibid., pp. xxx, xxxiv-xxxv.

4.    Ibid., pp. xxxix-xl, xli.

5.    Noah Ludlow, *Dramatic Life as I Found It* (New York: Benjamin Blom, 1966), p. 486.

were almost synonymous terms. And, though Field's mode of expression was sometimes sentimental (as when he described a number of the men on the expedition as "men to sigh over a love song and meet the red savage knife to knife"[6]) and at other times too unrestrained (as in the following: "Once more upon the prairie, yet once more! Once more a wanderer over that great ocean of grass that for long ages yet must remain a gigantic wonder of the mighty West"[7]), these weaknesses were by no means typical of his individual style. Indeed, it was even suggested that Thorpe's "Letters" were so generally believable that Porter himself was taken in by their supposed authenticity.[8] At any rate it appears that no one enjoyed the joke more than Field himself who, when he learned of Thorpe's parody, wrote a piece for the *Picayune* under the title of "The Concordia Intelligencer Man." In fine humor, Field begins by describing this individual:

> The greatest genius we had among us was a poor little fellow with an awful face. He looked like an animated embodiment, in semi-human form, of a thick fog on the Mississippi, at half-past three in the morning, to a man who had just lost his last dollar at poker. He claimed to be Irish, but we all suspected he was a Dutchman. He was about four feet in height, with a head like the decapitated upper part of a brass andiron, and he wore a hat that might have belonged once to Walter Scott; this he made tight upon his little odd-looking

6. New Orleans *Daily Picayune*, 30 May 1843. See *Prairie and Mountain Sketches*, p. 8.

7. *Daily Picayune*, 15 November 1843. See *Prairie and Mountain Sketches*, p. 8.

8. This particular charge, quoted from the *Planter's Banner* of Franklin, Louisiana, appeared in the 6 January 1844 issue of the *Spirit of the Times*, p. 534. There the statement was made that "Thorpe of the 'Concordia Intelligencer' has been running a great saw, and it has taken amazingly. Some time after Sir William Stuart left for the Rocky Mountains he commenced publishing a series of 'Sporting Letters from the Far West,' which purported to give an account of Sir William's party. Several papers commenced publishing him – the 'Spirit of the Times' among the rest – no doubt under the impression they were genuine." See also the 13 January 1844 issue of the *Spirit*, p. 546, for a further comment on the hoax.

caput by turning half of the rim inside, and stuffing into it, also, a number of old newspapers. His eyes, which he concealed however, in green goggles, were like two faded cherries, and his nose! .... if we remember rightly, when Hervio Nano was here in New Orleans his appearance in the *Gnome Fly* produced some such vague and gloomy impression upon us as this little crazy man's nose. He was decidedly brain-stricken but quite amiable and harmless in his madness. We could never ascertain whether his eye-brows were cut off or driven in; but no such universally considered necessary portion of the human face divine appeared upon his solemn frontpiece, and Crockett [the nickname given by Field to a member of Sir William's expedition named W. C. Kennett] declared they must have been scared away by the everlasting gaping upward of his cavernous nostrils. The sight of this nose produced dreadful notions of suicide in the mind, such as are awakened sometimes during long continuance of drizzly weather. "Old Cut-Nose," a Snake Chief, had a pipe, the bowl of which was made of the red clay common in the mountains, a face had been moulded upon it and the nose woefully disfigured in baking; it was an exact resemblance of this strange little being.[9]

Thus the man from the " 'Concordia Intelligencer' " is given the name of "Little Woeful," and he is known for the unbounded pity he feels for "everything in life that ever suffered pain."[10]

Thorpe was quick to pick up on Field's parry, and in his *Spirit* letter of 20 January 1844 he presented an extended dialogue between Little Woeful and Mat Field in which both characters are made to look ridiculous. Though Woeful is the principal narrator of this piece, it is signed — as are all of the sketches in the series — by a narrator who identifies himself only as "P.O.F.," a set of initials that Thorpe never bothered to explain.

The overall quality of the "Far West" sketches is very high indeed. At no point does Thorpe attempt merely to satirize the writings of Field. Though Field appears as a character in several

9.  *Daily Picayune*, 2 December 1843. The complete text of this sketch is reprinted as an appendix in *Prairie and Mountain Sketches*, pp. 220-24. It was reprinted by Thorpe himself in the 23 December 1843 issue of the *Intelligencer*.

10. See *Prairie and Mountain Sketches*, pp. 221-22.

of the sketches, it is the narrator, "P.O.F." himself, who endures most of the hardships of the expedition and who finds himself on the receiving end of most of the practical jokes. From the outset, Thorpe's target is general, not personal. On the subject of Indians, for example, he writes in the second of the *Spirit* letters that "We have had a great many savages with us one time and another, but most of them are more than half civilized, as they will get drunk and steal as quick as any white man I ever saw." As mentioned earlier, though, Thorpe's chief target was the notion of traveling for fun and sport. This theme is stated in most explicit terms in the last letter of the series. Suffering from numerous hornet stings, the narrator dreams

> that the learned members of the Royal Society, London, had issued a circular, offering a thousand pounds reward for a "perpetual motion," and a display of the most foolish thing in the world; and I dreamed that I gave to the society a journal of my adventures "Out West," and proved that I went out there for the purpose of "sport," and the society unanimously awarded to me the thousand pounds.

It is also to Thorpe's credit that while maintaining the flow of his satire, he accomplishes some very satisfying touches of individual characterization. "P.O.F." is himself a complex narrator, and Tar-pot-wan-ja should be regarded as one of the great characters (certainly the best Indian) in the field of antebellum Southern humor. The "Far West" letters themselves certainly represent Thorpe's most successful attempt at sustained comedy, and as a unified whole they rank on the same level as "The Big Bear of Arkansas" and "The Devil's Summer Retreat." It is only surprising that these twelve sketches have not been reprinted long before now.

The existence of Thorpe's "Letters" has been a matter of record for some time. They were first cited in Milton Rickels' "A Bibliography of the Writings of Thomas Bangs Thorpe," *American Literature*, 29 (May 1957), 174; and the listing reappears in Rickels' bibliography for his *Thomas Bangs Thorpe: Humorist of the Old Southwest*. The letters are discussed by John Francis McDermott in "T. B. Thorpe's Burlesque of Far

West Sporting Travel," *American Quarterly*, 10 (Summer 1958), 175-80. Rickels devotes one entire chapter to the letters in *Thomas Bangs Thorpe*, pp. 74-90; and McDermott makes a brief reference to them by way of introducing Matthew Field's piece on "The Concordia Intelligencer Man" (see n. 9 above).

Since the files of the *Concordia Intelligencer* in which three of the twelve "Letters" first appear do not survive, the *Spirit* versions must serve as copy-text in these instances. Specifically, these are the *Spirit* letters of 26 August, 9 September (the second letter only), and 23 September 1843. Inconsistencies, such as the spellings of "varmint" and "varment," "traveling" and "travelling," "inquire" and "enquire," have been left unchanged. Fourteen very minor emendations have been made: these involve, without exception, dropped letters and missing punctuation in the original texts.

LELAND H. COX, Jr.

[*Spirit of the Times,* 13 (26 August 1843), 303.]

### LETTERS FROM THE FAR WEST.

From the Correspondence of the Concordia (La.) Intelligencer. Crow Indians — Philology — Difficulties of Travelling — Yellow Stone — Anecdotes — Scotch Fiddle — A Fight — Crow Feet — False Alarm — Resume our journey.

I take advantage of a "half-breed," who is about leaving for "the settlements," to send you a line, a thing you neglected in packing up my stores, that you may know how we are all getting on. The chances out here for literary pursuits are rather bad, and for a desk I am obliged to use Sir Wm. Stuart's best pistol case, giving it a sort of *slant* by resting one end on the skull of a late buffalo bull, whom, I am told by one of the old trappers that compose the vanguard of our party, killed three Sioux Indians before he was killed himself. I must acknowledge that this rude writing desk inspires me with a hunting ardor, and makes me sweat all over to be in the chase. Speaking of the chase, it is expected that the "Crow Indians," who are thus named, from the fact that they *eat green corn*, and make a noise like the fish-hawk, will give us a chase, which is said to be very unpleasant: so you perceive the chase has its dark sides as well as its bright ones.

We have had a great many difficulties so far: the "dry season" being a constantly rainy one, and the warm weather, instead of setting in, set out, and left us freezing to death in the wrong time of the year. It is very unfortunate that the cold weather came on before we got our overcoats made; but we cannot get any cloth until we skin some *varmints*. I shall introduce technical terms as much as possible, as it has great effect in such descriptions I intend to give. Sir William Stuart thinks if we had not started on our trip until next year, the *calves* would have been twelve months older, and, consequently larger and more fit for game. I differed with him on the subject, but he said I was not hunter enough yet to know much about life on the frontiers. Our journey up the Yellow Stone was by water, but owing to the want of any water in the channel, we took it on foot, and left our boats at its mouth. This is a very beautiful stream, being composed, at this present writing, of sand bars, interspersed with gullies and overhung with small trees, which trees, considering the time they have had to grow, are remarkably backward. The name "Yellow Stone" is a corruption of the Indian title "Yaihoo Stunn," literally "the running water with green pebbles." I got this information from a trapper, who has resided several years above the Falls of St. Anthony, on the Upper Missouri.

I have a great deal of interesting matter, and many curious anecdotes to relate, two of which I will give here, and I would detail more, but I do not know whether this letter will ever reach you; if if don't, you will inform me the first opportunity. One night we were alarmed by a dreadful scuffle on the outside of the encampment: we all ran to see what was the matter, and found that one of the men and one of Sir William Stuart's servants had got to quarrelling; it seems that the difficulty rose from some remarks about a *Scotch fiddle*, which was in the possession of Sir William Stuart's servant; it would seem that "Scotch Fiddle" is a term that has more meanings than one, but I did not enquire what they were.

Mat Fields, as he is termed, is the *sowl* of the whole party: he has more anecdotes and drolleries than all the rest of the party besides. He says that Kendall, of the "Picayune," got a white horse on the prairies in Mexico 18 hands high, and that he was mistaken in Vermont, where he is now visiting, for an old Naraganset pacer; but I don't believe it, as he is a quiz. Mat is a practical joker, but got it rather hard a few nights ago. It was unpleasant weather, and we met around the camp-fire until late, telling stories. One of the hunters told a great many tales about cannibal Indians, particularly the "Black Feet;" he said they were the most savage fellows in the world, and would roast a fellow and devour him as quick as twenty-five hungry wolves would a buffalo. That night, about one hour before morning, Mat came into the encampment, with eyes staring out of his head, walking like a robber on a theatrical stage; he said nothing at first, but got out his pistols, which he stuck in his belt without loading, he then went and waked up Sir William Stuart and Mr. Audubon, and whispered in their ears: Stuart said "*hombog, mon*," and Audubon said, "There was no such a *bird* in a thousand miles." Mat insisted; we all got awake, an alarm was given, "*Black feet*" in the camp;" we rushed to our rifles and followed Mat. We shall never forget the laughter that followed. The "Black feet in the camp" turned out to be a nigger's, who had stuck them under and outside the tent in which he was sleeping. Mat said it was all a joke; however, we were all expecting that a fight would come off between us and the varlets (technical), but there was no such fun. We whipped the nigger, though, for airing his shins in such a public way. Order was restored, and we found the sun up, and prepared for our day's journey.

P. O. F.

P.S. The Sioux Indians, which I said was killed by the buffalo in the first part of my letter, should read, "three *Sioux Indian's dogs*."

[*Concordia Intelligencer*, 12 August 1843; *Spirit of the Times*, 13 (9 September 1843), 333.]

[CORRESPONDENCE OF THE INTELLIGENCER.]
LETTERS FROM THE FAR WEST.

*Prospect of sport; Frontier Temperence Society; a real wild Indian; his natural eloquence and its power; meeting with Buffaloes; their peculiar behavior; my first hunt; headwork; a joke of misfortunes.*

ABOVE THE YELLOW STONE, *June* 6, 1843.

In my last letter you could easily perceive that we were getting on the buffalo hunting grounds, in fact I thought for several days that I could hear the bulls bellowing in the night, but my companions told me it was only owing to my glowing imagination. The prospect of sport inspirited all of us, especially after the whiskey jug had been freely passed around, previous to the grand temperance society we shall form after we get out of liquor. We have had a great many savages with us one time and another, but most of them are more than half civilized, as they will get drunk and steal as quick as any white man I ever saw. Yesterday, however, we were blessed with the sight of a real wild chap, he came into the encampment looking like a corn-field scare-crow, dressed up in a coat of feathers; a man with us from Arkansas, said it would improve his appearance very much in his estimation if the feathers had been stuck on with a coat of tar; Audubon said he put him in mind of a sick Pelican, in the moulting season. This Indian was a brave looking fellow, though, he walked splendidly, evidently imitated Forrest the actor, in Metamora, or a parrot, I dont know which. He was short, thick set, and smelt strongly of rancid bear's oil, which he used as we do cologne; he is said to be the blackest Indian of his tribe; his name I learned, was Tar-pot-wan-ja, which means literally translated, *the tall white Crane*. I took to him naturally;

there was something that pleased me in his eye, and the grateful expression of his face, as I gave him a drink out of my canteen; I asked him if he ever had been in war, at the question he started back, placed himself in a most elegant attitude, a perfect representation of a corpulent Apollo, then tracing the sun's course with his finger through the heavens, he turned his face full towards me, uttered a gluttural "ugh!" took a plug of tobacco out of my hand, stuck it in the folds of his blanket, and quietly walked out of the tent, to attend to the sale of some venison at a dime a hind quarter; I never saw a more noble, and beautiful exhibition of savage life. Yesterday was an era in our history, the first of our seeing Buffalo, which are now skirting along the horizon as if we were in a great farm yard of fine cattle. Its a mighty great idea that a fellow owns as many of these monsters as he can catch, though the latter is more difficult than you would at first imagine. I was determined to be at last, first, as I was always before behind in every thing, so I mounted my horse unbeknown to my companions and sallied out, pretty soon I got near the reptiles, and oh! thunder and turf, such looking beasts as they were, no more like decently behaved cattle than I am like a flat-head. There they were, bless their souls, looking at me through their sweet little eyes, and seeming as willing to tuck me up with their fine little horns, as if I had been a bundle of prairie grass. Buffalo indeed, they all looked like Aesop's donkey in the lion skin, they were so shaggy in front the villains, and so slick and smooth behind. My horse at first did not seem to mind them, but all of a sudden he pricked up his ears; came to a stand still and snorted; as he did this, the buffaloes raised their elegant countenances, and stopped eating; the biggest ones sort of forming a half circle round me, and making obeisances by lowering their heads, and scraping their left fore feet in the ground. "Good manners to you," said I, taking off my hat, determined not to be out-done in politeness; as I did this, I thought I heard thunder; I just got a glimpse of some confused thing in a big dust, and here and there, a swab sticking in the air, that I now believe to be buffalo tails. My horse, all this time, was not idle; he took to his heels, started off, first splilling my gun, then my hat, bad luck to it, then me, and afterwards my saddle; I came to the ground under the impression I had been struck with lightening, but recovering myself I found that the top of my head had just come exactly on top of a buffalo skull, cracking it into three halves, and driving them into the ground. If you had seen me the next day, you would have thought I had painted myself in imitation of the savages; my face, particularly round my eyes, was of so many colors. It may be set down as a fact in natural history, that human heads are not generally as hard as a buffalo's. I gathered up my gun, hat and saddle, and walked towards the encampment. "Did you catch a buffalo bull," said one to me, as I presented myself, half dead with the fall, and the foot travel. "It was an Irish bull he was after," said Mat Field. "Out upon you, you unfeeling blackguard of a wit," said I, getting good humored in a minute. "It's Mat, is it, that cracks his wit, on my cracked head!" but I'll forgive him, hoping he may run his own against a live bull, that'll pay him for all his sins, bless his soul. Thus ended my first hunt, and as I shall go properly prepared to-morrow, I trust you will hear that I have done myself honor in bringing down as big a critter, as ever run over these big grass plots, called "prairies."

P.O.F.


P.S. – I am happy to say, as this letter did not go on the day I sealed it up, that I have had a fair view of the far-famed *one horned* buffalo, that has kept undisturbed possession of this country and has never yet been killed. He is known from the mouth of the Yellow Stone to the tributaries of the Columbia, as the "one horned buffalo of the prairies." I shall take great pains to learn all the anecdotes respecting him, particularly how he lost his duplicate horn. Sir William Stuart has put us all under "martial law," and some of the "young uns" make wry faces at it; but he is an old campaigner, and I think knows as much about the ways of this heathen world, as any one about here. So I sing "Scots wa ha," and go ahead.

[*Spirit of the Times*, 13 (9 September 1843), 333.]

## SIR WM. DRUMMOND STEWART'S HUNTING EXPEDITION IN THE FAR WEST.

[Correspondence of the Concordia (La.) Intelligencer.]

*Indian philosophy; start for another buffalo hunt; success; miraculous escape; troubles of frontier life; prophecy; a new bird; curiosities, etc*

ABOVE THE YELLOW STONE, June 16, 1843.

In my last I gave you an account of a fall from my horse, and the ornamental effect it had about my eyes. As an Indian's face is the color of a smoked copper kettle, you may hit them in the face, or run their skulls against a post, and you dont see any black eyes as a consequence; but with me, it was different. The only person that I saw when I started on my hunt, was Tar-pot-wan-ja's squaw, and she met me soon after I returned after the accident. Her curiosity was very much excited to know how I had painted my eyes in such beautiful colors, and she took it for granted I was imitating her ugly looking husband. Not content with mere looking, she insisted upon rubbing her fingers across the colors, and when she found them under the skin, she looked upon the whole matter as the effect of the "medicine man" who is of our party. She told her husband that my eyes resemble "bright shells, surrounded by rainbows." The Indian language is so figurative and beautiful, that I cannot resist the temptation of giving in full, their expressions whenever I hear them. As soon as I was able, I took advantage of the first hunting party which left our encampment, determined to redeem my lost reputation as a hunter, and distinguish myself, so as to put down some of my companions, who were continually crowing over me because they had killed buffalo. I mounted one of the baggage horses, that was said to understand his business, armed with two horse pistols, and decked out with a pair of old spanish spurs, of the same size as those worn by Mat. Field, though his are new, and of polished steel, and when he is lashing about in the sun, on his "mustang," you would think he had fire works tied on his heels; they are so beautiful.

We only rode a few miles before we came in sight of a drove of the curly pated varments, a few hasty orders were given, the party separated with a "whoop," and dashed off, I after them. My horse got within about two hundred yards of the animals, and in spite of my spurs, took the back track, and never again came within a quarter of a mile of them. From this awkward situation, I was relieved accidentally by Audubon himself, who came up with me on his return to camp, having found a rare bird, and wishing immediately to preserve it, so we exchanged horses; and now mounted on a regular "hunter," I felt as proud as any beggar on horseback ever did. Off I went like a streak — the rattling of my spurs seemed to alarm my steed, but when I stuck them in his flank, he seemed furious; it was only a few minutes before I was amongst a crowd of animals; who running and crowding together, striking their horns and snorting, made most dreadful noise. I might have been within a few feet of a fine bull, when I found that it was all I could do to keep my horse from running him down, and I could not get an opportunity to draw my pistols. In this situation I went a mile or two, and concluded *to quit*, when, to my astonishment, I discovered my horse was more willing to hunt than the others I had mounted were unwilling, and I expected very shortly not only to be between *the horns* of a dilemma, but to have both of them run into me. Another thing astonished me, my horse, who had everything his own way, finally succeeded in separating the object of his special pursuit from the herd, and off we went together on a private hunt, sure enough. How long we run, I don't know; when, horrible to relate, the big monster, with his tail stuck up in the air, and his tongue hanging down on the ground, came to a stand still, and so did my horse, but I did not; over I went on his neck, and would have next descended to the ground, had he not started forward to avoid a charge from the buffalo, that brought me way behind the crupper of the saddle. I rolled down the biggest hill of Ireland, "Old

Howth," but that was smooth riding, to bouncing about over a saddle, especially a Spanish one, that had a high goose-neck looking pommel that did dig into me awful. "Here is fun to travel, after three thousand miles," thought I to myself, beginning to say my prayers, for somehow the bull's horns seemed to be growing larger and sharper every minute, and I had all kinds of queer feelings that were caused by the draughts of cold air, I thought would soon circulate through my body. Pop, pop, said a pistol, and over I went on the ground with a force that made the contact with the skull mere imagination.

"Oh murther, murther!" I hollered; "killed with hard riding, and shot to death with a pistol."

"Oot o' the wa' mon, or ye'l git an Irish hist," sang out Sir William Stuart, and I opened my eyes and saw the wounded bull, gathering himself up to charge at me, he having been shot twice in the side. Before I could get out of the way, he made a dash – his horns struck about two inches from me, and he threw a complete somerset over my body, striking the earth with a force that made every thing shake again. This was considered the most miraculous escape ever known in the hunting grounds. The bull made no further efforts to make fight, but died off like a kitten.

It is a beautiful time I have of it, getting information for the "Intelligencer." Here I was surrounded by about twenty hunters, all grinning at me like so many hyenas, and all congratulating me on my good fortune. All I have got to say is, that horses on the prairie are the worst broke animals I ever saw, except the buffalo bulls, the varmints.

I got home that night, and slept, by sitting up, and nursing my poor body, that was more broken up than a whiskey jug, under a load of brick. This frontier life, ain't what it is cracked up to be, and a great many persons in Sir William's party *will say so when they get home.*

P.S. – The new bird Audubon caught, he has named the "Oxydendiaonicumtiorsurtimonium," that being the classical name, he says, for a poor little feathered creature no bigger than the end of your thumb. Besides, I have got some prairie grass in

my port-folio, and so has my horse in his, and they are both fatter for it. My next letter will be principally on scientific
subjects, and a particular account of the first scientific society
ever formed in this wild country.


[*Spirit of the Times*, 13 (23 September 1843), 356.]

## LETTERS FROM THE FAR WEST.

### CORRESPONDENCE OF THE CONCORDIA (LA.) INTELLIGENCER.

ABOVE THE YELLOW STONE, June 29, 1843.

*Face of the country; death of a buffalo; singular incidents in the*
*history of a dead buffalo; the manner of an Indian's death;*
*anecdotes; the best joke of the expedition.*

Two buffalo hunts I have detailed, in which I was engaged,
and both were very little to my notion — the first one having
been a hunt too little, and the second one being a hunt too
much. I have now a horse in training which is so gentle that I
am certain will permit me to have my own way, and that I shall
soon be able to write you something successful in which I was
engaged. The country in which we are at present travelling, is
one of the most extraordinary in the world, being decidely the
poorest, and yet producing the most. It is composed of broken
land, high clay bluffs, that wash into all kinds of fantastic
shapes, and look in the distance like old ruined Irish castles,
and small parcels of prairie. The River Missouri about here, runs
as fierce as a scared horse, tumbling about as if old Nick himself
was underneath it, rollicking it about, and leaving it no more
peace than a poor tenant has, that is in debt to a mean landlord's deputy agent. Here it is that the buffaloes try to swim
across the river, and get tripped up before they do it; in this
way hundreds meet with a watery grave, being thrown high and
dry on shore dead as hammers. It is a melancholy thing, to be

sure, to see the big varment on its back, as helpless as a chicken in the yolk, just insulted by every wolf and buzzard that chooses to stick their ill-looking bills into its side. Only a few days since a gigantic bull that had struggled across the river like a big saw-mill, but so fatigued that he could scarcely crawl, just managed to get up the bank of the river, about ten feet high, where he lay down regardless of my presence, and with an eye as peaceably disposed as a fawn's, just breathed his last quietly as a christian. In less than ten minutes, down wheeled a buzzard rattling about his ribs, with his beak and making a sound not unlike a brass drum. I moved a short distance off, when a couple of wolves pitched in, and tugged away at the animal's tongue. While watching these vultures, the body of the buffalo being almost poised on the edge of the bank, turned over, and rolled down hill — the wolves held on, and so did the buzzard. At first I thought the beast had been playing "possum," and had just laid down to make a *trap* of himself, but he was dead. I walked up to the carcass and found that both wolves had had a strong grip on the tongue, and as the body fell head first, and the wolves held on in the descent, the short horns of the buffalo were driven exactly through the wolves' backs, pinning them to the earth, and in their agony and fury, they got their heads together, and before they died, bit out each other's eyes, and nearly scalped themselves. The first turn over the bull made crushed the buzzard so flat between himself and the earth, that a gentle breeze blew his remains away as if they had been an old mourning scarf, tipped on one end with a red ribbon.

I mentioned these singular circumstances when I got "to camp," and it called forth from an old hunter the following incident connected with the death of Tarpot-wan-ja's brother. He and his brother were out hunting buffaloes with the usual Indian weapon, the arrow; they both were pursuing the same animal — Tarpot-wan-ja shot an arrow, and by some bad management of his horse, hit the buffalo in the head, just between the horns: the pain to the animal was so exquisite for the moment, that, though under headway, it raised its hind foot instantaneously to the wounded spot, caught the fetlock in its horns and rolled over on the ground like a ball – the same instant Tarpot's brother shot the animal through the heart, and he lay on the ground dead. The brothers went on and killed several buffaloes; on their return they stopped at the body of the one we have particularly alluded to, to take out its hump and marrow bones, when, to their astonishment, they found the hind leg of the animal still behind the animal's horns. Tarpot seized hold of the animal's head to unloose the hoof, just as his brother stooped to take hold of the tail, the movement of the head unloosed the leg, it flew back, striking Tarpot's brother on top of his shaved head, impressed the cloven hoof in his skull, driving his scalp-lock out of his mouth, and killed him instantly. Since that time, from the peculiarity of the Indian notion of vengeance, he is constantly killing buffaloes to avenge his brother's death. From these anecdotes of the terrible destructiveness of the animal, when dead, you can form some idea of their power while living. This story was told me by a chap who has acquired among the Indians the names of Ahn-ahn-ni-as, or "the teller of truth," so I believe it. When Mat Field heard it, he put this thumb to his nose and shook his fingers at Sir William who laughed heartily; they have already between them picked up many Indian signs which are not yet familiar to me. I will conclude this letter of anecdotes by saying that the scientific meeting did not come off, but will in due time. Audubon made a fine pun to-day, that pleased Sir William so much, that he treated all round with some choice "mountain dew," much to the great comfort of all of us. We were talking about buffaloes and their habits, particularly their fondness for water, in which they seem to live when near, when Audubon said that it had just struck him how the animal got its name, buf-fa-lo from the French "boeuf a l'eau." This decidedly the best joke, so far, of the expedition – so I think, except the idea of coming *out here for sport.*                              P.O.F.

P.S. The trouble of the Texans, and the Americans, and the Spaniards, relative to the Sante Fe Expedition, has roused up the Indians, who, not understanding the difference among white men, are apt to treat all alike, and for fear we may be taken for Spaniards, whom the Texans have advised to destroy, we sleep with our eyes open, and in our arms — that is the order of Sir William Stuart.

[*Concordia Intelligencer*, 23 September 1843; *Spirit of the Times*, 13 (14 October 1843), 392.]

*Correspondence of the Intelligencer.*

## LETTERS FROM THE FAR WEST.

### ABOVE THE YELLOW STONE, Aug.1, 1843.

*Difficulties of communication; Singular rocks; Audubon's remarks thereat; my own; Singular chase; Dilemma; Escape; Burial of a horse; Perils of Far West sport.*

The Post-office Department, in this heathen region, is very much neglected — the *runner* that will bring you this lettar, is so lame, that he will have to walk all the way. This tumbling over the prairies is a very flat piece of business, and a little diversity in the scenery was a great comfort to me. A few days since, the land became broken, and I determined to enjoy the novelty; I clambered up some queer looking rocks, and while thus seated, it slid off, and I rolled down about twenty feet into a sink hole. I scrambled out, when Audubon came along, and examining the rock carefully awhile, turned round to me and said, "these rocks are what a mineralogist would call a vertical dike of trap!" "They are that same," said I, "bad luck to their traps, and the dirty dikes at the bottom of them." "You are not afraid of bulls," said Audubon, laughing. "Bulls, indeed," said I, "is it the varments that must be continally pitched into my teeth, because I aint killed any." I was a little angry, and put off, determined to take the life of the first bull I met with, killed as I was with the sport of hunting them. An opportunity soon occurred; a night or two only passed when Tar-pot-wan-ja reported that buffaloes were in every direction round our camp; every one prepared himself for the morning hunt, and I among the number. Armed with great determination, and a good rifle, I thought I could not fail to do something; beside, I had at last got a good horse, one that had an eye like a fawn, and kept his ears and tail down, and would not budge if a buffalo gnat stung him in the nose. As was my custom, I avoided the hunting party, and went off by myself. I soon came up with the animals, and was very much surprised to find that while I was looking out for a big bull, a big bull was in my rear, looking out for me. Afraid he would begin the hunt, instead of myself, I gave a yell as much like an Indian as possible, and he turned on his heels, gave a fierce bellow, and started off with the herd. For a quarter of a mile, the run was beautiful, the prairies were covered with about two inches of water, and it made the animals in motion look like a mist, the water flew about so; on they went and I after them, until I was brought up short and immovable as if astride a log, by bogging down to my saddle girth in a swamp hole. The harder I thumped the beast, the more he stood still, and just went to eating the grass as quietly as if he was hoppled for the night. The morning was cold, and the fallen rain filled the air with mist, that blew over the prairies in scudding clouds, as the sun continued to rise. Here and there I could catch a glimpse of buffaloes on the edge of the horizon, and could sometimes see the horsemen dashing after them with a speed that seemed inconceivable, when I considered the situation of the horse I rode. About two hundred yards was the nearest point of hard land, and while contemplating what I should do, I was brought to a sudden resolution, by seeing approaching towards me the whole herd of buffaloes, presenting a front something like the inside of a half circle. My horse, alarmed, made a furious effort to extricate himself, turned over on his side, and me into the mire. I crawled out as a fly would from treakle, and made a push for the camp. The buffaloes, impelled on by the frightened, and pursued in the rear, were approaching me at a right angle with the direction I was running; it was a life matter entirely, and I just got beyond the extreme right of the wing, as it passed within twenty yards of me, clattering like a drunken hurricane. Confounded with my situation, the horrors of it was increased by the phenomenon, of what I thought to be the one horned buffalo, coming directly towards me, thus cutting off all chance of escape. Shutting up my eyes, I lay down, said my prayers, and determined to die like a man; a moment or two only elapsed, before I was roughly stirred up by what I supposed to be a buffaloe's horn, but it turned out to be the muzzle of Sir William Stewart's gun, just thrust into my ribs to see if I was dead. "A gude mornin' to you, mon," said he, calling up Mat Field to poke his fun at me. "And you are not the one horned buffalo after all," said I, opening my eyes and breathing more freely. "Not a bit of it," said Mat, handing me Sir William's flask. "There, *run one horn* into your own body, and commit suicide," he continued, like an angel, as he was; for the "Mountain dew;" had a very excellent effect on the prairie dew I had swallowed, I tell you. "I shall die between the jokes and St. Louis," said I to Sir William. "Pace to your sowl," said he, turning up the flask, but finding it empty, he finished his blessing with, "and purgatory to your bowels, you sponge." The buffalo in the mean time, had got nearly out of sight, and I observed, with consternation, that my horse had gone off with them. "Where did you leave him," cried several. I pointed in the direction, and we all started for the spot. Thunder and turf what did I see, the bog hole dry, and hollowed out like a bowl, at the bottom of which lay the *skin of my horse cut up into strips.* "Is that the burial that I would have got from the varments, if they had run over me? " said I, musing over the corpse. "The same," said every body. "Oh murther!" I exclaimed, "the idea of being killed and having nothing left of your body, but your coat and pantaloons!"                                    P.O.F.

P.S. — The necessity of sleeping in our arms has been removed, by the removing of the hostile Indians. We can now sleep in perfect peace, if the mosquitoes and gallinippers would not be continually eating us. This is a delightful country indeed, and if it was only situated somewhere nearer to a Christian land, would soon be filled up with decent people, like Tennessee, Kentucky, and other frontier States.

[*Concordia Intelligencer*, 30 September 1843; *Spirit of the Times*, 13 (21 October 1843), 405.]

Correspondence of the Intelligencer.

## LETTERS FROM THE FAR WEST.

ABOVE THE YELLOW STONE, Aug.17, 1843.

*Far West comforts; Indian names; Discovery of a strange animal, with a description, &c.; Yankee enterprise; Flat heads and curiosities.*

The last few days we have been traveling on what is known out here, as the "Kiln dried Forks," which are at this season of the year about three inches under water, much to our discomfort. Our party, however, has been enjoying itself very much; and I think, situated as we are, that we might *go farther and fare worse*, as I am informed that the whole country a few miles ahead, is entirely under water. The other night we sat out all night in the rain, as our baggage took the wrong fork, which is a greater mistake in the prairies, than taking the wrong tooth brush at a hotel. It would have done you good to see us enjoying ourselves out here, sitting Indian fashion, in a ring, soaked through, and smoking all over, like rotten straw stirred up in a cold morning. Sir William was terrible cross, particularly when the water gathered into small channels on his coon skip cap, and run off of his prominent nose in their course to the ground. Tarpot-wan-ja, who is like all aborigines, very expressive in his names, calls Sir William, from this peculiarity of face, "*Ah-gno-knoose*," and by this cognoman he is known for the distance of "six moon's" travel. We have had in our possession now three days, a very strange animal, and as *I never saw one like it* before, I conclude it is a new discovery, and one that will add immortality to my name. It is curious every way, and has created great excitement among the scientific gentlemen attached to the party. Audubon says it is decidedly the greatest *bird* he ever saw, and he has been drawing it off with a chord, ever since it has been with us; he has proposed several times to *kill it*, so that it might be preserved. He describes it as follows, on a paper handed to me to copy. *Characteristics — Brownish above, feet and all beneath white; ears, large; tail, hairy, and longer than its body*. Description — *Head, rather large, with pointed muzzle* — this last means they pointed a muzzle of a rifle at it, when it gave up, for fear of being brought down; *rounded above, and membranious*; can't say that I see any of these peculiarities about it. *Whiskers, numerous,* exactly to the original — as numerous whiskers as you would see on Count D'Orsay, or any other fop. *Fore feet, four toed*; right, of course — the four toes must be on the fore feet, *with five tubercles*, like the membranious beyond my comprehension. The *thumb is rudimentary* — what in the name of turf does that mean? *Tail, hairy and slender*, as much like it as two peas, *and subquadrate*, out of my depth again — *Molars tubuculated*. There is a description of the monster, and it looks quite a heathen and outlandish on paper, as it does on land, the varment. This critter affords us a great deal of amusement, as it frightened one of the horses after we first got it, so badly, that he came near throwing his rider and breaking his neck. This animal jumps by the means of its tail, and Mat Field says, will jump lower than he will higher, owing to his peculiar formation. To give you some idea of its agility, I need only to say that it, at one bound, cleared a pack of twenty-eight buffaloes, without touching them, and might have done better, if occasion required it. About two months ago some Yankee speculators passed us, on their way to Missouri, with twenty young buffaloes; they told us that they intended to show them off in the northern states, and that was the reason they only got *calves*, as they would meet with more sympathy in that part of the country. The owner of these animals were very much alarmed at the way Tar-pot-wan-ja looked at the fattest one; but kept on with his amusement of throwing a loop in a long bed-cord, over a tent pin; and I have heard that he intended to *laso* buffaloes in the States. The speculation is a good one; out here he could not laso a dead buffalo, if he was full grown. While we were at our last rendezvous, a party of strange Indians came into our camp, and exhibited some valuable gold and diamond trinkets, which, from their workmanship, were pronounced Spanish, and thought to have been lost by, or stolen from some rich Sante Fe trader. The Indians offered to exchange them for jack knives, which, from their ugly appearance, I thought they deserved. A bargain was soon made, and they marched off highly gratified, paying about fifteen hundred dollars for a few dimes' worth of knives. This strange conduct induced me to ask which tribe these Indians belonged to, when I was informed to the "Flat Head" tribe. Certainly they richly deserve the name, as the anecdote will show. I ought to mention that my cabinet of natural curiosities are daily increasing, and in spite of accidents continually occurring, I shall bring home with me some rare things. I have got a real Indian tomahawk, that has been much used, as its appearance indicates. The history of this weapon is singular, as it once belonged to an old hunter by the name of "Collins," who seems to have originally come from "Hartford, Ct.," as he has cut his name on the side. I also had a very fine "buffalo chip," which I had taken great care of, but having got my coat wet, it has injured it very much, and I shall have to look around for another specimen. In my next I shall have passed above the Yellow forks, and get into a more interesting country, which will be a great relief to me — the great fault of the Far West being, that there is too much of it.                                              P.O.F.


P.S. — I should have said that the strange animal jumped, at one bound, over a "pack of twenty-eight buffalo skins" — the meat having been taken out of them some time previous.

[*Concordia Intelligencer*, 14 October 1843; *Spirit of the Times*, 13 (4 November 1843), 421.]

*Correspondence of the Intelligencer.*

LETTERS FROM THE FAR WEST

ABOVE THE HEAD OF PLATTE, Aug.21, 1843.

*Interesting situation; Our appearance; Danger from the backwoods; Dresses; Singular appearance; Anecdotes; Reflections.*

It is an elegant way of living we have in this far west. Here is Sir William, as rich as a Santa Fe nabob, traveling about, talking Indian, and looking like Robinson Crusoe; and here is myself, back luck to my enterprise, out here too, dressed up in clothes made of skins, and looking like a scare-crow out of a corn-field. "It's sport we have," said Mat Field, with a big twine round his front tooth, trying to pull it out. "It's hu-wah-me-kas-haw," says Tar-pot-wan-ja, the villain, looking as comfortable as a setting hen. "It's all kind of scrapes that I am getting into continually," thought I, as I reflected on the elegant adventure of which I was the hero. You see it had rained some four weeks steadily, and my raw deer skin clothes, hair outside, were as loose and comfortable as an Ottomans. Six times since I wore them, have I been near being shot for an Elk, which makes my situation very pleasant indeed; but to the adventure. I was out on a hunting expedition, which took me a full days' journey from the camp, and was detained over night — sleeping on the ground in about two inches of water. In the morning I started for home, and to my great relief, the sun came out hot, and magnificent; if you could just have seen me traveling across the prairie, and drying slowly, and sending up steam like a locomotive. I ate dinner that day with great relish — the sun so inspired my appetite, and I indulged myself for the first time in some of Tar-pot-wan-ja's dishes, who was with me. It might have been three o'clock in the evening, when I felt a singular rush of blood to my head, a want of breath, and other unpleasant signs; presently my clothes seemed to grow *too small*, and kept tightening in an alarming manner. "How do people feel that are poisoned?" said I to Audubon. "Like a stuffed bird's skin," said he. "Then," said I, growing pale, "my mother's son will leave his bones among heathen." He enquired, with interest, what I ate for dinner, I told him some Indian dish; he rolled up his eyes with astonishment, and bid me hurry to the camp. I pushed on, all my alarming symptons increasing with violence, until it seemed as if my legs and my head would burst. When I got to the camp, I was so stiff I had to be lifted off my horse, and laid upon my back. A consultation was held within sight, but not in hearing, in which Tar-pot-wan-ja, pulling out a sharp knife, and shaking it at me, took a very active part. My feelings were indescribable. How I had offended the Red man, I could not imagine, for it was now evident he had poisoned me, and wished to finish the job, by cutting my throat. Not a soul pitied me, but looked upon the whole affair as a pleasant joke. "*Soak it out of him*," said Sir William finally; and to my horror, Tar-pot-wan-ja my enemy, and another Indian, took me up and laid me in a neighboring stream, just leaving my head out of the water. "They are all savages thought I," closing my eyes, and when I opened them the Indians were gone. "Is this the way to treat a sick man, pitch him into the river to die like a dog, for fear of a little trouble?" "Soak it out of him," indeed; its the breath they alluded to! Such were my thoughts, when, to my astonishment, I began to feel relieved — the blood seemed to leave my head, and limbs, and I began to have some power of locomotion — less than half an hour elapsed before I got up and walked as well as usual. I went to the camp, wet as I was, burning with vengeance; as I approached it, a general shout of laughter saluted me. "Oh you unchristian bastes that you are," said I, shaking my fist at the whole of them, "is it for you to leave a sick friend to die, you savages; but I've got well, and can whip the whole of ye." "*Not if you'r deer skin clothes dry up in the sun until you can't move*," said somebody, when the truth flashed upon me, that Tar-pot-wan-ja wished to cut me out of them, instead of out of my breath, and not "soak me out," as proposed by Sir William. My feelings altered at once, and I joined in the laugh; it only being one of those pleasant jokes peculiar to the *sport* of this part of the world. I find upon inquiry into accidents resulting from a precipitate use of deer skin clothing, that the most dreadful things have happened. An old hunter informed me that a whole party of white men, who were thus dressed, were caught by a sudden coming out of a hot sun, while eating their dinner; they were rendered helpless, before they were conscious of the reason, and sat staring at each other, with a buffalo steak in each hand, until they starved to death, their clothes not permitting them to move; and what made it more awful, after they were dead, damp weather came on — they melted down on the ground, and remained prostrate until the next sun shine — they then, as their skin clothing contracted by the heat, came up right again, in all imaginable positions, exhibiting one of the most melancholy spectacles that ever greeted the eye of humanity. The escape I made was miraculous indeed, for which I cannot be too thankful. And here, permit me to say one word, as I feel in a moral mood about the fitness of nature, the buffaloes it seems, from the inquiries I have made, are dressed in raw skins, as I was — hair outside — they are fond of water, and also fond of the sunshine. To avoid the fatal accidents that overtake the human species, they are provided over the shoulder with a *large hump*, containing nothing but fat. When indulging in the sun, this fat melts, runs over the skin, and keeps the water from penetrating the pores, so as to make the texture, when drying, susceptible to the sun's rays. Taking advantage of his beautiful law, I grease my clothes every morning with buffalo grease; and although they smell exceedingly rancid, and compel me to associate entirely with Tar-pot-wan-ja, still I had rather do this, than endanger my life, as I have already done.                                          P.O.F.

P.S. — The wild turkies of last year, were all killed by the rains, so that this season there are none to be met with; all sorts of game are very scarce. I bear up under my misfortunes, like a man, as I frequently hear the remark, I am *such game*.

[*Concordia Intelligencer*, 4 November 1843; *Spirit of the Times*, 13 (18 November 1843), 445.]

*Correspondence of the Concordia Intelligencer.*

LETTERS FROM THE FAR WEST.

ABOVE THE FORKS OF LAPLATTE, Sept.3, 1843.

*An encampment; sudden attack: its consequences; Far West dinner; Toasts, &c.; Storm; First trip in a canoe; Prospects.*

After the incident detailed in my last letter, relative to the danger of precipitately wearing deer skin clothing, our party traveled several days across the country, faring badly. We had little or nothing to eat or drink, our mules were fagged out, and it was determined that when we arrived at a convenient halting place, that we would rest for some days. Coming to the banks of a running stream, which were about ten feet high, it was thought a favorable location for an encampment, and in a few hours we were fixed in a manner perfectly agreeable. We made our tents by driving long poles into the banks, and resting them on forked sticks, then covering this frame with buffalo skins. About midnight of the second day, we were aroused by a whoop and a volley of shot and arrows — the balls did no damage — but the arrows, as they came sticking half way through the skins, looked rather frightful. Sir William rushed out, and gave the enemy a broadside in Scotch; they retreated a few paces, and talked back in Indian. A parley ensued, when it was discovered that a roving party of Kansas had mistaken our tents for those of their enemies — the Crow Feet — as this latter tribe are called "Prairie Dogs," because they lie in the side hills. The mistake was very natural, but as the party was small, and as some one observed only Indians, they were severly thrashed, to learn them better in future. The Indians were very submissive and seemed sorry for what they had done – the night following this adventure, we lost three horses, a chain, and a pistol; no doubt that is the way they took satisfaction for the injuries they received from us.

It is needless for me to say that our party was pretty sick of the Far West *sport*. Audubon had already packed up to return to the civilized haunts of mankind; we knew this from the fact that every thing was secured with lock and key that could be, to keep them from being stolen— a precaution generally unnecessary in savage life. Taking advantage of our resting-place we resolved upon having a good dinner, and perhaps the dishes may not be uninteresting to your readers. We had the breast of the wild turkey boiled as dry as a chip, which we used as bread; buffalo marrow for butter; bar ribs for pork; and prairie grouse christened chicken. To give the thing more the air of civilization, we all sat up bold, and in unnatural positions, and to make it still more "white folks fashion," we did not grease our faces in eating above our nose, and only used one hand when it was possible. Toasts were drank – one or two which I have preserved. By ------, *"The Far West – great country – like small pox, it need only be gone* through once to *answer every useful purpose"* – drank in silence. By ------, "Our sport out here – *like interesting Indians* – all in my eye," also in silence. By an old hunter, "The great diggins between the Yellow Stone and the mouth of the Columbia – *the only field* on which a smart white man can display his abilities." Great applause from Tarpot-wan-ja. By myself, "The Indian hunting grounds – like the Indians themselves, more interesting in ladies' books, than any where else" – three brays from one of the waggon mules. By Sir William, "Oot here, as much ahead of fiction as a sterling pound is worth more than a Scotch." Old Lang Syne, whistled by the party. By Tar-pot-wan-ja, – "Hoke-poke-humbug-ockenwocken-khantkumit ex sho," which literally translated means, "white man worth nothing after the whiskey is gone." The night following the dinner was exceedingly pleasant, until about midnight, when the wind rose and from a severe blow turned into a hurricane; for a while it passed over us, the bank of the stream keeping it off; but after a while it chopped round, and blew directly down the river — the rain also fell and put out our fires. The stream by which we were encamped, called by the Indians, "Shallahrille," from its great depth, rose rapidly; and lastly, to complete our difficulty, our tents blew over, our waggons were knocked down, our arms upset, sending the charge of two barrels of buck shot among us by exploding the caps. The morning dawned, and presented the worst looking set of fellows that ever appeared in these parts, and that is saying a great deal, when you reflect that the Indians live out here. After hunting about we found that we had saved most of our property, as nothing had floated off but a copper kettle and a box containing some old horse shoes, and a broken waggon tire. Sir William was anxious to obtain them, and commissioned Tar-pot-wan-ja and myself to take canoes and go after them.

To do any thing was a relief, so following the example of the Indian, I jumped into a canoe, took my seat in its bottom, and one stroke of my paddle sent me into the middle of the stream; the next instant I was balancing from side to side with a rapidity of motion that upset my stomach, and would have upset me had I not fallen into the bottom of the canoe. My gyrations afforded the spectators more amusement than it did me, and as I floated off they wished me a pleasant trip. I started up to reply, when I found to my horror that the least motion on my part destroyed the equilibrium of the canoe, and gave it a turn over motion truly alarming — in fact I had to keep my paddle perfectly erect like a mast, for fear it would tumble me over, and as I concluded I should be drowned I thought it was a *jury mast* erected over my remains. Down the stream I went, my feet close together, hardly daring to wink, when an eddy drew in my frail bark — it was a bark canoe — into a sort of bay, striking it against a log and turning me into the water as if I had been so much lead. I rose to the surface and snorted like a porpoise, seized hold of the tree, and flattered myself with the hope that I was born to be hung. A little reflection on my part and exertion got me safe ashore, and found myself about half a mile below where we had encamped, and on the opposite side of the stream. I walked back and found Tar-pot-wan-ja had already returned; with great difficulty I got across the stream nearly drowned, and a good deal sick, concluding I was the most unfortunate man of the party. After a days hard work, we got things together, and took a trail leading towards "the cross timbers," where, it is said, if the Blackfeet Indians are not in possession of them, and the wild turkies don't taste too strong of turpentine, living on pine burrs, we shall have some rest and enjoyment. P.O.F.

P.S. – It is possible Audubon may reach St. Louis before this letter reaches you; he is a great man, and one of the few white ones that ever made traveling in this part of the world advantageous to himself and his country.

[*Concordia Intelligencer*, 25 November 1843; *Spirit of the Times*, 13 (16 December 1843), 497.]

*Correspondence of the Concordia Intelligencer.*
LETTERS FROM THE FAR WEST.

ABOVE THE PLATTE, Sept.23, 1843.

*Hard traveling; significant sounds; novel ride; bear chase; bad fix; good shot; exciting sport; something new.*

The morning after the storm detailed in my last letter, we were proceeding slowly down the "Shallahrill," amusing ourselves with catching terrapins, a few which were to be seen, and for which as food, Sir William is passionately fond; when we most unexpectedly found ourselves in a soft, boggy soil, that gave way under our feet, and rendered our progress slow and painful. Here and there, were small clumps of stunted oak, and thick undergrowth, that seemed to spring up on the little ridges that presented themselves in this swampy land. About noon we halted at one of these little groves; clearing and cutting away a place sufficiently large for our use; we sat down and talked over the various adventures of the expedition, with such other associations as were called up. While thus pleasantly engaged, we heard a low whine, that altered finally into an immense yawn, that gave me an idea of the largest mouth I had ever conceived of; presently the mouth came to-gether — the teeth rattling most ominously as they met. The old hunters sprang instinctively for their rifles, and in a moment afterwards the ball of one sped its lightning way into the thicket — the sharp ringing sound was answered by a fierce growl, and a huge bear rushed passed us. Unfortunately I was directly in his course, and stooping down at the time, to see if I could discover any thing between the openings in the undergrowth, the bear, blinded with rage, he rushed between my legs, and carried me backwards some ten paces or more, when I fell off, and rolling down a steep bank, planted myself immovably in the mud — the bear kept down the edge of the ravine. The members of our party, as they pursued him — Tar-pot-wan-ja among the num-ber, hooting and yelling — were soon almost out of hearing, and I undertook to extricate myself from my unpleasant situation. It seems I had fallen into a puddle, made by the rain running down one of those narrow foot-paths, known as the track made by the buffalo and wild horses. The more, however, I exerted myself to get out, the more I got in, and at last I resigned my-self to fate, and the assistance of some of my friends. Presently I heard the shout of the hunters, and every instant it grew more and more distinct, and I was certain the bear had turned, and was coming towards me. Satisfied with having rode the animal, I was alarmed with the idea that if he should attempt to get on the high land, by running up the narrow foot-path, he might take the liberty of jumping *on me*. Dangers thickened — for, looking up, I just saw at the head of the foot-path, the hunting cap of Sir William, and the muzzle of his famous smooth-bore rifle called "Jeffries," that I knew was loaded with thirty buck shot, and *scattered like thunder*. Here was murther — buried alive to save the trouble of a funeral; but I had no time for reflection; the bear did come, and Tar-pot hallooing at his heels. He made a straight line for the foot-path, working his way through the mud like a turtle, his mouth open, it looking to me as large and fiery as a glass-house furnace. Sir William ran down the foot-path, and raised *Old Jeffries* to his eye and fired away. The shot, as they passed within a few inches of my head, made a noise like a flight of wild pigeons, but they caught the bear in the face and eyes, who, finding it all up with him, and seemingly determined to die game, rushed on me, seized hold of my deer-skin breeches, and shook them as clear of mud as if I had been laying on a feather bed; it need only be said, that to such attentions I was *insensible*. When I came to myself I was laid out on the grass, rather used up; but our party was in excellent *spirits*, a little of which being administered to me, I found I was more scared than hurt, and towards evening we were wending our way to the "Cross Timbers," so named, because when cut or blown down, they fall across one another.

My having rode the bear, which Tar-pot-wan-ja thinks was intentionally done, has raised me very much in his estimation, as there is a tradition in his family that his father jumped on a grizzly bear and never deserted him until he had given him a death stab behind his ear. We have a new-comer to our party — a sort of nondescript half breed, who has lived much of his life at Santa Fe, and a tremendous fellow with the lassoo; he calls himself *Don Desparato el Triumpho*, and to hear him rattle it off, with the guttural sound of the Indian and Spanish mixed, would put you in mind of an expert fellow, calling the roll on the head of a base drum. He is expert in frontier life, and "jerked" the bear that so awfully *jerked* me, which he most ingeniously did, by cutting of the whole of the meat from the bones in one strip, and fixing it on the bushes to dry, very much as you would a bed cord.                P.O.F.

P.S. — I send you with this, a very faithful drawing, taken from the inside of Tar-pot-wan-ja's buffalo robe, in commemoration of his bold attempt, to shoot a buffalo at the distance of *three miles*, a feat, except by him, never before attempted.

[*Concordia Intelligencer*, 16 December 1843; *Spirit of the Times*, 13 (27 January 1844), 569.]

LETTERS FROM THE WAR WEST.

[CORRESPONDENCE OF THE INTELLIGENCER.]

CROSS TIMBERS, October 2, 1843.

*Throwing the Laso; Unintelligible Jokes; Far West Fun; Singular Phenomenon; New way to catch Wild Game; Escape from Indians; Scientific failures; Prospects for immortality.*

In my last, I mentioned the addition to our party of the famous laso thrower, *Don Desparato*; as a catcher of wild horses, and even deer, he has no equal. The day following my ride on the bear, we halted on our way to the "Cross Timbers," upon a very beautiful hillock that, but for its extent, might have been taken for an Indian mound. Desperato, who was idle, and vain of his accomplishment, amused himself by throwing his laso over "Spanish quarters," which he did with great precision at thirty yards, and in that way won a pocket full of silver coin. Sir William proposed for amusement to turn one of his saddle horses loose on the plain, and that Desparato should, at full gallop catch the horse with the laso by the hind foot. The thing was encouraged, and was soon ready for execution. The Spaniard mounted his "Indian poney," that, from its small size, compared with the big saddle on his back, looked at a distance as if it was standing under a shed, and gave the word. I let go Sir William's horse, and hit him a severe lick to send him ahead; but the animal, instead of running off, turned round, and walked back to the baggage wagons. We were not to be thus disappointed, and at the suggestion of several, I mounted the horse myself, and putting whip to his flanks, dashed off, down the hillock, but circling round the base, so as to give all the party at the top, a fair chance to see the Spaniard catch the horse by the *hind foot*. On he came, shouting like a Pawnee, and making the diameter of my circle, of course he soon came up, threw the laso, and missed. A shout of derision followed this failure, and as my blood was up, I laughed myself, and went on the harder. Now my horse had the heels, and I bothered him tremendously; I could hear him muttering big words, that I knew was Spanish, for swearing. Presently he came near me again and threw his laso; I felt a slight tap on the head, heard a great shout and laughter, then my respiration stopped, and I realized a shock over my whole system, that felt as if I had been caught under a falling tree. Respiration returned, and on opening my eyes, there sat Desparato on his poney, I on the ground, the laso round my neck, and he holding on the opposite end of it, grinning at me like an enraged monkey.

"Halloo!" said I.

"Senor Necio!" he growled.

"Let me up," cried I, with alarm, seizing hold of the laso. Hereupon he gave it a jerk that tightened it up, and I concluded the dog intended hanging me — the motion, however, exposed a piece of tobacco that was in my pocket — so, getting down, he very quietly took the quid, released my neck, and mounted his horse, and rode towards the party on the hillock. I was so bruised by the fall from my horse, and so sore about the neck, that I could with difficulty get up the hill. "Haw, haw, haw," uttered all the party when I got among them.

"Villians!" gnashed I, through my teeth.

"Don't get mad, that was a *Spanish joke*," said somebody.

"And he don't understand the language well enough to enjoy the wit of it," said every body.

For the fifteenth time since I have been out here, I saw there was no use at being offended at merely being killed, if it was done in fun, so I joined in the laugh; but in my heart execrated Spanish jokes and lasos'.

As was anticipated by some of our old hunters, the "mast," which means the fruit of the forest trees, is very scarce, and we find ourselves, since our arrival here at the "Cross Timbers," nearly starved. Nothing is found in the woods but the Pine burr — the tree which bears it, flourishing here in its most magnificent grandeur. As we relied principally, upon the wild turky for food, and they having been compelled, from necessity, to eat these pine burrs for food for a long time, they become so impregnated with turpentine, that they caught fire whenever we attempted to roast them, and burnt up. I really believe we should have starved to death but for the ingenuity of an old fellow with us, who said he was originally from Bunkum, North Carolina. He took some dozen turkies, well cleaned, covered them with about six inches of dirt, and then built a large fire over the pile. In the course of the day, small streams of clear tar were seen running out of the heap, and when evening came, the turkies, shrunk up to the size of chickens, were taken from "the kiln," and eaten − tolerably fair food, but, as might be imagined, *very dry*.

This singular impregnation of wild game, with the article of food on which it exists, has been strangely overlooked by naturalists. I would in this connection, relate a singular escape made by a party of hunters connected with these "turpentine birds." It seems that while they were out hunting they were attacked by a large number of Soshonees, and surrounded. Protected by a small skirt of woods, they entrenched themselves for the night, expecting in the morning to have their scalps hung on long poles, and dried in the smoke like Dutch herring − an idea, by the way, that makes my head ache − just to think of. Well, in the night there came up a terrible storm, in the midst of which, the lightening struck a tree near the white hunter's camp, on which were roosting several of these pine burr fed turkies. The birds, as the lightning descended, were instantly on fire, and flying towards the Indians, fell blazing, and hissing among them, such an exhibition struck them with consternation, and supposing the white men had the means of destruction they were not acquainted with, the Indians fled, and left the hunters in peaceable possession of the country, and, I am sorry to add, they were found afterwards starved to death, from the great inclemency of the season.

As may be imagined, a person of my enquiring mind and aptness to learn, would pick up many many useful hints in this wild country. I have among other things, as leisure permitted, practised much to get the art of preserving birds and animals. Now Audubon will take either, and in an incredible short space of time, make the expressionless mass of skin, teem with life, as if the bird or beast had been suddenly petrified in some graceful action. But, some how, I cannot get the hang of it -- my quadrupeds look like sausages, and my birds like a roll of dough. I have got a crane with a neck as big as his body, and a wild cat that resembles a gigantic weasel.

Sir William says he would not trust me to stuff a pillow. I intend to keep my "specimens" as works of art if not of nature, and when I get home, if they are mistaken by some natural history society for *new species*, of course I shall be mum, and they will receive unpronounceable names, and my memory will be handed down to posterity, preserved in a dead language.

P.O.F.

P.S. – Tar-pot-wan-ja is very anxious for me to stuff for him a buffalo skin; he says if I will do it, it will be "Knochanee-shokbou-nahoola," which literally translated, signifies buffalo made ugly will be handsome "heap."

[*Concordia Intelligencer,* 30 December 1843; *Spirit of the Times,* 13 (20 January 1844), 557.]

LETTERS FROM THE FAR WEST.

[CORRESPONDENCE OF THE INTELLIGENCER.]

CROSS TIMBERS, October 23, 1843.

*Alarming Pantomine; Its consequences; The result; Hunt for a Bear; Incidents; Getting up a tree; Keeping a promise.*

In my last I wrote particularly about scarcity of food, and the singular manner we kept from starving. We might have been encamped two weeks at the "Cross Timbers," and thus faring badly, when, one night as we lay grouped round the camp fire, thinking of our distant friends, and the comforts of civilized life, Tar-pot-wan-ja, who, as is usual with him, sat resting his chin on his knees, and thinking of nothing; suddenly threw up his head, leered round with his eyes, and distending his nostrils like the ends of two speaking trumpets, snuffed up the cold air, and uttered a most significant *ugh*! Now it so happened that nobody was at the fire but fellows from the settlements, as *green as myself*; and knowing something was wrong, I, by signs, asked him what was the matter? Tar-pot. replied, with a most agreeable smile, by going through the motions of shooting a rifle, *cutting his own throat*, and then *pulling off something*, which we presumed to be a scalp. "It is all up with us," was the general exclamation, particularly as our Indian friend shut up his eyes and seemed to resign himself to his fate. The effect of all this on "Mat" was truly awful; his hair fairly crawled about his head, while mine rose like the quills on the fretful porcupine. "Good by, Woeful," said Mat to me, without winking, for his hair just at that moment had retreated to the back of his head, and drawn the skin on his forehead so tight he could not.

"Good by; I ain't used to scalping, and I expect it will strike in and kill me; it is worse acclimating than yellow fever; ain't it Woeful?"

I acknowledged the impeachment, and told him I had been killed so often *in fun*, since I had been out in the "Far West," that I thought to have it done seriously would be quite a relief.

"I think," said "Mat," philosophizing, "that people have lived after being scalped."

"They do that thing in Texas," I replied, for I recollected of hearing such cases in that country; "And if we live through it," I suggested, "we will have our bumps mapped off, and labeled, and make a fortune by illustrating the science of phrenology."

"I think," said Mat, moralizing, "scalping is nothing; it is merely the knife of the savage, anticipating for a few days, the scythe of time."

"That is all," I groaned, putting my hands on the top of my head.

"Quien sirve nos libre, San Carlos," shouted Don Desparato to his horse.

"Them's my sentiments," said Mat, musing. "That was a cruel allusion to *St. Charles* just at this time, Woeful, wasn't it?" he continued, as if his feelings were wandering back to temporal things.

"It is just the time to call on the Saints, when you expect to be scalped," said I.

"Well," said Mat, in desparation, "I don't know any, but St. Charles, and St. Louis, and I have called on them *so often* they have got used to it."

While this conversation was going on, Tar-pot-wan-ja had stealthily and Indian-like left us, gun in hand, and when our expectations of the coming foray were at the highest pitch, we heard Sir William's yager, "Old Jefferys," and immediately a shout from Tar-pot., and a second and third discharge of fire arms. A long, low groan, and a struggle among the bushes follow-ed, and every thing was silent; presently in came our faithful In-dian draging a dead body, and throwing it down beside the fire, we heard him sharpen his knife on his gun barrel. Mat and I both opened our eyes at the same time to see the scalp taken, when, lo and behold, a half grown bear cub, lay before us, and the mysterious signs of Tar-pot., that alarmed us so, merely alluded to his smelling the scent of a bear, and the shooting it, cutting its throat and skinning it. As the truth flashed upon our minds, Mat and I breathed as simultaneously as the puff of a double engine.

"Did you ever, Woeful," said Mat, "see a man before that could *voluntarily* move his hair about his head as I can?"

"Or make it *stand up* as I can?" I suggested.

"We showed great presence of mind, Woeful, did'nt we?" said Mat, looking very comical.

"Certainly," said I; "we would have been killed if the Indians had really come, as dignifiedly as the Roman Senators."

The following morning we breakfasted upon bear meat; and as the animal was small, "Mat's" share and mine, lay be-tween a small piece of the neck, and two paws; we took them and ate away voraciously, Mat tearing the meat between his teeth, as they do flax through a hatchel. I insinuated that the meat was tough; Mat acquiesced, suddenly stopping, his eye lit up in fine phrenzy, and twinkled with humor, when he uttered the following impressively: "Woeful, its a piece of *grizzly bear*." "I think it is, as the French say, a *"fore paw*," holding up my particular piece.

Hereupon we both lay down on the prairie and laughed and kicked our heels into the earth, until we raised a dust like a herd of running buffaloes.

After our breakfast, an old hunter suggested that whenever there was a young bear killed, a cub or two more, and the old one were about; and it was suggested that we set out in pursuit of them, to the great edification of Tar-pot., who had been anxious to be at the work at the early dawn of day. The sun shone out beautifully, and a more merry party than we were, never buckled a horse-hair girth. Guns were loaded with care, and, unlike good bear-hunters, we started off with a shout. We had no dogs, and depended entirely upon the "signs." Tar-pot. and the old hunters would see marks and tracks, where I could see nothing; however, we came on the bears — an old one with one cub; — they were hidden away in the hollow of a pine tree; a smoke was soon raised and applied to the hole, and as we had smooth ground, Sir William said the bear must not be murdered, but *run down*. Very soon the old bear broke out, and rushing past us with a growl, set off at a killing pace. We all followed her in the rear, shouting and yelling; she was very fat and soon tired, and entrenching herself in a small skirt of wood, backed up against a large tree, and squared off as if for a boxing match, in the most scientific manner. We all dismounted, hitched our horses, and determined to make the best fight we could without powder and ball. It would be impossible to describe the feats of valor, and agility that followed; but the bear, in the contest, got the worst of it, and got wounded, and then got desperate, and pitched into us regardless of danger or death. Now Mat. and I were unconsciously merely looking on, and standing some distance from the thick fight, when the infuriated animal, with a hog-like *wugh*, broke after us. "Take to a tree," shouted a dozen voices, as we broke for some stunted pines, up which we sprang, and climbed into the branches in an instant. Here we clung with a hug for dear life, shutting our eyes to the danger about us. An hour might have thus passed, which seemed an age, when I heard Mat. say "Woeful, what an escape; suppose these pines had not been at hand to have got into?" I opened my eyes, and discovered Mat. few yards of me, and both of us with our toes within an *inch of the ground* — the young pines had insensibly bent towards the earth by our weight. It was a most ridiculous figure we cut, and both of us promised never to say any thing about it.                                    P.O.F.


[*Concordia Intelligencer*, 10 February 1844; *Spirit of the Times*, 14 (16 March 1844), 33.]

## LETTERS FROM THE FAR WEST.
### [CORRESPONDENCE OF THE INTELLIGENCER.]
### BEYOND THE CROSS TIMBERS, Oct., 1843.

*An amiable mule; Tar-pot-wan-ja's astonishment; Transmigration; New troubles; Fun alive; A fix peculiar; A dream; End of the days' work.*

Our party hailed with pleasure the announcement that we were to leave the "cross timbers," and take up our line of march towards the fine country lying beyond them. We packed up with alacrity, and as the bright morning sun in long reaching rays, lit up the prairie, we were in motion. Every thing went ahead, but a long eared mule in one of the baggage waggons — a stubborn representative, that did honor in this respect to his respectable progenitor, whoever he was. Don Desparato pounded him on one side, and Tar-pot-wan-ja, voluntarily, for an Indian never works by compulsion, labored on the other.

"Fire-consume-your-heart," said Desparato in Spanish, hitting the brute across the head.

"Ah-whooh-hah!" grunted Tar-pot., as he followed the example; here the mule laid down, and turning his head over his harness collar, and eying his tormentors very cooly, gave a loud bray, extended himself at full length on the ground, and seemed inclined to go to sleep under the hands of his tormentors, as a Turk will while under the process of shampooing. All this seemed to amuse the red man highly; between every blow, he would place his extended hands over his ears, and flap them, as if in imitation of wings; then laugh heartily, and hit the mule again. Desparato in the mean time, gathered some light wood, kindled a fire around and near the beast's body, and as the curling flame increased in force, and the rough hair began to singe, and smoke, while the animal paid no attention to it, Tar-pot's. enthusiasm extended into admiration; his vivid imagination pictured the animal possessed of a soul of some Indian warrior, who defied blows and the faggott — kicking the fire about the prairie, he rushed forward and embraced the animal; muley not understanding the nature of the hug, got upon his feet and commenced kicking in a most violent manner. Tar-pot. sprang out of the way of the dangerous heels, fully convinced that a mule and an Indian were of the same identical breed.

In time we fairly got under way, and the horsemen, including myself, instead of following the wagon trail, took a short cut through some low, swampy land, covered by what is known out here as the "scruboaks;" they are the same kind of trees I mentioned as peculiar to the "yallah stun" in one of my first letters. When we got fairly among them, we noticed them covered with little balls of earth, as we thought; but upon close examination they proved to be hornet's nests, which, disturbed by our intrusion, commenced issuing out in formidable numbers. Now a hornet is decidedly a very passionate yellow coated insect, and pitching into us with a vehemence truly commendable, attacked us in the front and rear. A general *scrub race* commenced — the horses flew through the low growth of brush, the tallest of which only came up to their breasts, as if they were pursued by torches of fire. Sir William Stewart's grey horse, which was the most powerful animal, snorted like a hurricane;

while Desparato, swearing in Indian and Spanish, threw his arms about like a wind-mill. Tar-pot-wan-ja, Indian like, took it more coolly — he and his horse seemed above complaining, except as evinced by the poor animal's tail, that kept whirling around like a piece of fire works. On we went, knocking at every step, the little mud balls on the ground, as rapidly as if we were dropping potatoes from a cart, while the inhabitants, first astonished, would for a moment confusedly crawl about, and then with un-erring instinct make a straight line for the luckless invaders of their homes. My horse, not at any time one of the best, coming to a hole in the earth, caught his foot and fell to the ground; before I could recover myself, my companions were some distance ahead of me, and the hornets, to my horror, instead of pursuing on, turned back and made a general attack on me. My horse, infuriated by the hornets, would keep running around me, kicking and snorting, and raising up new enemies every instant; I finally mounted and pushed on, enveloped in a cloud of burning stings. Whatever might have been my troubles in my search of sport out in the Far West, this excelled every thing in my unfortunate experience. I fought and knocked about, expecting every moment to fall from mere pain, when my horse again stumbled, and threw me in a hole about five feet deep, — the hornets buzzed above me for a moment like a thin mist, and then, as if afraid to descend, where I lay, separated to their dilapidated nests. Bruised and poisoned, I felt some relief from the absence of the hornets; no part of my body, but my face and hands, was much stung. Presently my face began to swell, my eyes closed up, and I was left in total darkness. In this situation, covered head, neck and heels with mud, for the hole into which I had fallen, was, at its botton, composed of it, exhausted with pain, and sightless, from the swollen state of my face, I gradually swooned away and lost myself. While thus, I dreamed that the learned members of the Royal Society, London, had issued a circular, offering a thousand pounds reward for a "perpetual motion," and a display of the most foolish thing in the world; and I dreamed that I gave to the society a journal of my adventures "Out West," and proved that

I went out there for the purpose of "sport," and the society unanimously awarded to me the thousand pounds. Taking the money, I awoke with joy, and discovered that my eyes would open — that I was much relieved of the pain in my face, and that the sun was just setting. Crawling out of the hole, as the chilly air of the night came on, I found the hornets benumbed with cold; I lit a fire by flashing powder in the pan of my pistol, and sat down beside it, and from the fix I was in when thoroughly warmed, I resembled a huge hornets nest, from my close resemblance to a ball of mud. About midnight, I discovered the camp fire of my fellow travellers, about two miles off, and made towards it, the most miserable dog that ever went sport-seeking in the Far West. P.O.F.

# An Unknown Tale by
# George Washington Harris

The probable existence of an undiscovered story by George Washington Harris was first mentioned by Donald Day in his unpublished doctoral dissertation, "The Life and Works of George Washington Harris" (Univ. of Chicago, 1942). Day found his clue in W. T. Porter's "TO CORRESPONDENTS" column in the New York *Spirit of the Times*, 19 (12 January 1850), 553:

> W.A.S. – Will you send us another copy of the "Courier" containing G. W. H.'s Christmas story? Someone has 'boned' the first copy, 'blame him!'

Day did not locate the story, however, and concluded that it "was not reprinted in the *Spirit*. . ." (p.22). Subsequent Harris scholars have also failed to uncover the Christmas story. How Day and the others could have overlooked it is inexplicable, because only two weeks after the reference in the "TO CORRESPONDENTS" column, the story did appear in the *Spirit*, 19 (26 January 1850), 584. It was entitled "HOME-VOICES – A TALE FOR THE HOLY-TIDE" and was signed "G. W. H."

Backtracking from the *Spirit*, one finds that the story was first published in the Buffalo (N. Y.) *Daily Courier*, 16 (25 December 1849), where it was simply signed "G. W. H." That this "G. W. H." is Harris is supported by the appearance of the names "Geo. W. Harris" and "Geo. Harris" on lists of general delivery letters being held at the Buffalo Post Office at the time the story was written. (The lists were published in the Buffalo *Morning Express*.) Very little is known of Harris' whereabouts and activities during this period, but it appears likely that he was in Buffalo, perhaps working for one of the railroads or steamboat lines. Furthermore, since Porter reserved the pseudonyms and initials of favored correspondents for their exclusive use, Harris' authorship of the story seems certain.

"Home-Voices" is entirely atypical of Harris' other known fiction. It is written in the worst tradition of nineteenth-century sentimentalism and has little intrinsic merit. However, the story does raise some intriguing questions about Harris. Does the story reveal a hitherto unrecognized side of Harris' nature? In his best work, Harris shows himself to be a tough-minded realist — even, at times, a misanthropist. "Home-Voices" hardly represents this same George Washington Harris.

Does the story reflect an attempt by Harris to manufacture fiction for profit? Throughout his life Harris moved from job to job, and there is some evidence that he was a poor businessman. His writings until this time had brought him little financial reward, and "Home-Voices" might have been an effort to break into the commercial fiction field. If this is true, however, the *Daily Courier* was an unlikely place for Harris to have published the story. Almost no newspapers of this time paid for original fiction; if the *Daily Courier* did, it was an unusual paper.

"Home-Voices" is also of interest because it is clearly patterned after Charles Dickens' "A Christmas Carol," first published in 1843 and a standard holiday tale by 1850. Harris was familiar with at least some of Dickens' writings; the unpublished book-length manuscript that Harris was carrying at his death, for example, was entitled "High Times and Hard Times" after Dickens' novel *Hard Times*. When Harris tried his hand at the popular tale, it was only natural that he should copy Dickens, one of the most successful professional authors of the day.

Harris' reasons for writing this story are unclear. If he was attempting to sell a slice of his talent for money, it is to his credit that he appears to have done so only this once. As Harris' only known attempt to write outside the genre of humorous and sporting literature, "Home-Voices" is an interesting literary artifact that should be preserved and studied.

The text below is taken from the *Spirit* appearance; the only available copies of the *Daily Courier* text are mutilated and unreadable beyond transcription. An emendations list records all editorial corrections of the text, both accidental and sub-stantive.

WILLIAM J. STARR

## EMENDATIONS

The table below records all emendations made in the *Spirit* text. The page-line citation refers to the text reprinted below. The first reading in the entry is the emended reading from that text. The emended reading is followed by a bracket and then by the erroneous reading from the *Spirit* text.

| | | | | |
|---|---|---|---|---|
| 162.10 | arm. ] arm | | 167.1 | creditor? ' ] creditor? |
| 162.17 | all ] al | | 167.9 | losses, ] losses |
| 162.28 | fellow. ] fellow | | 167.18 | transactions. ] transactions |
| 162.31 | from ] fr m | | 167.37 | snow bird ] snow-bird |
| 163.4 | the ] t e | | 168.13 | favor ] fav r |
| 163.17 | trowsers ] trow ers | | 168.16 | by ] bv |
| 163.24 | fear ] ear | | 168.22 | more ] mo e |
| 163.27 | good ] g od | | 169.2 | that ] hat |
| 163.27 | hear. ] hear | | 169.12 | core. ] core |
| 164.8 | grocers', ] grocers,' | | 170.8 | him, ] him |
| 164.16 | HOME. ] HOME | | 170.9 | fascination? ] fascination! |
| 164.24 | objects, ] objec s | | 171.17 | which ] whic |
| 164.26 | pockets' ] pocket's | | 171.21 | raisins ] rai ins |
| 165.1 | stone. ] stone | | 171.24 | question ] ques ion |
| 165.15 | cherub. ] cherub | | 171.25 | Mrs. ] Mrs |
| 165.15 | shoulder ] sh ulder | | 171.33 | valuables. ] valuables |
| 165.22 | sewing. ] sewing | | 171.33 | was a ] was |
| 166.4 | passage. ] passage | | 171.34 | at ] a |
| 166.20 | snow bird ] snow-bird | | 171.35 | ware, ] ware. |
| 166.26 | bald. ] bald | | 172.19 | re-appeared ] re appeared |
| 166.36 | Day, ] Day,' | | 172.27 | presence ] pre-ence |
| 166.36 | as ] a | | | |

# HOME-VOICES — A TALE FOR THE HOLY-TIDE.

Probably but few persons who saw Tony Prockett, as he wrought his way through the snow drifts of that Christmas eve, doubted that his was a jovial and pleasant sort of heart enough, though it did beat beneath a rough frieze spencer; for, as he toiled along, presenting the top of his head to the driving storm, and ever and anon plunging that part of his system into the stomachs of wayfares whom he met, or getting it in forcible contact with innumerable umbrellas, you might have heard that he trolled a simple ditty, as if confidentially to the monstrous goose he carried beneath his arm. Not one of your sophisticated airs, but some honest, jolly, old time ditty, having for its burden something about 'Christmas coming but once a year,' and then the rhyme to this was 'good cheer,' which chorus, as it seemed, occurring frequently, in the course of the song, and indeed, going to make up nearly the whole of it, at each repetition became more cheerful and enlivening, until, just as Tony was passing a shop where they sold all manner of curious toys and sugar articles, it broke out into a long, hearty troll, while, at the same time, the singer stopped to examine the devices of the confectioner, displayed behind the glass.

But either it chanced that the fanciful frost-work on the window panes was too thick to allow a perfect view, or else there was something inside that, more than the rest, excited Tony's curiosity, for, after standing by the window long enough to sing his jovial chorus three or four times through, he made a plunge for the door and entered the shop. And now it was, that, in the bright blaze of the gas light, one discovered and appreciated the full jollity and good nature of the honest fellow. On his head, squeezed down so tightly that, when it came away, every hair projected in a wrong direction, he wore a remarkable cap, the fur of which, from being very long and filled with the driven snow, caused the whole apparatus to resemble a gigantic cauliflower. His shaggy coat, too, was filled with the frozen particles, so that when Tony made his entrance, he fairly glistened, like an iceberg.

Shaking part of the snow from his person, and stamping his feet with a hearty vehemence, Tony laid down his goose, very carefully, under the counter and turned his blooming countenance toward one of the bland clerks who dealt out the sugar curiosities. It was the influence of that look, I know it was, that set the bland clerk off in a perfect paroxysm of smiles, which, being reflected from Tony's beaming countenance, with tenfold interest, became, after a short period of time, a full blown and jocund laugh.

'Good evening, sir!' said Tony, addressing the bland young man, 'Merry Christmas, almost — was near forgetting it — bless me! if I had for the first time in fifty years!' and the reflection, on the possibility of such a horror, quite overcoming him, he continued to ejaculate 'Bless me!' for the space of a minute, after which time, finding himself soothed, he again smiled upon the bland clerk, and assured him that 'it was all right, now.' — Then, after fumbling, for some time, in his trowsers pocket, Tony produced his spectacles, from a highly polished steel case, and, putting them on, desired the bland clerk to 'go ahead,' which the clerk, apparently well acquainted with the form of expression, did, by displaying, upon the glass show case, various toys and playthings for children. — Over these, Tony became intensely amused, chuckling, rubbing his hands, holding his mouth until he was apoplectically red in the face, for fear of disturbing the other customers, and, every once in a while, in spite of all precautions, breaking out into a broad laugh, which would have done any one good to hear.

It seemed a matter of great study, with Tony, the selection of such toys as he desired, but, after a period of fervid excitement, he at last succeeded in straining his pockets to a capacity capable of admitting one or two wooden horses, some mechanical mysteries, in the form of water and wind mills, various pockets of candy and a curious musical instrument, to hear which blown, was to abandon hope forever. With this addition to his luggage, Tony started, after once more smiling at and with the bland clerk and again expressing his gratification at not having forgotten 'Merry Christmas.'

Still carolling that merry song, still breasting against the fast driving storm and stoutly plunging through the rapidly accumulating drifts, the merry old fellow pursued his way toward HOME.

By gas lights, half dimmed beneath their heavy blankets of pure snow; by brilliant shop fronts, gorgeous with ribands and laces; by fruit stands, with red apples piled to fearful heights; by grocers', where the air was faintly odorous of citron, raisins and lemons; by meat shops, with great quarters of red beef suspended, and ticketed at ruinously low prices; by heaps of oyster kegs, smelling deliciously of salt water; by theatres and ball rooms and concerts; by taverns filled with laughing men; by groups of boys at snow ball; by livery stables resounding to the tinkling of small bells; by each and all of these, and many other pleasant sights, passed Tony Prockett, eager to catch the voices of his humble HOME.

Here then, at last! How light and pleasant seems the little house, as half a dozen pairs of sparkling, happy eyes are turned upon the new comer. How joyously rings forth the merry laugh, as Tony shakes the wonderful cap, full in the faces, first, of wife, and then, of little ones! Then, what a getting off of that coat and a laying aside of the goose, with many a futile effort, on the part of Tony, to attract the attention of the children to imaginary reptiles and other unreal objects, upon the walls or under the table, by which ineffably adroit device he was to conceal for them the nature of his pockets' contents!

But ever still the burden of that song was on his lip, and ever still the voices round him spoke to him of HOME.

Then tea was ready, and, taking the least of the little ones upon his lap, he said a short grace, and then, at odd intervals through the repast, when he could spare time from burning his mouth with a hot spoon and choking the baby with crumbs of bread, he hummed the same air, or repeated the words, processes which continued to afford him the highest satisfaction, as often as they were indulged in.

Surely, you had said, this is a HOME worthy the sacred title, had you but seen it on that Christmas Eve, after the meal was finished and the family seated round the hearth stone. To the pleasant gurgling of the father's pipe, the glancing knitting needles of the mother kept clicking time, as she plied her busy fingers. Around a table, farther from the fire, were seated the four scions of the house of Prockett, engaged in various occupations, the most absorbing of which, and by far the noisiest, was that which employed master Tony, junior, a youth, of whom it might well be said, the unkindest thing to be done for him would be to make him any fatter, for he was already so very much too large for his garments, that it would have been difficult to pinch him anywhere. His face was very red and his eyes and hair very black, so that as he stooped over the table and scratched dreadfully upon a hard slate, with a hard pencil, he seemed, noise and all taken into the account, anything but a cherub. His younger sister, over looking his shoulder, made bubbles with her mouth and occasionally would wet her chubby little finger and rub out the designs he had so painfully elaborated, when he, as if to give the lie, forever, to his wide awake and never touch me look, would quietly kiss her pouting lip and ask her, as a favor to him, to rub them out entirely. The second of the family perused a pleasant work on grammar, and the eldest, a fair, delicate girl, was busy with some mysterious sewing. But, least of all, while, still, by no means modest in pushing his claims to notice, hopped and twittered on the table, one of the smallest specimens of that small breed of birds, whose life is spent amid the snows and storms of winter. Hopping, now upon the hand of one, perching then upon the head of another; now flying off to tap against the darkened window and again returning to nestle in the bosom of the eldest girl, the brave little fellow drew great enjoyment from his eccentric course.

He was a pet of the eldest daughter, who had found him, in distress, upon the door step, had nursed him, and when she had offered him his liberty he had declined to be free, by clinging to her with his tiny grasp and piping shrilly. So she had kept the estray, and, though the world was before him, for his choice, he still clave to the hand, that had relieved his wants.

Such were the individuals that made the groupe beneath

the shade of Tony Prockett's roof-tree, and listened ever and anon to the soft burden of the little chorus that he sang.

A knock came, at the door, followed by the entrance of some person and a great stamping of feet in the passage. At sound of this, Tony turned pale and laid up his pipe, while his wife, gathering together her little flock, vanished, with them through another door. Before the stranger entered, the burden of the song was stopped and the snow bird had flown to his perch upon the clock, for safety.

And then, the stamping of feet having ceased and the friction upon the mat which succeeded, having grown less vigorous, Tony, with a serious face and by no means alert step, moved to the door of the room and opened it for the admission of the visitor.

Not with the ordinary courtesy of a salute was it that the new comer greeted his host, but rather with the air of a superior being, haughtily acknowledging Tony's marks of respect and seating himself by the hearth, without a word. The bright light that had made the room so cheerful before, seemed now to darken almost into gloom, and the snow bird chirped a dismal note.

The stranger was a man, apparently ten years the junior of Tony Prockett, yet larger and stronger, and with a face that showed the workings of some vile sentiments and passions. His hair, too, was grizzled upon the temples, and the top of his head was bald. Though, in all these respects, far from resembling Tony, they bore the same name and acknowledged the same parents. The difference in their dress was equally striking, for while the elder of the two was habited in a plain and inexpensive suit, the other was clad in fine cloth and wore an ostentatious amount of jewelry. The one was poor, but much beloved; the other rich and hated, not for his riches but his want of virtues.

'Well, Anthony,' the latter began, when he had warmed and rubbed his hands before the fire, 'to morrow will be what you call Christmas Day, and on that day, as you are probably aware, there will be due from you to me a certain debt. Shall

you be prepared to meet it, or must I still continue your cred-
itor?'

'Brother Henry,' the elder replied, in a subdued and faltering voice, 'with barely means to keep the life our parents gave
me and to support the few whose lives depend on me, I borrow-
ed of you, at your own desire, the sum for which you ask me
now. By your advice and counsel, I embarked with you in spec-
ulations, where, for a time our success seemed certain. Reverses
came; the rich man, able to support or to redeem his losses,
came from the trial unscathed; that was you. The poor one, saw
his little all, slip from his grasp and found himself at middle life,
surrounded by creatures relying on him, forced to begin the
world anew and still involved with heavy debts; that was I. And
bitter, brother Henry, was the day when the poor man saw his
mite go to help fill the coffers of the rich one, while wife and
children asked for bread with doubt and trembling!'

'I am a business man, Anthony, and shape my dealings by
the known laws of business transactions. Were I to be moved by
such rhetoric as this, those men who hold me now in good respect, would mark me as a lunatic and I should suffer by the act.
You know me too well to hope to succeed by such arts. What
fools call "Charity" is waste, and waste is sin – '

'Hold, Brother Henry,' the other rejoined; 'I have asked
and shall ask no charity or lenience at your hands. You say well,
I know you better than to expect, even were I capable of asking it. The debt I shall pay – shall even desire your indulgence
so far as to request you will take it before you leave the house
– and take with it the recollection of how it was obtained, by
days and nights of toil unceasing and severe – by deprivations
such as you have never known, but not one cent of it by fraud,
extortion, or deceit. Take with it, too, the remembrance that it
is my all, and that thus, for the second time, you leave me
worse than poor while making yourself richer –.'

All gone, now, the faltering voice and trembling accent; –
the interview, dreaded for years, was but a trifle after all, to a
just man, wronged, and Tony Prockett felt the strength of his
position. The snow bird, too, looked down upon him from his

perch and seemed to encourage him with that little, twinkling eye. Henry, never before accustomed to this strange manner in his meek brother, scarce knew what reply to make him, so absolutely monstrous was the crime of which he found him guilty. At last, he found speech, and in a sneering tone proceeded.

'You desire me to receive the debt before I leave the roof that shelters you and your pauper family. — I need not say how gladly I accede to your request, for not many days can elapse before this hearth will be cold and these dependants of yours, testing the beauty of that charity which you make so prominent an article of your creed. I know your circumstances, and, but for your insolence, might have been induced to show you some favor. All such throughts, and I wonder that I ever entertained them, I banish, now, forever, as unworthy a manly nature. Let me have the pleasure of signing a receipt.'

'Henry, my brother, do not add to my affliction by cursing the house which you have desolated — only that one favor I ask at your hands. You who have never known a Home — who live but in the cold embraces of your own selfishness — cannot in never so remote a degree, comprehend the sorrow you might have warded off from us. My own race is nearly run, but I leave more behind me who might — such is the nature of man — at some future day desire to seek retribution for this. It shall be my daily duty, while yet their minds are capable of entertaining such advice, to teach them to forget the wrong already done, save for the lesson it may be to them in doing right —' and here the bird, still perched upon the clock, looked down, and chirruped out a little song, it seemed of hopefulness, and now, the burden of the old chorus occurred again to Tony Prockett.

The money was paid over — the unnatural brother had taken his leave, and now the subdued hum of the children's voices in the next room — Hush! what was it that they murmured so softly? That old — old supplication — 'Forgive us our trespasses as we forgive those who trespass against us.' Tony sank in his chair, and the snow bird, coming fearlessly down from his perch, alighted on his shoulder.

\* \* \* \* \* \* \* \* \* \*

Still raged the storm, as the younger brother tramped through the drifts, bending his steps toward the shelter that he was used to call *his* Home. Bitterly the wind howled past the street corners, and sharply it whirled the snow flakes in his face and sported with his garments. Still the same joyous sounds of boys at sport, and jingling bells — the same bright lights in windows, and the same hilarity and happiness abroad, as when poor Tony plodded through the storm that night. But what were all these to that seared and thankless heart? No innocent mirth or hallowing associations had ever wrought on it. Suspicion, revenge, jealousy had only harbored there and bitterness was at its core. He passed a church, where a pealing organ sent up its strains of thankfulness, and the Holy Symbol glistened in forms of light, but turned from them with a jeer. But one thought possessed him — his Brother's ruin.

There was a small fire burning on the hearth when he reached his home, and, locking his door, he seated himself by that, to brood in secret over his revenge. But ever and anon, as he pondered, there flitted across his mind some recollection of that piercing little eye that had looked down upon him from the clock. The more he strove to blot it from his memory, the more fixed and piercing it became, until, turn where he would, that little point, more like a diamond than an eye, was fastened upon him with a fascinating power. He cursed the bird, and wished that he had killed it where it stood; but still the same, unwinking eye, on every side. Knowing it for an illusion, he wondered was he getting crazed? — or, fearful thought! was he dead, and this some keen torture wrought to punish him for sin? He dared admit none to his secret, for there were none whom he could trust — and then he thought of what his brother told him — that he had no Home! Still the little piercing eye — upon the wall — the door — the iron safe — within the grate; what would he not have given to have that dreadful presence removed! He went to bed — there the horror was still greater, and he rose in an agony of torment, hastening to re-light his lamp. Pacing the room, he beat his hand upon his forehead, groaned aloud, screamed, and when some one about the house, hearing his cries, came to the door, he laughed out that it was nothing but an ugly dream – that was all!

But a dream that would not leave him, curse or scream, or mutter as he might. Every where that awful presence – so keen, so bright, so unchanging. At last, out into the street, to roam, he knew not where, he cared not, either, so he lost himself to that.

What was it that led him, to set his face again toward his brother's House? Was it the power of that fascination? – did the terrible eye move on before him, its magnetic influence drawing him still towards the hearth he would have desolated? That way he went, however, and, somehow, as he neared the place, the diamond spot grew dimmer, dimmer still, until, when standing upon the very threshold, it disappeared!

And with it went the influence it had exerted to bring him there, and he turned to leave the spot, cursing his folly. But there it was again – brighter, keener, more implacable than ever!

How many times he followed the dread influence even to the door, and then, upon its disappearance, retreated, in the hardness of his heart! But each time less stern than at the last, 'till finally, exhausted, perhaps, with cold, but certainly with his brain near crazed, he softly opened the door, and entered his Brother's HOME.

Tony slept before the hearth, and on his shoulder perched the snow bird with the unchanging eye fixed on the stranger. But not now to him a malign one – not now the terrible apparition of his waking vision – but tenderly gently drawing him toward the wronged and innocent brother, whose lips even then murmured the chorus of the little Christmas song.

And as the bell told out the hour

'That to the Cottage as the Crown
Brought tidings of salvation down.'

Henry knelt by the side of Anthony and sobbed out tears of sorrow and repentance, while the snow bird flitted about the room, making music with his tiny wings.

There is an old song — a very old one, but whether it was Tony's favorite we cannot state, as he never pretends to sing above a whisper — which runs —

'And all the bells on earth shall ring,
On Christmas day, on Christmas day,
And all the bells on earth shall ring,
On Christmas day in the morning.'

And on *that* Christmas morning they *did* ring, or some of them, at least, and for the first time in his life, Henry Prockett knew what it was to hear music in the peal of bells. How fresh and smooth he looked, as he took his way through the snowy streets, and how people stared to see him smiling on the boys at play, and stopping to ask the prices of all manner of articles, such as he had never thought before of buying, and sending them home, too, that is, Tony's home, by cart and basket loads, and paying out shillings, and even larger coins, without the least compunction, nay, even with a chuckle which, though it was new to him, really became him very much! He was beside himself upon the subject of turkeys, and a very bedlamite in the matter of oysters; but when it came to oranges and nuts, and raisins, and curious devices in sugar, and marvellous toys, and beautiful gift books, you would have given him up forever. And then, as if he had not done sufficient to establish beyond all question his title to a straight jacket, he must crown and consummate his lunacy by the purchase of a silver tea sett for Mrs. Tony, when, having done all he could possibly think of, he ran as fast as his legs could carry him to Tony's home, and there seated himself with an asseveration that he intended to spend the day. But it probably occurred some half score of times, that while he was pondering, and gazing at the fire, or the snow bird, he would suddenly start up and dash out of the house, returning very much blown, in the course of half an hour, with some new addition to the stock of household valuables. At one time it was a small cheese, at another, a few nutmegs, now a broom or two, and again a whole cupboard full of tin ware, according to his convictions of the wants of the family. Having at last nearly immolated himself with a half dozen of skewers, which he attempted to bring home in his pocket, at the same time that a patent rat trap in his hat went off with a tremendous noise, he became subdued, in this respect, and remained quiet for the rest of the day, making himself a very Momus for the children, who thought they never had seen or heard anything half so good as Uncle Henry's stories and imitations.

Were it required of me to tell of the festivities following upon these happy events, I should despair. How at dinner, Uncle Harry, with tears in his eyes, told the story of the snow bird, for the twentieth time, while the bird himself pecked at his bread unmolested — how Tony attempted to sing the whole of his song and broke down at the first line — how Mrs. Tony and Miss Tony senior *did* sing a simple old carol, which was many times encored — how they danced and played at games until midnight, and how Tony junior, having executed many novel airs upon that subtle instrument of music before mentioned, was finally inveigled to bed by a cunning stratagem, and re-appeared again, in white garments, within three minutes — all this I leave for your imagination to fill up.

My tale, such as it is, is done. The snow birds flit and twitter among the boughs outside my window, the odor of green wreaths fills the atmosphere about me, bells jingle merrily and children play before my door, but the mimic characters that these have conjured up, are vanished from my sight. Yet, though like spectres they have come and gone, perhaps their airy presence has left no harm behind, and there may be those will not the less enjoy, to day, the blessings of that religion which, like the linden leaf, tossed by the storm, shows brightest in adversity, for having been reminded by these simple creations how much of happiness we owe to an appreciation of our every day HOME VOICES.

G. W. H.

# Johnson Jones Hooper's
# "The 'Frinnolygist' at Fault"

*Wheler's Magazine*, published in Athens, Georgia, from July 1849 until January 1850, was in most ways typical of Southern literary periodicals of its time. It had high aims, a modest format, limited financial backing, a small list of subscribers, and a brief life.[1] In two respects, however, *Wheler's Magazine* was unusual: it sold for a low subscription price, and it paid money to its contributors.[2] These two characteristics, in conjunction with one another, likely had much to do with the rapid demise of the journal. During its brief run, however, *Wheler's Magazine* did manage to publish important work by several well-known authors, Northern as well as Southern.

In the fourth issue of *Wheler's Magazine* (October 1849), editor C. L. Wheler noted in his "Editor's Lounge" column that "We shall hereafter pay a fair compensation for *Original Tales*, whether by profossional [sic] or amateur writers" (p. 97). In this way, Wheler was able to attract writings from such authors as James T. Fields, T. S. Arthur, James Russell Lowell, J. M. Legaré, John Neal, William Gilmore Simms, Henry Wadsworth Longfellow, and Johnson Jones Hooper.[3]

---

1. A useful account of the publication history of *Wheler's Magazine* is found in Bertram Holland Flanders, *Early Georgia Magazines: Literary Periodicals to 1865* (Athens: Univ. of Georgia Press, 1944), pp. 110-18.

2. Subscriptions to *Wheler's Magazine* sold for only one dollar per year, according to a note "To the Reader" on p. 22 of the first issue of the journal (July 1849). Subscriptions to most comparable periodicals of the time ran between three and five dollars. C. L. Wheler's policy of paying for the material he published was quite unusual in the South: Flanders remarks in *Early Georgia Magazines* that "This is the first instance where a Georgia editor is recorded as paying for contributions" (p. 118).

3. For a list of contributors to *Wheler's Magazine*, together with

Scholarly attention has been given to some of these writings. Simms contributed two items: a poem entitled "Stanzas," and a lengthy "Letter to the Editor of Wheler's Magazine" which discusses the role played by periodicals in the cultural development of the South. This letter, an important one, has been republished in Simms's collected correspondence.[4] Longfellow's contribution, entitled "A Lay of Courage," is a translation of a Danish poem by Ove Malling. This Longfellow item was unknown until 1935, when it was discovered and republished in *American Literature*.[5]

Hooper contributed a sketch, titled "The 'Frinnolygist' at Fault," which has not been republished since its initial appearance in the January 1850 issue of *Wheler's Magazine*.[6] Hooper's reasons for contributing the sketch to the magazine were likely personal as well as pecuniary. Wheler probably contacted Hooper through their mutual friend, T.A. Burke. Like Wheler, Burke lived in Athens and tried more than once to establish a successful periodical.[7] He edited and published the literary and humorous journals *Mistletoe* (1849) and *Horn of Mirth* (1849-50), and he compiled the humorous anthology *Polly Peablossom's Wedding* (Philadelphia: A. Hart, 1851). Burke was a friend and admirer of Hooper; *Polly Peablossom's Wedding*, in fact, is dedicated to Hooper. Burke also included one of

citations to the better poetry and prose published in the periodical, see Flanders, *Early Georgia Magazines*, pp. 115-116.

4. *The Letters of William Gilmore Simms*, ed. Mary C. Simms Oliphant, Alfred Taylor Odell, and T. C. Duncan Eaves (Columbia: Univ. of South Carolina Press, 1953), II, 515-23.

5. See Flanders, "An Uncollected Longfellow Translation," *American Literature*, 7 (May 1935), 205-07.

6. The sketch, however, was known to exist. Flanders refers to it on p. 115 of *Early Georgia Magazines*, and W. Stanley Hoole notes its existence on p. 213, n. 71, of his biography of Hooper, *Alias Simon Suggs: The Life and Times of Johnson Jones Hooper* (Univ. of Alabama Press, 1952; repr. Westport, Conn.: Greenwood Press, 1970).

7. For information on Burke, see Flanders, *Early Georgia Magazines*, p. 109.

# WHELER'S MAGAZINE.

| New Series.] | JULY, 1849. | [No. I....Vol I. |

## PERIODICAL LITERATURE.

### Letter to the Editor of Wheler's Magazine.

BY W. GILMORE SIMMS, ESQ.

*Dear Sir*—You are pleased to ask at my hands a leader for the first number of your contemplated periodical. I am scarcely in a condition to serve your purpose. Even were my abilities such as would fully justify your application, or permit me to suppose it anything more than the mere compliment,—the tribute rather of your personal good feeling than of my merit,—I have not just now the requisite leisure to attempt compliance with your wishes. My whole time is consumed in labors which are imperitive, as they occur under the severest exactions of duty ; and the constant exercise at the desk deprive pen, ink and paper of all those attractions which they would otherwise possess for a mind whose strongest passion is that of letters. But I have every disposition to promote your objects ; and, if the brief and hurried considerations which are here set down will contribute in any degree to your design, they are cheerfully at your service.

Of the advantages and importance of Periodical Literature there can be no question. It has been recognized in all countries that have made any progress in civilization, as contributing largely, first to the provocation to proper exercise of the domestic mind, and next, as enabling this mind to determine and mature the standards of a just judgment and a becoming taste. What has proved true of other countries must certainly prove true of ours.— What has been beneficent to the intellect of other communities, cannot fail of doing service in the South. In fact, there are special reasons why a Periodical Literature is more important and necessary to the South than to most other regions. The very sparseness of our population, which renders it so difficult a matter to sustain the Periodical, is the very fact that renders its existence and maintenance so necessary.— The great secret of mental activity, in most countries, is the denseness of their settlements,—the size and frequency of their great cities, and the constant attrition of rival minds, which can take place nowhere so constantly as in the commercial and populous marts. Wanting in these fields of attrition and collision, the mind of the South-

---

Figure 1. The first page of the first issue of *Wheler's Magazine* (July 1849). Simms' letter to the editor was the lead item.

# MAN.

BY G. A. WORTH, OF NEW-YORK.

THE human mind, that lofty thing!
　The palace and the throne,
Where Reason sits, a sceptred king,
　And breathes his judgment tone;
Oh! who with silent step shall trace
The borders of that haunted place,
　Nor in his weakness own
That mystery and marvel bind
That lofty thing, the human mind!

The human heart, that restless thing!
　The tempter and the tried;
The joyous, yet the suffering,
　The source of pain and pride;
The gorgeous-thronged, the desolate,
The seat of Love, the lair of Hate,
　Self-stung, self-deified!
Yet do we bless thee as thou art,
Thou restless thing, the human heart!

The human soul, that startling thing!
　Mysterious and sublime!
The angel sleeping on the wing,
　Worn by the scoffs of Time;
The beautiful, the veiled, the bound,
The earth-enslaved, the glory-crowned,
　The stricken in its prime!
From heaven in tears to earth it stole,
That startling thing, the human soul!

And this is Man!—Oh, ask of him,
　The gifted and forgiven,
When o'er his vision, drear and dim,
　The wrecks of time are driven,
If pride or passion in their power
Can chain the tide or charm the hour,
　Or stand in place of Heaven.
He bends the brow, he bows the knee—
Creator! Father! none but Thee!

For Wheler's Magazine.

# THE "FRINNOLYGIST" AT FAULT.

## AN HUMOROUS SKETCH.

BY J. J. HOOPER, AUTHOR OF "SIMON SUGGS," ETC.

SEVERAL stories have been told, I know, in the newspapers, founded on the idea of the mistake on the part of a Professor of Phrenology, in regard to the degree of combativeness of the person submitting to his manipulations; but as I was "personally present" and witnessed the scene I shall attempt to describe, the readers of this miscellany have assurance that what I shall relate is, at least, a Sketch from Real Life.

During the session of the Alabama Legislature, in Montgomery, in December of 1847, on a very cold, blustering night, a party of gentlemen were assembled in the bar-room of the new and splendid "Exchange Hotel," engaged in—(shall I tell it, in these the days of the triumphs of Temperance?)—discussing a couple of baskets of champaigne which WASH TILLEY had produced in honor of the occasion of the opening of the lower story of the aforesaid "Exchange." It was a most hilarious scene. There were the "mad wag," George A—n, of Sumpter; John W—n, of Louderdale; Joseph S—l, of Mobile, and B—s and H—r, of the *Journal*. Besides these, there was a friend of mine whom I shall call *Mac*, a generous, noble-hearted fellow—brave as a lion, but with a heart that could cover the universe with its charity. His single foible was an occasional indulgence in too much wine. His friends all loved him dearly, in spite of that and his ugliness—for he *was*

Figure 2. The first page of Hooper's sketch, from the January 1850 issue of *Wheler's Magazine*.

Hooper's sketches ("Shifting the Responsibility. A Hard Shell Story") in a later T. B. Peterson reprinting of *Polly Peablossom's Wedding*.[8]

Burke and Wheler seem likewise to have been on friendly terms: they contributed to each other's magazines,[9] and Burke acted as publishers' agent for *Wheler's Monthly Journal*, the unsuccessful 1848 predecessor of *Wheler's Magazine*.[10] When Burke's own *Mistletoe* suspended publication in March 1849, he turned over his list of subscribers to Wheler. Wheler fulfilled Burke's obligations by sending issues of *Wheler's Magazine* to *Mistletoe* subscribers for the remainder of 1849.[11] The Hooper-Wheler connection, then, was very likely made through Burke.

Hooper had originally agreed to write a series of sketches for *Wheler's Magazine*. In the October 1849 issue, Wheler proudly told his subscribers, *"It gives us pleasure to announce that we shall commence in the first No. of Vol. II, a series of HUMOROUS SKETCHES, by the author of 'Capt. Simon Suggs,' etc."* (p. 100). Hooper's "The Frinnolygist' at Fault"

8. The sketch originally appeared in William T. Porter's *New York Spirit of the Times*, 21 (5 Apr. 1851), but was not published in the 1851 first impression of *Polly Peablossom's Wedding*. In 1969, Garrett Press issued a photo-offset reprint of a T. B. Peterson reprinting which does contain the Hooper sketch. On its copyright page, this Garrett Press reprint erroneously identifies itself as "a photographic reprint of the 1851 edition published in Philadelphia by T. B. Peterson." The 1851 first impression was published in Philadelphia, but by A. Hart, and, as noted, did not contain the Hooper sketch.

9. Wheler contributed to the January and February 1849 issues of Burke's *Mistletoe*. Burke contributed to the July and October 1849 issues of *Wheler's Magazine* under the pseudonym "Aleck," and to the November 1849 and January 1850 issues under his own name. The "Aleck" items — both humorous sketches — are attributed to Burke in the table of contents for the entire vol. 1 of *Wheler's Magazine*.

10. Burke is named as "Publishers' Agent" in an advertisement on p. 16 of the first number of *Wheler's Monthly Journal* (15 Oct. 1848).

11. "Notice to the Subscribers of 'The Mistletoe,' " Wheler's Magazine, 1 (Oct. 1849), 100. See also Flanders, *Early Georgia Magazines*, pp. 110-11.

duly appeared in vol. 2, no. 1 (January 1850), of *Wheler's Magazine*, but that was the last issue of the journal ever to appear.[12] The remaining sketches in the series, if they were written, were never published, at least in *Wheler's Magazine*.

In "The 'Frinnolygist' at Fault," Hooper taps a vein of comic Irish material frequently found in newspaper humor of the day. Other Southern writers — Henry Clay Lewis, George Washington Harris, and Simms, for instance — also drew on humorous Irish material;[13] in fact, the connections between the comic Irish "Paddy" and the backwoods scalawag hero might be examined with profit. In "The 'Frinnolygist' at Fault," Hooper depends, for much of his humor, on comic Irish man-

12. Three files of *Wheler's Magazine* survive. Until 1973, the New York Public Library and Duke University Library held the only two known files, both of which contain vol. 1 complete (six issues, July-Dec. 1849) and the first issue only of vol. 2 (Jan. 1850). Rutgers held only vol. 2, no 1. A third file was acquired in 1973 by the special collections division of the Newman Library, Virginia Polytechnic Institute and State University. This file likewise contains vol. 1 complete and the first issue only of vol. 2. In the Newman file, the entire run of seven issues is bound up with the title page and table of contents for the whole of vol. 1. Also bound in is the 15 Oct. 1848 issue (the only known copy) of *Wheler's Monthly Journal*, the predecessor of *Wheler's Magazine*. The fact that all three surviving files of *Wheler's Magazine* end with vol. 2, no. 1, indicates that this issue of the periodical was almost surely the last ever published.

13. Lewis, "Cupping an Irishman," in *Odd Leaves from the Life of a Louisiana "Swamp Doctor"* (Phila.: A. Hart, 1850). Harris, "A Snake-Bit Irishman: An Original Tennessee Hunting Incident," *New York Spirit of the Times*, 15 (17 Jan. 1846), republ. in *High Times and Hard Times: Sketches and Tales by George Washington Harris*, ed. M. Thomas Inge (Nashville: Vanderbilt Univ. Press, 1967); Harris rewrote the sketch as a "Sut" sketch and included it as "The Snake-Bit Irishman" in *Sut Lovingood. Yarns Spun by a "Nat'ral Born Durn'd Fool.* (New York: Dick & Fitzgerald, 1867). Simms, *Paddy McGann; or, The Demon of the Stump*, initially published in sixteen installments in *The Southern Illustrated News* (Richmond), 14 Feb.-30 May 1863; republ. in vol. III of *The Writings of William Gilmore Simms*, Centennial Edition (Columbia: Univ. of South Carolina Press, 1972).

nerisms and dialect, and he also ridicules the then-popular pseudo-science of phrenology. The basic theory of phrenology is that there are a group of separate faculties in the mind, and that each of these faculties is seated in a particular "organ" of the brain. Supposedly, the phrenologist can judge the development of each faculty by examining the shape of a person's skull. The subject's personality and intelligence are thereby revealed. Much of the humor in Hooper's sketch comes from Stephen O'Cargin's "reading" of the configuration of Mac's excessively ugly and misshapen head. The final punch line brings Irish dialect and phrenology together in a pun: Stephen claims to have angered Mac by touching the "Aurgin of Stame" (organ of steam/steam-organ) on his skull.

"The 'Frinnolygist' at Fault" is republished below for the first time since its original appearance in *Wheler's Magazine*, 2 (January 1850), 25-28. The text printed here is identical to the *Wheler's* text except for one emendation: in the first sentence of the next-to-last paragraph, "unclion" has been emended to read "unction".

JAMES L. W. WEST III

For Wheler's Magazine.

## THE "FRINNOLYGIST" AT FAULT.
## AN HUMOROUS SKETCH.
### BY J.J. HOOPER, AUTHOR OF "SIMON SUGGS," ETC.

SEVERAL stories have been told, I know, in the newspapers, founded on the idea of the mistake on the part of a Professor of Phrenology, in regard to the degree of combativeness of the person submitting to his manipulations; but as I was "personally present" and witnessed the scene I shall attempt to describe, the readers of this miscellany have assurance that what I shall relate is, at least, a Sketch from Real Life.

During the session of the Alabama Legislature, in Montgomery, in December of 1847, on a very cold, blustering night, a party of gentlemen were assembled in the bar-room of the new and splendid "Exchange Hotel," engaged in — (shall I tell it, in these the days of the triumphs of Temperence?) — discussing a couple of baskets of champaigne which WASH TILLEY had produced in honor of the occasion of the opening of the lower story of the aforesaid "Exchange." It was a most hilarious scene. There were the "mad wag," George A — n, of Sumpter; John W — n, of Louderdale; Joseph S — l, of Mobile, and B — s and H — r, of the *Journal*. Besides these, there was a friend of mine whom I shall call *Mac*, a generous, noble-hearted fellow — brave as a lion, but with a heart that could cover the universe with its charity. His single foible was an occasional indulgence in too much wine. His friends all loved him dearly in spite of that and his ugliness — for he *was* ugly, and took a pride in being considered excessively so.

The night waned apace, and the later it grew the more uproarous became the mirth. Decanters rattled, bottles clashed, glasses clinked; and every now and then the whole company *roared*, in concert with M — n, the chorus of *"Carry me back to Ole Virginny,"* the popular Ethiopian melody of the day. Everything was getting topsy-turvy; Wash in vain essayed to get a hearing in regard to the "deuced fine times they used to have up at the 'old Hall,' in '36, when a gentleman considered it an insult to be charged less than six dollars for a bottle of wine;" the "old Colonel" had a friend by the button, in a corner, giving him a desertation on the most approved Parisian mode of *cooking ducks*; and Ned H — k was endeavoring, at the top of his shrill treble, to make a group comprehend how a *North Carolinian* might have been born in Ireland — when "all at onst, of a suddint," a tall figure strode into the room, took an oratorical position in the centre, long enough to observe that it wore a florid complexion, yellow *snaky* locks, and a battered hat — and remarked interrogatively, in most unctuous *brogue*:

"Is there iver a gintleman here wud let me have **the** faalin' ov his head, to help a poor man in his thrubbel, and amyuse the good company?"

"Hollo! Ned H — k!" shouted some one "here's a country-man of yours who wants to 'faal' your head!"

"The divil fly away wid him for a countryman of mine! Does he say *he* came from North Carolina?"

"No, be the powers;" put in the stranger; "and its yerself, me friendly, that's from across the saas, as well — wid yer tongue as maaly as a petatie!"

"Well, well," said Ned, by way of changing the conversation; "what do you want? Do you know that this is a company of *gintlemen*, convaned for social purposes?"

"Me name, me petatie-faced friend, is Staven O'Cargin, Frinnolygist and so forth — at yer service, gintlemen — (bowing to the right and left) — "and in the *ould* counthry a kump'ny ov *gintlemen* be it *one* more or *one* less, is vary much the same thing. I'd be faalin' one ov yer heads, by yer lave, jist to illusthrate the science and to kape things asy along wid the bar-keeper."

The proposition of Mr. O'Cargin was acceded to, by acclamation. He was made to imbibe a glass of brandy, and our friend Mac was drawn up to a chair in the middle of the room, much against his will, and seated before the Phrenologist. He looked particularly dull on the occasion; his eyes were half closed, his nose seemed swollen at the end, and his huge lower jaw seemed to require an effort to keep it from sinking on his breast. All this Mr. O'Cargin seemed to take in, at a glance; and rolling up his cuffs, and making a flourish with his arms, he placed one of his hands on the top of Mac's head:

"Riv'rence, gintlemen, here's riv'rence. At laste, here's the hole in his head where the augrin should be! He's no more riv'rence than a cow, gintlemen, an' he'd make fire-wood of the Thrue Cross. But we'll pass on.

"Ah, self-estame. He's *that* be sure, as big as a turnip. Yes, gintlemen, he's the augrin of *estame* and the augrin of *'stame*" — touching Mac's nose with his forefinger — "beautiful! He'll dhrink like a fish and sthrut like a paacock!"

The crowd laughed uproariously, encored and stamped,

and Mr. O'Cargin thought himself privileged to proceed in a sort of burlesque examination.

"Ide-yality, gintlemen. His frin's must watch him. If iver two little idees or one big one gits withinside his skull, crack it'll go — hard as it is."

Another roar from the company made Mac 'wring and twist' in his seat. He was really a fellow of fine intelligence, and the Phrenologist was going "bloody murther" on his character. Still he bore it very well, only showing his annoyance (as was usual with him) by the energetic grinding of his tobacco with his large, unhandsome lower jaw. Mr. O'Cargin proceeded:

"Adhasiveness, me frin's. He's that illegant, too, but it's connected with another aurgin I mintioned a little ago. His adhasiveness goes by *stame*. He'll *stick by* a bottle of whiskey till — its *dhry!*"

The uproar was now prodigious, but still Mac said nothing. When the noise subsided, "drinks all round" was proposed, and Mac and O'Cargin took brandy together. The former then re-seated himself, and the Phrenologist continued:

"Destructiveness, gintlemen. The craythur is not *destruc*-tive, and by the same token," (changing to another organ,) "he's not *con*structive aither. He could n't set a rat thrap!"

"That's true," said Ned H — k; "and it's the first time you've struck his character, at all!" This was the opinion, too, of all present.

"Niver fear, gintlemen," said O'Cargin, looking round and taking an attitude; "me science is the touch-stone of karakter, intirely; and whin a man's dhifferent from what me science ses he is, it's for the raason that he's a bloody hypikrit and desavin' the worl'!"

"Go on!" roared the crowd.

"Well, thin, gintlemen, here's combativeness;" and he made a step backwards from his subject, but keeping his left thumb pressing on the organ indicated; "and I'll show you his karakter in regard ov that. *He's a coward.*" Mac's jaw ground convulsively. "It's well he did n't go to Mexico! He'll run from his own shadder some sunny day, and kill himself in the attimpt to git clear ov it!"

There was a loud laugh at this, for Mac's character for courage had often been tested, and a truer heart than his never faced danger. O'Cargin however, went on — the muscles of Mac's face and arms twitching and jerking at a terrible rate, and the mastrication of his tobacco being continued with increased energy.

At length the examination was over, and Mac rose.

"You say I'm a coward?" he remarked, his face whitening as he spoke.

"Thrue for you!" replied O'Cargin.

"Take that!" roared the infuriated subject, aiming a blow at the Professor; but his friends, anticipating the movement, caught and held his arms, but with much difficulty, for he struggled like a giant.

O'Cargin was "dumbfounded" with astonishment.

"I did n't say he was a *coward*," he exclaimed, in terrified tones: "at laste I didn't mane it. He's a *paceable* man, was me manin'!"

"I'm not a 'pacable' man, you slandering villain!" cried Mac, bursting from those who held him, and making for O'Cargin furiously.

"Will nobody *hould* him?" yelled the Professor, as he "made play" for the door.

"I'll make you run from something heavier than a *shadow*, you Irish rascal!" roared Mac, loud above the tumult of the crowd.

"I'll *sware* he's a paceable man," screamed O'Cargin, as he slipped (being cut off from a retreat to the street by the door's being locked) with wonderful celerity through the crowd, evading his pursuer.

"And I'll swear I'm *not!*" returned Mac, furiously rushing on.

At last, as Mac, was about to seize him, the Professor sprang over the counter, and amid the crashing of glasses, the expostulations of the bar-tender, and the shoutings of the crowd, crawled under it and ensconced himself between two barrels. In a moment, the ludicrousness of the affair came home to Mac, and he joined the rest in coaxing O'Cargin to come out.

"Divil thrust yer smooth talk," said the Phrenologist.

"O, come out," said Mac; "I was wrong to get mad — come out, and let's make friends."

"I don't know," replied O'Cargin, "how to thrust ye. Ye've sich divilish aurgins — aich gives the other the bloody lie, and I'm afraid o' ye."

"Well, but, surely," exclaimed Mac, "some one of my organs must predominate over the rest."

"Well, thin, may be *one* of 'em does."

"Which is that — my combativeness? asked Mac, laughing.

"I'll niver say that — it was yer self-estame that acted on yer combativeness the minit ago."

"Which is it, then? — speak out."

"Belikes ye'd be mad if I said it."

"No danger," said Mac; "out with it, and out with yourself, or I *will* get mad."

"Well, then," said O'Cargin, as he slowly emerged, looking quizzically into Mac's face, "it's the aurgin I touched awhile wid me forefinger — it's the *Aurgin of 'Stame!*"

Three cheers were given, with great unction, at this "palpable hit;" and amid roars of laughter from all sides, Mac, O'Cargin and the rest proceeded to drink, while Ned H — k proposed, with infinite glee, as a sentiment —

"GOOD LUCK AND THE AURGIN OF STAME!"

# South Carolina Writers
# in the *Spirit of the Times*

In all the study devoted to the New York *Spirit of the Times* as vehicle for the humorous and realistic literature of the antebellum South, scholars have directed most of their attention to the Old Southwest as the source of this type of writing. The states of the Old South have been practically ignored, and no state has suffered more from this neglect than South Carolina. Indeed, the second oldest and most settled of the Southern states after Virginia might seem an unlikely environment to produce contributions to a literature usually associated with the rough-and-tumble society of the American frontier. Yet a search of the New York *Spirit of the Times* and *Porter's Spirit of the Times* shows that more than one hundred South Carolina sketches appeared in their pages during the twenty-nine year period from 1832 to 1861, with the most intense concentration occurring in 1846 and 1847, when eighteen were published. Many of these sketches, it is true, do not exhibit sufficient literary merit to redeem them from a deserved oblivion. However, as the four sketches which follow should clearly indicate, a number of the South Carolina contributions to the *Spirit* are good enough to justify serious critical attention. And they also suggest that a comprehensive study of the entire body of humorous and realistic writings from the Old South states would reveal that this type of writing was a phenomenon of the entire South and not merely of the Old Southwest.

A complete bibliography of South Carolina contributions to the two *Spirits* may be found in Stephen E. Meats, "A Bibliography of Contributions by South Carolinians to the New York *Spirit of the Times* and to *Porter's Spirit of the Times*" (Unpbd. M. A. Thesis, Univ. of South Carolina, 1968). Additional information on South Carolina humorous and realistic writing may be found in the following articles: Leland Cox, "Realistic and Humorous Writings in Ante-Bellum Charleston Magazines," *South Carolina Journals and Journalists*, ed. James B. Meriwether (Columbia, S. C., 1975), pp. 177-205; Donald McNair, "Backwoods Humor in the Pendleton, South Carolina, *Messenger*, 1810-1851," *South Carolina Journals and Journalists*, pp. 225-232; Nancy B. Sederberg, "Antebellum Southern Humor in the *Camden Journal*, 1826-1840," *Mississippi Quarterly*, 27 (Winter 1973/1974), 41-74; and James L. W. West III, "Early Backwoods Humor in the Greenville *Mountaineer*, 1826-1840," *Mississippi Quarterly*, 25 (Winter 1970/1971), 69-82. Norris Yates, in his *William T. Porter and the New York Spirit of the Times* (Baton Rouge, 1957), mentions or discusses six sketches by South Carolinians, but indicates the South Carolina connection for only two, those written by Pierce Mason Butler while he was living in Arkansas; see Yates, pp. 82-83, 125, 126, 184, 198.

In editing the four sketches which appear hereafter, I have followed the original texts exactly except for corrections of obvious typographical errors and accidents and elimination of small capital letters in proper names and place names. The texts printed here are based on those appearing in the American Periodical Series microfilm reproduction of the New York *Spirit of the Times*.

Much more could certainly be said by way of introducing the South Carolina sketches which follow. Such critical commentary might highlight the interesting variety of subject matter, the peculiar characters, the narrative techniques, the authenticity of dialects – might probe for weaknesses of conception and design, failures of imagination and execution – might even attempt to isolate traits of work and author uniquely South Carolinian. But perhaps the best thing to do when presenting such new material is to withdraw quietly into the background, like Thorpe's framework narrator in "The Big Bear of Arkansas," and let the principals speak for themselves.

STEPHEN E. MEATS

*"NATURAL ANGLING, OR RIDING A STURGEON" was reprinted in the* Spirit of the Times, *15 (24 May 1845), 145, from a now lost issue of the Columbia* South Carolinian. *The author of this sketch and of the one following, "THE VEGE-TABLE SHIRT-TAIL," was Adam G. Summer, who wrote under the pseudonym "Vesper Brackett." Summer (1818-1866) was a lawyer in Newberry, S. C., for several years after he was admitted to the bar in 1840, but sometime near the beginning of 1845, probably early in February (his inaugural editorial address is reprinted in the Charleston* Mercury *of 10 February), he went to Columbia where he became owner and editor of the* South Carolinian. *Except for one brief period in 1847, Summer conducted this newspaper until 29 December 1848, the date he announced the termination of his connection with the paper. While editor, Summer published a number of sentimental sketches and tales in his paper under the pseudonym "Vesper Brackett," and agricultural articles under his own name. After leaving the* South Carolinian, *Summer farmed on his plantation, "Ravenscroft," in Lexington County, S.C., and in the early 1850's was elected to several terms in the state legislature. Throughout 1853 and part of 1854, Summer edited the* Southern Agriculturalist (Laurensville, S. C.) *with the aid of his brother, William. Beginning in 1857, Summer lived for a brief period in Florida but returned to South Carolina in time to serve in the Civil War. He was married in 1865, only one year before his death. Summer is also reported to have written for the* Southern Quarterly Review, *the* Southern Literary Messenger, *and the Newberry* Sentinel, *but no contributions by him have been found in these journals; two Summer items have been seen in* The Magnolia. *John Belton O'Neall included one of Summer's sentimental sketches in* The Annals of Newberry *(1859). In the text reprinted below, two obvious typos have been corrected from the original* Spirit *text.*

# NATURAL ANGLING, OR RIDING A STURGEON.

---

## BY VESPER BRACKETT.

---

Fishing is not the same wild and exciting sport it was, when our rivers were untamed, and instead of the subdued and present worn appearance, their banks were pictures of nature in her most romantic and captivating garb; and when the chief charms of *divine divertisement* consisted of the break-neck adventures and real peril of the pursuit. Now-a-days, woe to them! anglers must fish with quaint bait, recommended by that venerable piscatorial saint, great Izaak; and though they submit to the modern innovation of a generous Limerick hook — the remainder of the tackle must be arranged by the book — and taciturn demeanor is always to be observed, even though they angle under a Niagara; for the sage hath said, that silence in the fisherman is conducive to great success. This fastidiousness has, in my opinion, driven the most princely fish from our waters; at least, I can in no wise account for their disappearance, unless *these patent draw out Conroy's*, with their thousand yards of gossamer gut, have caused the surprising immigration. Where now can we snare the vigorous rock-fish, or the tasty and gentlemanly trout of a dozen pounds weight? All gone! and it has really come to pass that fifty pounds of small-fry, taken in one ramble at some breeding place, is a capture astonishing to boys, and talked of for a week at least.

Belton Tinkerbottom was the last fisherman of the old sort whom I knew, and he was a hook well tied on. I saw him, in our last excursion, draw in a thirteen-pounder with "a love of a reed," cut by my own hands — selected from a million on Hampton's Island — and a line twisted by his own skill, with a grace that would have taught a nibble or two, to the patent spring-pole gentry of the present times. He did it in a native American style, which was, of course, original, and methought when his line whistled in the eddying circles of Cohees' dashing currents, that the river-gods who dwelt thereabouts, must have been in trepidation, lest their peculiar divinity should not entirely protect them from the skill of the sturdy angler.

There are many angling stories told about Tink, but the best came under my own observation. Even at the risk of prolixity, I must favor you with it: — We were just ready to leap into our little dug out, with lines all properly measured and tied on, when — after admiring the first Limerick hook he had ever beheld, it was transferred to his mouth for safe keeping, until we should reach "*trout pond*," a beautiful eddy between two sluices in Cohees, which, good reader, is a romantic shoal in Broad River, South Carolina — Tink stumbled, his foot pressed the rod, and before he could gain an upright position, he was hooked most endearingly through his right cheek. *The Trouticide* had tied on *that hook*, and he would not permit me to cut it loose from the line, for he said he was determined to fish *with that hook*; and, of course, as there was no chance of further sport in his being both bait and angler, I was forced, at his request, to cut it out of his cheek, which operation I performed with my old jack-knife, and with such surgical grace that we made a glorious day's sport, and though he was the largest fish caught by *that hook*, it carried the *take-in* deep amongst the finny patriarchs on that occasion, and it contributed but little to lessen his beauty, for Tinkerbottom's mouth was the best natured feature in the world, and never was known to object to any dilation, in any manner whatever. Soon after this occurrence he was hooked by Father Time — who once and a while hunts up even anglers — and is now, I sincerely hope, revelling amid the wonders of the strange waters to which he has been translated, or perhaps is discussing with the aforesaid St. Izaak, the comparative merits of *natural* and *artificial* fishing.

The immediate predecessor of Tinkerbottom was Honyucle Hallman, who was still more natural in his warfare on the finny tribe. Catting was his great *forte*, and the needle fins saw perfect sights the days he thought proper to invade their domains. He caught cats to please his wife, and extenuated the awful crime in those days by saying "Sally loves cat-fish, but I love shad," and always insisted, that "a man who wishes all his fellow-varmints well, will only eat fish in the shad season," and as for perch, brim, and *sich like*, Honyucle would as soon have been caught eating mud-suckers or pond roaches. He would condescend to fish for rock and trout, as he said they had a gentlemanly flutter, and tried honestly to save their lives. He lived for the shad season, and angled for sport alone, and to see him hook a magnificent rock-fish with his long float line — to mark his varying countenance, and to judge of his excitement by the velocity with which he rolled the quid in his cheek, was enough of the sport for an observer. You might have noticed a thousand attitudes before he finished his capture. Honyucle never went on the principle of satiety; one rock-fish was enough, and when that one was secured, like "old Washington," (the sobriquet of an aged eagle who frequented this part of the river,) he retired from Cohees. Another favorite of Honyucle's was spearing sturgeon as they lay on their pebble beds, among the shallows, during the warm days in the month of May. In fact, this was whale fishing in miniature, with all its excitement attended with some peril, for frequently the pierced fish would dart off with such velocity that his canoe would be upset; and amongst the rapids of Cohees, with a boat fastened to a sturgeon, that circumstance is not altogether as funny as some might suppose. But in time sturgeon grew shy or wise, or perhaps the water was not sufficiently clear in the proper season for him to see them, and Honyucle pined away; he grew morose, and waited for the next season with hope, anticipating that some change would manifest itself in the realm of sturgeon-*dom*. February, March, April — glorious season of shad — flew by, and each day found him with his nets among the shoals — wind or rain — as regularly insinuating his skill among the salt water visitors as "old Washington" and his white-headed partner went to the raft of drift-wood, in the middle of the river, from whence they generally picked up their daily rations of dead fish and terrapins.

Though moderate success always attended his efforts, he

grew moodier as the spring tide brightened, and frequent spells of the "blue dipper" gave his wonted communicativeness a singular feature of interest. Speaking of success, Honyucle was no "*water-haul*" man — he was a perfect seducer of fish, and it was the belief of the honest Dutch in that neighborhood that he could charm them, owing to certain secret powers by him alone possessed. If the "green-haired maiden of the sea" could wile the Spanish mariner to

> "Isles that lie
> In farthest depths of Ocean; girt with all
> Of natural wealth and splendor — jewelled isles,
> Boundless in unimaginable spoils
> That earth is stranger to." Simms' Atalantis.

with a voice "like the winds among a bed of reeds," Honyucle in his turn enchanted the water divinities, and his achievements with rod and line always scattered grief in the realms below, even if it was not agreeable to the scaly captives. Settled melancholy begets peevishness in meditative minds; and Sally's ingenious inquiries failed to extract the cause of his gloom. The clack of his mill seemed to knock this unusual feature deeper into his soul every day, and he scored and tolled a thoughtful man.

May-day, in the south, you have enjoyed, my dear P***er, but as you have never seen Cohees, with its sparkling sluices flashing in the warm and mellow sun-light — the ancient wave-worn rocks, on which the heron race in light-blue and snow-white garbs delight to rest 'mid their aquatic wanderings, the vines bending to the water's edge, and casting shadows of fairy-like greeting on the tide beneath, with cliffs rising abruptly from the shore, crowned with flax-colored shoots of the late-springing hickory, a green pine-forest standing like sentinels in the rear; and below this, on a level almost with the water, is a little kingdom, yet another realm of nature comprising the beautiful river Laurel, the dwarf cedar, the stinted river ivy, and thorny leaved holly with its red berries still unshed, and con-

trasting with beautiful effect its green foliage, forming a shelter-
ing covert, and letting in just enough sunshine to keep the
prickly cactus, the creeping periwinkle, and other modest
daughters of the floral kingdom – from languishing. As you
have never enjoyed this scene of enchantment, you will pardon
my asserting its kindred to magic, because it was the first impression which invaded the "bad humor" of Honyucle. All this
was *goose-grease* to his discontended soul, and it

> "Called up sweet fancies form his pliant hope,
> And stirr'd the languid spirit into life,
> Surveying the blue waters and his home."     *Atalantis.*

He saw the fish leaping from the bright river, the skimming
swallows fluttering o'er its shining surface; he looked up at the
sky, "old Washington's" savage scream arrested his attention,
and high up, poised upon the air, with his bald pate, glittering
like a jewelled crown, and the grey down of his pinions reflect-
ing the beams of the morning sun in brilliant effulgence, he
marked with admiration the rapid whirl of the old patriarch of
Cohees, who darting downwards like a stream of light headlong
into the foaming surf beneath, vanished for a moment; then
emerging, rose heavily from the bed of the river, and flapping
his wet wing, with a glittering prize in his talons, sailed slowly
towards his time-honored and uninvaded eyry.

Honyucle's gloom relaxed – there was no straining for
contentment visible in his countenance, and he sallied forth,
trout rod in hand, once more to enjoy his accustomed sport.
On foot he entered the river, and picking his path among the
rapids, now wading a rapid sluice to the depth of his waist, now
leaping from rock to rock; and anon peering into the chrystal
waters, as was his custom when on a piscatorial scout, he suddenly seemed transfixed, his body became motionless, and he
stood as firm as if his brawn had been moulded from the en-
during granite on which his form rested. Beneath him in the
waves lay a large sturgeon, unconscious that the foe of his race
was so near; but the deadly sturgeon-spearer was unarmed, and
his usually eager excitement was tempered into admiration.

There lay the fresh water monster, and the more Honyucle looked at him the ruddier grew the crimson glow of the scales on his sides in the sunny water. In the red gills, opening with the regular breathing of the fish, he saw proper reins to hold by,

> And a thought, for a deed,
> Cast him on the water steed!

Slapping his hands into the gills of the sturgeon, who, not relishing this obstruction of his respiration *by poking straws* into his *side nostrils*, instantly contracted them, and having thus secured his rider, darted with the rapidity of fright down the rocky and jagged sluice. A few flights and the shallows were passed; at one time Honyucle's head might have been seen, and then he was quickly drawn below the water, and thus alternately hope and despair agonized or cheered his wife, who stood sole witness of the scene on the distant shore. After traversing with the rapidity of lightning the downward course of the river, several hundred yards, one hand of the drowning man was released, and the water was violently lashed by the tail of the infuriated sturgeon, who now, instead of keeping a straight course, circled round several times, still dragging Honyucle by his side. His left hand had become entangled in the throat or gills of the powerful fish, and the sturgeon became incommoded by the broad hand of Honyucle; round and round they went, the prisoner having only a chance now and then to gasp for breath, was tremendously thumped by the lashing of the sturgeon's tail.

At this period of the *melee* the blood from the torn cartilage of the throat of the fish was ejected with great force, and the red tide of life mingled with the agitated waters; another struggle, and conqueror and victim floated side by side on the surface of the river. One more ineffectual attempt to free himself, and the last flutter of the dying sturgeon, faint and weak as he was, threw them on a low rock, and he was thus providentially rescued from the death which so imminently threatened him. His wife leaped into a canoe, and rowed hastily to him to give whatever succor was in her power, and when he was released from the dead fish, it was ascertained that his wrist was severed to the bone; his body was covered with contusions, and his legs were terribly lacerated by the tail of the bruiser.

This adventure cured Honyucle of grieving after the scarcity of sturgeon, and though he continued a devotee of the rod to his dying day, he always avoided the scene of his ride.

South Carolinian.

*****

*"THE VEGETABLE SHIRT-TAIL; Or, an Excuse for Backing Out," was also written by Adam G. Summer (see the headnote for the previous sketch); it appeared in the* Spirit of the Times, *16 (5 September 1846), 325. It is on the basis of this sketch that Summer's pseudonym, "Vesper Brackett," was identified. In the "To Correspondents" column in the* Spirit *of 4 August 1849, William T. Porter disclosed that the shirt-tail story was written by "Maj. A. G. S. of S. C." Two obvious typographical errors have been silently emended.*

## THE VEGETABLE SHIRT-TAIL;

Or, an Excuse for Backing Out.

---

BY COL. VESPER BRACKETT,
OF SOUTH CAROLINA.

I wont tell you, my dear "Tall Son of York," how I just happened to be staying a spell at Deaves's Sulphur Springs, in the State of Buncombe, N. C. — nor need I tell you that I was liver-beset, which *disagremens* did not attach itself to my 'innards' as 'similar like' appendages do to the celebrated bipeds of Strasbourg — but I must be allowed to just knock you down, with the full born *idee* that of all the *humanities* I ever saw crowded into one skin, "Pot Runnels" was the fullest. "Pot," as you must know, is the abbreviation of "Potley," which, in turn again, is "the short" for "Bartholomew," and the owner of this *convayniant* soubriquet wasn't above turning his availabilities to almost anything which was required of him. I found him a useful scenery guide, and he was a first rate hand to turn squirrels, for he was so "onmarsifully onhansome" that the little animals would never stay on his side of the tree, and I was sure to get a fair shot.

Pot told me on one of these rambles, that he was never "outened but a single twice in his life." "Kunnull, I tell you — one time by a leetle sivil *Ingineear*, who warn't so darned sivil as he mout a been. Don't you think, Kunnull, he tuk devantage of the squerrils by pokin a long brass spy glass at 'em, when an honest man would have hunted 'em with his native eyes? Kunnull, this Cincinnati Rail Road man — all the way from Charlestown, and a blasted fool at that, with no shakes in his head but matical levels — could draw a squerril up to the muzzle of his double-barril with the wicked thing, and then he'd shoot 'em, without even saying, by your leave, Mister Squerril. A dubble-barril, Kunnull, is onchristian enuff; but bringing the nutcrackers right on to your nose with a glass, was sartingly the work of the devil. I axed Klingman, our Kongressman, and he says he is a rale *Ingineere*, and has quit squerrils and does nothing but hunt Injuns on the pararies, and that he got so good with his cussed glasses that the President had some big long ones made for him, and he drawed the Rockey Mountings, and the "Great Fighting Oregon," so close to the Fedderl City that all Kongress can look through his Reports, and see everything laid down. He was wonderful, Kunnell, and when Klingman told me he was a rale Army Kunnell, and had writ books bigger nor a Columby Orator, and laid off rivers and mountings by draft, just like Kunnell Seaver laid off his new house, I was *outened* the first time, for I never consated little Freemount would ever come to any thing."

"But your second *outening* — how was that, Pot?"

"Well, Kunnell, that was worser, by a jug full. I reckon you know Miss Flekins over the mounting, the place where Old Cordes says he always sends Billey to get butter-milk for his *ask-ma*? Well, if you don't, it's that little dubble-cabin, where there is a most outdacious site of gourd vines growing on the strate fence before the house, and where there is a pile of chips and an ash bank, which shows that the Widow has some fire to keep folks warm in the winter. That's the place, and Winey Flekins wasn't slow before she throwed herself away though, I tell *you*. Well, I sorter lickered arter Winey, and puts in shoots for her name at every shootin match in our diggings, and thought I'd go over and see her one Saturday afternoon. Our Buck was about the shiniest of the oxen-kind in these parts, and so I put on my bran new flax shirt mammy just had got done, and I started over to see the galls. You see, Kunnull, folks under twenty didn't wear briches up here before you folks tuk to coming to the Springs. Well, when I got there, there was the galls a spinnin and ironin on the *piasar*, an Buck, he had a nack of tearin loose, so I was afraid to go in and leave him hitched but helt him, and sat on the fence a talkin to the galls all about courtin, and going to meetin, and sich likes, and I tell *you*, in less nor an hour I was in an orful fix. Oh! Kunnull, I was in the catechism strong, I tell you. Don't you spose I looked mean when I felt the darned steer a likin the salt sweat off of the back of my neck? I thought I'd fall, Kunnell, for I mistrusted — for it was a new shirt, made from right green flax — and sure enuff, the beast had *smelt the weed* in it, and eat the whole backwards off, smack smooth up to the collar, and 'twarn't no more nor an apern, no how, left. I didn't know what to do, I tell you. But the wust must come to the wust, said I. You think I done wrong, or could be called a coward for backing out, in a decent way? Well, sir-ree, I dun nothin else. But before I started I told the galls I'd sarve 'em like the Chineese do their King: I'd retire from their presents with my face towards 'em, and not offar them a dignity. Well, didn't the galls take it nice? — Winey, she snickered some — but I was sukseedin to the fraxshun of a nat's heel, when Buck got gaily, and whirled *'right about backwards face,'* as our Cap'n says, and it didn't take me till Sunday morning to jump astraddle of him and clare out. But, Kunnull, the galls seed it; and at the next shootin match Bill Spires called me a *'wegeble shurt-tale,'* and we had a fite about whether flax was a *wegeble* or not. I

swore it was a *small grain*, and I flogged him, shirt-tail or no shirt-tail, and so it must be a small grain. Don't you think it is, Kunnull?"
Columbia, S. C., August, 1846.

\*\*\*\*\*

*"A FISH STORY" was published in the* Spirit of the Times, *16 (12 September 1846), 342. Its author, John A. Stuart, was the only South Carolinian other than Pierce Mason Butler to have a sketch published in one of William T. Porter's two collections of humorous writings. Stuart (1800-1852) was a native of Beaufort, S. C. He graduated from the South Carolina College in 1817 and was admitted to the bar in 1822. In 1827 he became editor of the Beaufort* Gazette *and assumed an editorial stance strongly in support of States' Rights. He soon became an out-spoken proponent of his brother-in-law, Robert Barnwell Rhett, the South Carolina politician who was perhaps the leading advocate of secession in the South. In 1831 Stuart moved to Charleston where on 1 October he started* The State Rights and Free Trade Evening Post. *He served as its editor until he announced his resignation on 20 October 1832; on 31 October, he took over as editor of the Charleston* Mercury *from Henry Laurens Pinckney. Although he continued as official editor of the* Mercury *until his retirement on 3 January 1845, in reality he had been active in the office only sporadically for more than two years previous to this date. After he turned the* Mercury *over to J. Milton Clapp, his assistant of seven years, Stuart returned to Beaufort permanently. Stuart's one other item in the* Spirit, *an insignificant extract from the* Mercury, *appeared in 1843; he also contributed articles to the* Southern Literary Journal. *Six printer's errors in the original* Spirit *text are silently emended in the text below.*

# A FISH STORY.

By J. A. Stuart, Esq., late Editor of
the Charleston "Mercury."

Beaufort, S. C., Aug. 30.

Old Lignumvitae and Mulatto Peter, were the two most inveterate fishermen of our island. No other old man of that day could remember when the old bachelor was called anything but "Lignumvitae," and Peter, though some sixty years younger than his master, was, at the time of our legend, a man well stricken in years. Age cooled not their devotion to sport, but only riveted the chains of habit. Their nets were heard at eve and early dawn lashing among the mullets of Salt Water Bridge; their light wood torch, as they went striking on frosty nights, moved like a broad meteor along the waters of "Deep Hole;" and in sheephead season, they served as a landmark to the coasters, as they kept their daily low water station on Pigeon Point, like "anxious cranes silent and watching." They were slender as their fishing canes; and, except when a sheephead fixed on their never missing hooks, flashed up his broad bars of ebony and silver, so motionless were they in their intentness, that the king-fisher would frequently perch on their heads.

On a drizzly cold evening in November they pushed off their paddling canoe in pursuit of a school of trout that were taking refuge from the porpoises, among the mud-flats and sand-banks of Pigeon Point Creek. Peter made fine hauls with his net – and his master, armed with the *grains* attached to his wrist by a short hand line, was dexterously pinning the finners, now perpendicularly and anon pouncing his unerring weapon upon them at the distance of ten or twelve feet. This sport had continued some time, when a porpoise loomed darkly under the bow; the old gentleman either was angry at the interruption, or deemed his a fish of less calibre, or could not resist the temptation of so fair a hit. In went the grains! and over went Old Lignumvitae. "Porpus, Massa! don't strike!" screamed Peter.

The words fell on empty air. 'Ere they were uttered the old man was flashing like a rocket's tail, deep through the channel of the creek. One whirl round the boat, and as he caught at the marsh on the margin, and tore it up by the roots, — "Pete!" cried the old gentleman; "Old Lignumvitae gone to day!" — gobble! gobble! gobble! he choked and went down; a frighted bass flounced out on the mudflat; "Pete!" cried the old man emerging, ("the ruling passion strong in death") — "mind that fellow!" gobble, gobble, gobble! and up the creek they swept; the water boiling like a cauldron. The porpoise wheeled on his wake and ran down his hanger-on as a steamboat would a yawl; and back they came almost on Peter and the boat. Peter instinctively flung his net at the porpoise. He might as well have flung at the winged lightning; the fish plunged on with the speed of added terror; the old gentleman darted into the air: the bullets of the net rattled on his head, and his shoes flew off into Peter's face. "Old Lignumvitae is gone to-day!" groaned the old man in his extremity. Plunge! gobble! gobble! gobble! Away they whistled, and splashed, and flounced, and flourished, succeeding each other in rapid alternate leaps; porpoise up, Lignum down — porpoise down, Old Lignum exalted; entrance and exit; submersion, emersion! quick as thought — hurry skurry! duck and drake — whiz!! The old gentleman could scarce breathe; his right arm was strained forward by the fatal tow line; his left was pinned close to his side by the pressure of the element through which he was careering, and the brine foamed between his unsheltered nose and chin, as through the beak of a shear water. Once in his airy flight, he snatched a moment to slip a plug of pig-tail from his breeches pocket to his mouth; in a moment breeches pocket he had none! For as the porpoise did not merely swim and rise as if only to blow — but absolutely bounced along the water like a cannon ball, and leaped like a stag, Peter all at once thought he saw his master stretching outrageously as the fish vanished, and the legs of the old man spread against the horizon in his white nankeen inexpressibles. The fact was, the breeches were coming off — for Lignum wore no suspenders. The porpoise gave a whirl to the right, the old man flew to the left; they spun for a moment on the vexed waters like a rocket, or whirligig; the old man cast a magnificent somerset, and the white nankeen inexpressibles flew off into the air. "Gor amighty!" cried Peter, "he cut him in two!" Eased of a portion of his draft, the porpoise sped faster than ever and with Old Lignum at his tail, hissed and brustled, and flew through a fleet of paddling canoes that had just turned Pigeon Point. The negroes squatted into the bottoms of their boats, some swearing 'twas a water spout; some, (seeing fish and man confusedly,) that it was a mad mermaid; and some that it was the devil, carrying off an overseer in a whirlwind. At length they came to the Point, and the porpoise was now going with such straight forward, regular velocity, that Old Lignumvitae was kept above water, skimming and scudding along the surface on his stomach, like a wild duck alighting on ice; when behold! the cutting sight of a black battalion of oyster shells, with their sharp serrated edges, stretching directly athwart their course! One lash of the tail and the porpoise bounded across. "Oh! my g — s!" cried the unwilling follower. But the shells cut the line — and Old Lignumvitae was safely stranded on the bank. The porpoise went merrily to the ocean, and was long after famous as "Old Will" among the fishermen; and identified by his blunt fin, which they said was injured in this very scuffle.

Peter paddled up and found his master — whom experience had taught to take a lesson from every incident — manufacturing his first pair of suspenders from the fragment of the grains' line.

"Peter!" said the old man getting into the boat as his faithful servant cried, "Tank farer!" and gave a long whistle; his eyes opening to the size of a dollar! "Peter never take in hand more than you can well manage, or you will catch yourself, Peter!"

"And maybe lose yourself too," said Peter. "Whew!!!" and he whistled and paddled.

"I've lost the grains," said Old Lignumvitae.

"Drat de grains!" muttered Peter.

"But the bass, Peter?"

"I got um!"

"And my breeches, Peter?"

"Got um, too – but tobacco gone!"

Notwithstanding this miraculous escape, fate had determined that the fish should have retribution; for the very next year, while the old man and Peter were fishing near the Fort, a Devil Fish seized their anchor, and dragged them to sea. They were never heard of after, though some of the old negroes say they have seen their ghosts in a phantom canoe on very dark nights, and in September gales.

*****

*" 'SINGED POSSUM'S' FIRST LOVE" appeared in the* Spirit of the Times, *17 (25 September 1847), 363. The same author also contributed two sentimental poems to the* Spirit; *his pseudonym, "Glenvarlock," has not been identified. There were five typos in the original appearance; they are silently emended here.*

## "SINGED POSSUM'S" FIRST LOVE.

### BY A NEW SOUTH CAROLINA CORRESPONDENT.

———

"Now, now, while 'tis youth, pluck the roses of love."
Gerusalemme Lib. Canto XVI.
"Go it while you're young!"
Jonathan's Translation.

———

It was almost dark. I had ridden far, and was now urging on my wearied horse in search of a shelter for the night. The ground was covered with snow, and the wind came in fitful blasts, shaking the icicles from the trees, and sprinkling rider and horse with the frozen shower. The path became still more obscure and difficult to follow; and the idea of spending such a night in the wilds of Tennessee, and leaving my bones to bleach in the wilderness, uncoffined and unshrouded, was anything but pleasant. Thoughts of home and kindred dear, "o'er the far blue mountain," only increased my uneasiness, and rendered me still less willing to furnish a meal for the vulture and the wolf. However well grounded, my apprehensions were nevertheless not destined to be realized. My reflections were agreeably interrupted by the discovery of a man in advance of me whom I was rapidly overtaking, notwithstanding the hurried application of his heels and the "butt" of his rifle to the flanks of his horse, in his vain attempts to raise a "canter." Our horses were soon "neck and neck" – the usual salutations passed, and we rode on together for a house, which my companion in homespun assured me was not far distant.

"Wal, squire," said he, as soon as we had exchanged one or two common place  observations, "you arn't from them gall-bustin big cities at the north, is you? Though them ingan-eaten fokes does come this a way wunce on a while!"

On my assuring him that I was not a "Yankee," but a South Carolinian living near the sea board, he resumed,

"That are a darned flat country of your'n, squire. Sich sand I never seed afore. I were down thar in '33, with a load o' bacon. I druv six hosses, ere a one on 'em good enough for a President to ride. Them hosses went over Paint Mountain and Saluda Gap like nuthin, and didn't stop to wind their bellowses – but darn me if they didn't stall gwine down hill in your Calina sand. That sand are killin to hoss flesh and human natur. When I got thar I felt sorter humsickish – it were all peticler flat, not a mountain. I could see a darn long shot down the road but it were all sand. I swar I b'leve if thar had been unly one good hill to a pulled up, I'd a felt betterer. But I gin it up. I sold out to a darned punkin-faced squatter up to his knees in sand, for a leetle less than nothin rather than go on to Charlesting. It a'most busted me quite; but blast me if I b'leve I'd av ever seed hum ef I hadn't turned back. The sand were gittin bilin hot – the last night I were thar I lay down about 9 o'clock, and 'twarnt long afore I woke up with sich a koorious feelin all over, snakes and wildcats! but may I never eat meat agin, if the sand hadn't burnt off my hair and whiskers, and the misketers was all over me brushin off the sinders. When I come'd hum, the nabers called me "Singed Possum;" darn that sand to everlastin stigmatize, sez I. One place I passed were called "Frog Level," but if I had the christ'nin it, blast me if I didn't baptize the whole on it Frog Flat, from Hamburg to Charlesting. No offence to you, squire; your State mout do for them whats used to it, but it's agin my natur; my cons'tution wouldn't stood it no time at all. I were raised about 80 mile above this in the mountains, at the head of Big Limestone; not fur from Rackoon Hollow."

My companion was here interrupted by the loud barking of a dog, and the gleaming of a light from a cabin, which he said was the only place within ten miles where we could be accommodated for the night. Our hail was answered by a rough-looking woodman, who, after various interrogations and a rigid scrutiny of our persons and faces, agreed to shelter us for the night. Having placed our horses under a shed and supplied them with provender, we entered the cabin. Supper was already on table, so, as soon as we had warmed at the fire, we assisted the family of our host in despatching the ham and eggs and biscuit, with a bottle of peach brandy in lieu of the more desirable coffee.

Our landlord, Timothy Trink, was a short, surly, and incommunicative ruffian, who, I was afterwards informed, had been, under a different name, connected with the notorious Murrel. His wife appeared to be better disposed, though excessively indelicate; and their two daughters, Kate and Phyllis, 16 and 18 years old, Amazons, completed the domestic circle of Mr. Timothy Trink. They all appeared more or less annoyed by our presence, and spoke but little. I therefore determined to cultivate my acquaintance with "Singed Possum," and for this purpose, after supper engaged him in conversation. The squalid poverty, rude manners, and suspicious looks of the Trink family appeared in no way to disturb my "singed" friend. Taking an extra "quid," and throwing a fresh log on the fire, he thus did his "tale unfold" –

"I'se about 27, come next June, and a purty-sized whapper, as you obsarves. My idication warn't looked arter as it jist ought to 'av been: but I sez nuthin agin them what ought to 'av seed to it. No man are worth shucks what'll talk agin his mammy and dad, sez I. So, as I were sayin, I were a sorter wild, like, a leetle of the tallest feller for fun in the settlemint. I were afeard of nuthin. I could out-fish, out-hunt, out-run, out-drink, out-laugh, out-yell, out-court, out-fight, out-play, and out-eat anything. Thar were nobody like me in them diggins 'till I got on trail of a love scrape. I were one day down at a meetin in Rackoon Hollow, whar the new Circuit rider were to hold forth. His name were Rogers, and when he talked you'd a thought his tongue were iled. I were ridin the same hoss I has now, and he wanted to swop with me; so we swopt hosses, and I were sucked; he were too smart for me, thar. Dog my cats if I'se ever gwine to swop hoss flesh with another Circuit rider. He were into me a feet; he warn't anythin else; but I went in the meetin to hear him cavort. His darter Nancy were thar, with the butifulest red ringlits, and the witest face, and sich anuther set o' ribbins, golly! how I loved her rite off. The fellers soon seed how the cat jumped, and gin me a clean room. So arter meetin I tuk Miss Nancy Rogers up behind me to see her hum, and all along the way I were pourin out the saftest kind o' soap. When we lighted at her house nobody were home yet from meetin, so I sot down close to Nanny, and sez I –

'Nan, does you knows I love you?'

'Yes,' sez she, 'I reckon.'

'And, Nan, does you love me?'

'Yes, I reckon.'

'And will you be my wife, Nan?'

'Yes, I reckon.'

'Will you jine hands to-morrow night?'

'Yes, I reckon.'

'May I kiss you, Nan?'

She pouted her lips, Squire, and I gin her what we call a

half-hour buss. I swar, her lips were sweet as maple-sugar, and I does not knows how long I'd 'av hung on to 'em, but somethin touched me on the shoulder, and thar were the circuit rider, with his big gray eyes a starin at us. My dander riz, and I'd a gin him a leetle thunder and lightin in no time, but Nan begged for him. He were in a perfect hurricane of a humor, too, and I kept peticklar wigilant. He axed me how I could feed a decent 'ooman, and I showed him these ere corn-pullers. He gin up, and all were fixed; only he spiled our 'greement for the weddin, as he 'lowed I'd have to go down South with a load o' bacon fust, and when I come back with the needful, I were to marry the gal. I knocked under to him, but I met with a little the worst luck, as I were tellin you. I were singed and exploded, — that darned Calina sand; and when I got back almost to hum, I were told that Nan were gwine to marry Ned Daykins, a fat-bellied hound what war n't worth a tallow candle, or a spoonful of ile to his homny. They b'leved me to be down South, but, darnation, I were fixin' a solemncolly infair for 'em. I were in a blaze, a rigler volcaner of blue brimstone; the whole Massissippi couldn't a cooled me. Ned Daykins were like a mice playin with the sweet-meats wile the cat were away; but the cat were thar, only under cover like, waitin to spring.

When the night come for it, I were at the circuit rider's, with a dozen of the tallest chaps in the Hollow to see fair play. Ned and Nancy was on the floor ready to be tied, and they looked all-fired sheepish when I stepped up to 'em and sez, sez I —

'This ere gal were mine, as you all knows, and this ere lump o' slush are guilty of a darned sight o' larseny and mean-ness in takin my place, and so,' sez I, 'we'll fought it out, and the best man takes the gal, if he wants her. Move the gal in the corner,' sez I, 'and now, Ned, darn you, stand to your rack.'

He gin me a few licks, but dod rot me if the fourth lick I let 'im 'av didn't send his front grinders down his guts, and make him holler ''nuff,' like a screech owl. 'Now,' sez I, when I seed the warmint wur done fur, sez I, 'Mister Rogers, I reckon you'll go on with the surremony, seein as how the right man

are here now.' With that he comed forad, and Nan took hold on
my hand, gigglin and friskin like a monkey on a apple wagin.
Darn me if I didn't love her arter all, when she shuk her red
ringlets about and pouted her lips — but 'twere no go; she
hadn't oughter been so changeful like. So when the circuit rider
axed me if I'd jist have 'er and keep 'er for a wife, I sez, sez I —
'No, sir-ee, I'll take anuther load o' bacon to Calina fust,'
sez I, 'and more,' sez I, 'you is a darnation white-livered cheat,'
sez I, 'what's too darn mean for the sun to shine on; hang you,'
sez I, 'and your darter too! I gin up your gal, and your hoss to
boot — so you kin jist git my hoss Brimstone, and I'll darken
your door no more forever and a day arterwards.'

He were petickler scared, and jist a leetle of the maddest. I
I jumpt on Brimstone, and were off — the 'ooman folks yellin
like Injins, and as I gallopt past the hog-pen I seed the chaps rol-
lin Ned Daykins in the softest bed imagible. I were off to Alabam, whar I got a gal not quite sich a frisk as Nan, and I've been
livin with her these six years. I haint seed Nan since, but,
'though I has three children, and a purty smart 'ooman for a
wife, I can't forgit the circuit rider's darter with her red ringlets,
and sweet maple-sugar poutin lips. I'se jist been on a visit to the
Hollow, but I seed nuthin of 'em; they must a moved out West,
I reckon; they were a mighty movin people anyhow."

By this time the Trinks were all asleep on a large pile of
straw in a corner of the cabin, and "Singed Possum" joining
them without ceremony, was soon snoring in deep bass. Wrap-
ping up in my cloak, I stretched myself on a bench before the
fire; but reflection on my companion's singular story banished
for a long time the drowsy god. Poor Singed Possum! His was
*love in the backwoods.* The blue heaven of Italy, the swift-gliding
gondola of Venice, the flowers and vines of sunny France, the
fountains and castles of Spain, which invest their love-scenes
with so much romance, were all wanting here in the western wilderness; and yet the passion was the same, though not so re-
fined or sentimental, in Singed Possum and his affianced Nancy.
'Twas the same, only somewhat modified, which Coleridge cele-
brates in his Christabel:

"Alas! they had been friends in youth;
But whispering tongues can poison truth;
And constancy lives in realms above:
And life is thorny; and youth is vain;
And to be wroth with one we love,
Doth work like madness in the brain."

In the morning I continued my journey towards Knoxville, bidding farewell to "Singed Possum," who turned off to the left *en route* for "Alabam," singing as he went —

"Git out de way, de people's risin —
Who's for Clay and Frelinhysen?"

Charleston, S. C., Sept. 15, 1847.          GLENVARLOCK.

# A New Mock Sermon

The mock or burlesque sermon is an important sub-genre of antebellum Southern humorous writing. It seems to have flourished in newspapers of the 1840s and 1850s, but few examples have been resurrected and published in modern times. The best-known mock sermons today are William Penn Brannan's "The Harp of a Thousand Strings,"[1] and another sermon, of uncertain authorship, entitled "Where the Lion Roareth and the Wang-doodle Mourneth."[2]

"Another Water-Proof Sermon," republished below, is certainly in a class with "The Harp" and "Where the Lion Roareth." In fact, certain parallels suggest that "Another Water-Proof Sermon" may actually have been written by Brannan. According to Brannan, Waterproof, Louisiana (a notoriously rowdy river town full of thieves, prostitutes, and gamblers), was the scene of "The Harp of a Thousand Strings." No text of "The Harp" that I have been able to locate makes mention of Waterproof, but in a dialect letter supposedly written by Jabez Flint, the preacher who delivered "The Harp," Brannan (the author of both sermon and letter) mentions that the sermon

1. The text of "The Harp" most frequently reprinted in modern anthologies is from the New York *Spirit of the Times*, 29 Sept. 1855. George Kummer has ascribed the sermon to Brannan in a sound article entitled "Who Wrote 'The Harp of a Thousand Strings'?" *Ohio Historical Quarterly*, 67 (July 1958), 221-31.

2. The standard text of "Where the Lion Roareth" is printed in *The Harp of a Thousand Strings; or, Laughter for a Lifetime*, ed. S. P. Avery (New York: Dick & Fitzgerald, 1858), pp. 224-26. Both "The Harp" and "Where the Lion Roareth" are included in the anthology *Humor of the Old Southwest*, ed. Hennig Cohen and William B. Dillingham (Boston: Houghton Mifflin, 1964; reissued Univ. of Georgia Press, 1975), pp. 355 59.

was originally preached "to the benighted heathen of Water-proof."[3] "Another Water-Proof Sermon," then, may very well be Brannan's work, published to follow up on the wide success of "The Harp."

Other parallels reinforce this speculation. The humorous devices of the two sermons are similar. In both, the preacher (for obvious reasons) cannot reveal the exact source of his text. Too, both sermons make fun of the various denominations of the "christun persuashun." In "The Harp," the denominations are likened to various animals – Episcopalians to turkey buzzards, Methodists to squirrels, and Baptists to possums. In "Another Water-Proof Sermon," the denominations are compared to different kinds of "licker": Episcopalians are like "shampain wine," Methodists like *bust head* whiskey, Catholics like "Coneyac Brandy," and so on. Finally, the styles of the two sermons are quite similar – the frequent pause for breath indicated by "ah," for instance – and the dialect forms and spellings are very much alike. Brannan may not have written "Another Water-Proof Sermon," but whoever did write it was obviously familiar with "The Harp" and used it as his model.

A noteworthy feature of "Another Water-Proof Sermon" is its bawdiness, a characteristic not found in either "The Harp" or "Where the Lion Roareth." References to the "Piscopallans," who have "tall churches and monstrous orgins," and to the "Catholick preest," who "keeps large nunneries full uv Saint Peter," show that the author of the sermon was not above some raunchy joking.

"Another Water-Proof Sermon" is republished below from the 9 July 1859 issue of the Macon, Georgia, *State Press*, where it was credited to the *Madison Pioneer*. No attempt has been made to backtrack the sermon to its first appearance in print. The sermon was located in the *State Press* by George R. Ellison. The text is republished here with no emendations.

J.L.W.W. III

3. The letter, written by Brannan to prove that he was the author of "The Harp," is reprinted by Kummer on pp. 229-30 of his article, cited in note 1.

## ANOTHER WATER-PROOF SERMON.

*Preached by Elder Blow, of Waterproof, La.*

MY DEAR BRETHERING AND SISTERN: — I appear
before you to-day, a minister uv the gospil; and I've no doubt
that afore the foundation uv the world ah, I was predestinated
to preech the glad tidins uv the Prince of the New Jerusalem,
ah. I believes in the doctrins uv the Saints, an uv thar final
preserverance. An enny doctrin that teeches you to believe
otherwise, can't be found within the leds uv the Bible, ah. I am
proud to say, my brethering an sistern, that I am a old-fashion-
ed chrishtan uv the Hardshell Baptist persuashun, as I have
chosen fur my tex a passage uv scriptur that's found in the leds
uv the Bible; an I could tell you what it is, but I don't know
myself, ah. But, whenever you do find it, the words will be
these:

"Give strong drink unto him that is reddy to perish, and
wine unto those that be uv heavy hearts."

Now my brethering and sistern, thar's a great many kinds
uv licker in this world, as is mentioned in the tex, and these different sorts uv sperits may be likened to the various
denominashuns uv the christun persuashun, ah. In the first
place, we have the bright and sparklin shampain wine, that cums
from furrin parts, ah. This is a costly licker, an is used by them
as is troubled with the big-head, ah. It is a mity fine sperits, an
keeps a scissin, a popin, an a effervessin.

It is just so my brethering an sistern with the Piscopallans,
ah. They is a highfaluten an 'ristocratic set of onbeleevers, ah.
They have fine pews, tall churches and monstrous orgins. Thar
is hoss racers gamblers and chicken fiters among 'em ah. They
is a mity proud people and believe in the Postolic Accession,
and they keeps going up frum big preacher to another, until
they get up to nuthin'. They resemble St. John's beest with
sevin heads and ten horns, fur in speekin uv horns the text says:

"Give strong drink unto him that is reddy to perish, and
wine unto them that be of hevy hearts."

Again my brethering and sistern, thar's another kind of licker that depraves the appetite, corrupts the sensibilities, nauseates the stomach, consterpates the bowils, depresses the feelings, destroys the health, perduces sick bed ake and vomiting ah. This kind of strong drink is commonly cauld whisky. But, in different localitys, it has various congelations. In Rackensack, it is called *rot gut*; in Tinnysee, it is named *red eye*; in Illinoys, it is denominated *bald face*; and in Texas, whur I live, it is termed *bust head*. Now this strong drink my christun and dyin friends, may be liken unto *M*ethodis pursuasion; for they is a people that sturs up things with a short stick ah. They is death on campmeetins and preechin up thar free grase and parden to all. They sprinkles in place uv baptisen, and with thar shoutin, an sermonin, and fallin frum grace, they gets obstropulous and hungry with heviness of heart, for tex says:

"Give strong drink unto him that's reddy to perish, an wine unto them that be uv hevy hearts."

Agin, my dying congregashun, thar is yet anuther kind uv drink which if it don't do enny good, it can't do enny harm. It is Ginger pop ah; an thar is a grate deel more water nor ginger in it ah. It is like the Camelite, fur thar is more water in them than enny thing else. They even carries thar doctrines so far as to reject glorius old burbin ah. They my christian friends is at subjects fur the track, and mishionary scieties; but no whar within the leds uv the Bible, can enny tex be found which tells you that you can enter into the gate uv the New Jerusalum on water alone, for the tex says:

"Give strong drink unto him that is reddy to perish, an wine unto them that be hevvy uv heart."

And yet my heerers thar is one powerful strong drink found in all stores, groceries, hotels, an 'pothecary shops. It is Coneyac Brandy. It is made outen everything an bears a great price, ah. Your worthy speaker, my brethering and sistern, knows it well, ah. It makes a man feel his keepins, ah, and when under its influence he is mity apt to let the cat outen the bag, ah, an confess to things that he oughtnt to tell. This licker may be likened to the Romin Catholicks; bekaus when they gets with thar preest an under the influense of spirets, they confess thar sins. A Catholick preest, my friends, is a great man, as he keeps large nunneries full uv Saint Peter it may be supposed he is allers ready, for the tex says:

"Give strong drink unto him that is reddy to perish, an wine unto them that be hevvy uv heart."

Thar is furthermore, my beloved follerers uv the meak and loly, another monstrous mean drink, outlandish in name, abominable in smell, bitter in taste, and horrible to drink uv. It is Lager Beer ah. This kind uv strong drink fuddles the idees, upsets dijestion, obfuscates the understanding an leads the drinker thereuf into the ways uv sin an uv death. It may be likened to the Mormons. They is wus than the Babblonish idolaturs that fell down and worshipt the goldin image which Nebicatsnezsur the king had sot up. Jo Smith was thar proffit, and they believes that Brigham Young possesses imaculist powers. They has a grate number of wifes, which is kontrary to dyvine teechin, fur one man that is a true christian can manage but one woman at a time without keepin hisself in bylen watur, fur the tex says:

"Give strong drink unto him that is reddy to perish, an wine unto them that be uv hevvy hearts."

"An lastly, my dyin friends, thar is a glorious strong drink ah, that will do yer hearts good. It enlivens the feelins, opens the heart to deeds uv luv ah. You can drink it foruver without makin a beest uv yourself. It is old Peech Brandy, the best uv all strong drinks. This sperits, my christian heerers, may be compaired to the old Hard Shell Baptists ah. They never deviate from the old track. No fallin from grase among um. When they once makes the eddy, they keeps clear uv the breakers uv whisky, the quicksands uv Shampayne, the whirlpools uv Jimmaky, the sholes uv Ginger pop, the waves uv Coneyack, and the siroccos uv Lager Beer. But they steers right unto the havin uv old Peech Brandy, an thar my dyin friends, the wins may houl, the lightnins flash, the thunders roll, an the yeth quake, the old Hard Shell Baptists will set thar megs. But it makes no difference, my brethering, when we get to heaven, how we get thar. The luvers of Shampayne takes the ristocratic car uv Piscopalionism, the disciples uv whisky prefers the high pressur dubble biler steam bote uv Methodism, the drinkers uv old Jimmaky takes thar passage in the reglar packit uv Presbyterianism, the suckers uv Ginger pop expects to wash their way into life everlastin in the cause uv Camelism, an whenever enny uv them gits thar, you may then sing "the Camels is coming."

The swiggers uv old Coneyack expects to make thar trip to Jerusalem Land in the motley raft uv Romin Catholervism, while the swillers uv Lager Beer is willin to go to heaven in the flatboat uv Mormonism ah. But the Baptists, the glorious old Hard Shells, they is willin to enter the gates uv heaven by faith alone, as they intends to travail thar in the old wagin uv Baptism. An I hopes, my christian an dyin friends, to meet many uv you thar. But I am afraid I shant ah, fur I see that sum is reddy to leev an is gettin dry ah, an the tex says:

"Give strong drink unto them that is reddy to perish, an wine unto them that be uv hevvy hearts."

# Another New Mock Sermon

"Parson Stovall's Hair-Suit Sarmon" was published in the *Spirit of the Times*, 4 (7 September 1834), 225. This sketch is significant because the *Spirit* issue in which it appears is the only issue from the 1834 volume to survive; this issue is privately owned and is not reproduced in the American Periodical Series microfilm. The sketch is also significant because it is the earliest known appearance of the type of popular humor piece later known as the burlesque backwoods sermon and is the only such *funeral* sermon on record. The person under whose name this sermon was published, Parson Noah Ezra Stovall, was actually a backwoods preacher for a circuit of small free-will Baptist churches near Moonville, S. C., in the 1830's and 40's. Little is known of the facts of Parson Stovall's life, but the legends of his career in the South Carolina up-country, as reported in Judge Abner Follet's *Chronicles of Moonville* (1876), suggest that such sermons preached at funerals and upon other occasions were not unusual for him. It is now beyond our ability to determine if the following piece is an authentic Stovall sermon, taken down as preached to record it for posterity, or if some now unknown author merely made it up and signed Stovall's name to it to poke fun at him.

A. S. WENDEL

## PARSON STOVALL'S HAIR-SUIT SARMON

My beluvid brethering and sistren: it is wif a sad and hevvy and overhanging hart that I appears afore yew to-day to oversee the layin-away ove our beluvvid backslidden brother, Deekin Bodymount, whom lies afore us as fresh a corpse as ever was, layin thar a livin moniment to the evil that men does lives arter em while the good come offen a turd, like thar bones. Now my brethering, I aint come afore yew to-day to yellowgize Brother Bodymount, fer we all knows on his shortcomins; I aint gonter dwell on his wikked ways, fer twouldn't do no good; I aint even gonter tell the peeculyar sarcumstances over his passin, jist two days ago over to Sister Agnes Mabel Becky's (shame, Sister!), how he slammed the door on thet thar long beard ove his'n as he was a makin a shall we say monst'ous hasty ex-cape fum thet thar house. No my brethering, I aint gonter dwell on the sordid facks ove Brother Bodymount's life amungst us, cause we and Brother Bodymount's widow, settin here amungst us, knows it all, and caint be no more edificated than we already is.

I am gonter take this 'casion, howsomeyer, to use Brother Bodymount as a objeck lesson to hole up afore all ove yew: see him a-layin thar, thet monst'ous bushy growth fum his face a-coverin' right near all ove him, includin' them new undertakin' close: an' ef yew c'd see his eyes, my brethering, yew'd see eyes thet was old an' red an' cust yew fer findin' him out; ef you c'd see his mouf, my brethering, yew'd see a mouf thet were scornful and hard: *ef* yew c'd see em, my brethering, *EF* yew could. But yew caint, *fer he is hidden in the bushes.* That's right, my beluvvid brethering: *fer he is hidden in the bushes.* Ah! thar's a lessun for us all in thet, aint thar, brethering? And right thar, beluvvid, right thar, is the pint ove hit all, the pint I wants to make and has beeen comin tu fer some time now. And rightcher I turns to what I has chose as the tex fer this solum occasion. It am in the holy scripters, sumwhar atween the leds of the book known as the Book of Regurgitations, and when you finds it you'll find that it says: "Let them that hath beards hear what the *spirrit* seth unto the bushes: Shame unto them that culti-

vates hair: fer they hath not strength nor length elsewhere; woe
unto them that flees from a razor, fer they shall be cut off in
the latter day" — ah! Minds me of that blessid scripter that was
so ably expectorated by our older and wiser brother in the
gospill, "Fer they shall g-naw a file": not *might* g-naw, ner *can*
g-naw, my brethering, but *shall* — ah! Let us think on them
things.

Now, my brethering, they's diffrunt kinds ove hair, as you
all knows on: they's fine hair and ove course hair; they's red
hair and brown hair, straight hair and cully hair; they's false
hair, they's splittin' hairs, and they's puttin' on hairs; they's the
hair ove the dorg, which am the wuss one ove them all, thet
done in Brother Bodymount — Ah! *Shame* unto them that cultivates hair; fer they has not strength nor length elsewhere; *woe*
unto them that flees from a razor, fer they shall be cut off in
the latter day — Ah!

And my brethering, they's also diffrunt kinds ove beards,
which we all sees witness to evry day. They's long beards and
short beards; they's fat beards and they's skinny beards; they's
long full beards and they's skinny shrivelled up beards; they's
straight beards and cully  beards; they's greybeards, bluebeards
and beard the lion — But ah! my brethering and sistren! —
they's all *ugly* beards, onnatral and again reason — they am a
abomination ontu the yeath. They is those that tells yew beards
is flowing and byootiful; but *I* say they is abominations. They is
those that tells you beards is a mark of vi-rility; but *I* say they is
a waste of nateral juices. They is those thet wears liplint only,
mustachers, that strains the flies outen whisky; *I* say that they is
luke-warm and halfassed and shall be spewn outen the mouf —
they *shall* g-naw a file, my brethering — ah! Then they is them
that wears leetle pointy beards on they chins — they is soft and
skinny and given to mean and evil ways; they's given to strokin
they chins and givin way to evil passions Ah! Then they is them
that puts on they face what they aint got on they head — they
is full of lies and deceits. Then they is also them, my chirrin,
that hes full flowin beards, that creeps like grayed over moss
over they sholders an' limbs an' down ontu the extremes ove

they bodies – and they is the wuss ones ove all: they pertends tu be wise when they is foolish; they pertends to be strong when they is weak; they pertends to be long when they is short – oh yes, my friends, *they* is the *wust* ove all - *fer he is hidden in the bushes*! Ah! Let them that has beards hear what the spirrit *seth* unto the bushes: *Shame* unto them that cultivates hair, fer they has not strength nor length elsewhere; *woe* unto them that flees from a razor, fer they shall be cut off in the latter day! –

Say to me, Preacher, whut 'bout Sampson? Sez I, what about 'im? Sampson hed a beard, got 'im trubble. Say to me, Preacher, what about Abe Linkhorn? Sez I, whut about *'im*? Linkhorn hed a beard, used it to cover leetle bumps on his cheeks – fer he is hidden in the bushes! Ah yes! my brethering. Sampson hed a beard – whar *he now*? Abe Linkhorn hed a beard – whar *he* now? Deekin Bodymount had a beard – *whar he now*? – Ah! Let them thet hes beards hear what the *spirrit* seth unto the bushes: SHAME ontu them thet cultivates hair, fer they hath not strength nor length elsewhere; WOE untu them thet flees from a razor, fer they shall be cut off in the latter day – Ah!

Parson Noah Ezra Stovall

# The Porter-Hooper Correspondence

*by*

EDGAR E. THOMPSON

Johnson Jones Hooper — lawyer, newspaper editor, politician, sportsman, and humorist — rose to fame during the 1840's and 1850's as one of the foremost writers of the antebellum southern humor genre. Hooper's character, Simon Suggs, became well known across the United States and in England as a rapscallion con artist par excellence, and Hooper assumed a high position as a writer and humorist. But Hooper most likely would have gone virtually unknown except in the region of Alabama and surrounding states had he not gained the attention of William Trotter Porter, editor of the New York *Spirit of the Times* and connoisseur of rugged backwoods tales. Because of Porter's interest, many of Hooper's sketches and sporting articles appeared in the *Spirit*, thereby gaining a national audience, and through Porter's efforts and influence, Carey and Hart of Philadelphia published *Some Adventures of Captain Simon Suggs* (1845) and *The Widow Rugby's Husband* (1851), both of which were collections of backwoods Alabama humor, and *Dog and Gun: A Few Loose Chapters on Shooting* (1856), which was a manual for hunters.

Porter and Hooper appear to have been friends from 1843, when Porter noticed " 'Taking the Census in Alabama' by a 'Chicken Man of 1840' " in Hooper's *East Alabamian*, to the New York editor's death in 1858. Porter obviously saw a rare genius for backwoods humor in Hooper and fervently sought more material from him for the pages of the *Spirit*. The two editors exchanged newspapers regularly, and by 1845 a correspondence had developed which continued through the mid-1850's However, the only known extant portion of their correspondence is in the *Spirit*, primarily in two forms — notes from Porter to Hooper and notes by Porter about Hooper. These notes appeared mainly in three sections of the *Spirit*. Most were part of the "To Correspondents" section in the top left corner of every front page where Porter addressed friendly messages to his many correspondents and contributors and reported on business arrangements for which he acted as agent. "To Correspondents" also enabled *Spirit* readers to have a more personal involvement with the paper, its editor, and its correspondents and contributors. Other notes by Porter also appeared in a section entitled "On Dits in Sporting Circles," which included miscellaneous messages and comments about friends of the *Spirit*, and in "New Publications, etc." which was devoted to information about new and forthcoming publications. Still other notes appeared in other sections of the *Spirit* and in numerous introductory notes to Hooper's sketches.

The importance of Porter's notes to and about Hooper lies in two main areas, content and frequency. The notes often contained praise for Hooper and his writing and announced forthcoming sketches. Porter considered *Simon Suggs* "the best half dollar's worth of genuine humor ever enclosed between two covers," and, in anticipation of the arrival of "Daddy Biggs's Scrape at Cockerell's Bend," Porter said of the Alabama humorist, "There wont be a button left on the jackets of the readers of the 'Spirit,' if we scare up many correspondents like Hooper!" He also noted that Hooper's "keen perception of the ludicrous and the comic, is only equalled by the facility by which he displays in bold relief, striking features of character or incident. His style is forceful, playful or ornate, by turns, and he possesses, in an eminent degree, the happy faculty of rendering his portraitures instinct with life." Later, as Hooper wrote fewer sketches, Porter solicited contributions from him by requesting a friend of Hooper to " 'stir him up' for that new story" and asking on another occasion, "why in the world doesn't he write more?"

Porter also commented from time to time on his friend's activities, other than political, in Alabama and spoke favorably of Hooper's newspapers. He reported Hooper's moves from one editor's chair to another, mentioned sporting events in Alabama, and answered questions on sports which Hooper asked from time to time. Occasionally he mentioned Hooper's health, wishing him well. Several notes concern business arrangements for paper, guns, books, and other items, for which, on one occasion and possibly on others, Porter neglected to charge his friend the usual five per cent fee. A few of Porter's comments involve private jokes such as the antics of the "Muscat Club" of Hooper's boyhood, a group of boys who evidently enjoyed playing mischievous pranks and juvenile games.

The frequency of Porter's notes indicates that Hooper was a major *Spirit* correspondent and contributor for whom Porter had great regard. Messages concerning Hooper appeared many more times than those concerning most other correspondents and contributors, suggesting that the private correspondence between the two editors was quite frequent. That such a personal correspondence did exist is evident in such comments from Porter in the *Spirit* as, "Will make the necessary enquiries, and write you at length," and "Mr. Hooper, in a very courteous private letter to us, needlessly apologizes for what he is pleased to term his 'miserable performance' in the original sketch of 'Daddy Biggs'. . . ." Also, the frequency of the notes parallels the progression of their friendship. Many notes appeared between 1845 and 1849; however, as Hooper's interests began to change from backwoods humor to politics, a subject which Porter refused to treat in the *Spirit*, the correspondence between them declined gradually until only one or two notes a year appeared, and in 1856 and 1857 no communication was evident.

The basic inadequacy in the Porter-Hooper notes is that they offer only a partial, superficial view of the relationship between the two men. Since their original correspondence does not seem to be extant, a study of their private communication and an accurate picture of their friendship is impossible. However, the notes do provide insight into the types of matters about which they corresponded. The notes also indicate that the Porter-Hooper relationship included a mixture of fun and business and that each man was interested in the activities of the other. The number and frequency of the notes indicates that their private correspondence was quite large. In fact, the quantity of the numerous messages which obviously passed between them indicates that Hooper was one of the most important of Porter's many correspondents. Since notes to and about Hooper appeared much more frequently than those to most other correspondents, it is safe to assume that Hooper was as close a friend and correspondent as T.B. Thorpe, another correspondent and humorist, whose messages also appeared very frequently and who edited the *Spirit* after Porter's death. The notes to and about Hooper also support his position as a successful writer of fiction and a serious sportsman, and they reflect the transition Hooper passed through as he began to shun his fiction and the Simon Suggs image and to center his writing efforts on the hunt, the turf, and politics. Porter's notes do not serve as a substitute for the actual correspondence between the two editors, but they do reflect the relationship between the two men.

The following transcriptions of Porter's notes to and about Hooper provide a complete and convenient illustration of their friendship as it was recorded in the *Spirit* from 1843 to 1855, the year Porter's health began to fail and the year before he ceased editing the *Spirit*. Items are arranged chronologically, and each appears exactly as it was published in the *Spirit*. Notes from "To Correspondents," "On Dits in Sporting Circles," and "New Publications, etc." are indicated by TC, OD, and NP respectively; other titles are provided in full. Explanatory notes are provided to indicate the location of Hooper's sketches in the *Spirit* and to clarify as many names, terms, and abbreviations as possible.

For additional information concerning the location of Hooper manuscripts, one might consult the following sources: Johnson Jones Hooper Papers, Alabama Collection, University of Alabama Library, University, Alabama; Thomas Hill Watts Papers, State of Alabama Department of Archives and History,

Montgomery, Alabama; Thomas Addison Burkes Papers, Georgia Historical Society, Savannah, Georgia; John DeBerniere Hooper Papers, Southern Historical Collection, University of North Carolina Library, Chapel Hill, North Carolina; Griffith John McRee Papers, Southern Historical Collection, University of North Carolina, Chapel Hill, North Carolina; William Porcher Miles Papers, Southern Historical Collection, University of North Carolina Library, Chapel Hill, North Carolina; Journal of the Provisional Congress of the Confederate States of America, Chicago Historical Society, Chicago, Illinois; William Stanley Hoole, *Alias Simon Suggs: The Life and Writings of Johnson Jones Hooper*, University, Alabama: The University of Alabama Press, 1952; Marion Kelly, "The Life and Writing of Johnson Jones Hooper," M.A. thesis, Alabama Polytechnic Institute (now Auburn University), 1934; Edgar E. Thompson, "The Literary Career of Johnson Jones Hooper: A Bibliographical Study of Primary and Secondary Material (With a Collection of Hooper's Letters)," M.A. thesis, Mississippi State University, 1971.

Information concerning William T. Porter manuscripts may be found in Norris Yates, *William T. Porter and the Spirit of the Times*, Baton Rouge: Louisiana State University Press, 1957. Yates indicates that manuscript material may be found in the New-York Historical Society Library; the New York Public Library; the Henry Carey Baird Papers and the Carey & Hart Record Books for 1845-1846, Historical Society of Pennsylvania, Philadelphia, Pennsylvania.

* * *

1. TC, 14 (18 January 1845), 553.

    The second chapter of Hooper's "Capt. Suggs, of Tallapoosa," was received yesterday, too late for this week, in which is recounted how young Simon "did" his father – the "hard shell" Baptist preacher – out of his "spare change" and "the fastest piece of hoss-flesh, accordin' to size, that ever shaded the yearth," by his skill in "scaring up a Jack!"[1]

1. "Captain Suggs of Tallapoosa," *Spirit*, 14 (11 January, 1845), 547.

2. OD, 14 (15 February 1845), 606.

Mr. Hooper, the accomplished editor, *en amateur*, of "The East Alabamian"[2] — the author of "Taking the Census in Alabama,"[3] of "Capt. Suggs, the Shifty Man,"[4] and other sketches unsurpassed for their wit and humor, is to become an occasional correspondent of the "Spirit of the Times." The last number of that paper contains the following paragraph, from which it will be seen that the writer's modesty is in keeping with his sterling merit: —

Our acknowledgements are due to the editor of the N. Y. "Spirit of the Times," for the very complimentary notice of ourself and "Simon Suggs," which we find in the last number. It is not the first time that Mr. Porter has given us more by far, than our deserts; and we shall be glad to show our appreciation of his kind notices, at our earliest leisure.

The original of "Simon,"[5] will be "lifted kleer off the ground," when he learns that he has been embalmed in the columns of the "Spirit." He will not believe it however, unless he have occular demonstration.

Capt. Suggs *shall have* "occular demonstration" if he wishes it, by furnishing his address. But our readers and the world of letters have yet to be informed of the great treat in store for them. Hooper writes us a line which has caused us as great joy as that afforded to Pedro (in Cinderella) by the "wonderful news" of the "royal proclamation," brought "by a royal post," which was "proclaimed about the city by sound of trumpet and drum." He is to send us, in a few days, "DADDY BIGGS'S *Scrape at Cockerell's Bend!*"[6] There wont be a button left on the jackets of the readers of the "Spirit," if we scare up many more correspondents like Hooper! Our private opinion is that the "Spirit" can just naturally beat the world, in the way of correspondents! "It takes us, and *we* can't hardly!"

2. *The East Alabamian*, La Fayette, Alabama, was a weekly newspaper edited by Hooper 1843-1844.

3. " 'Taking the Census in Alabama' by a 'Chicken Man' of 1840," *Spirit*, 13 (9 September, 1843), 326.

4. "Simon Suggs, the Shifty Man," *Spirit*, 14 (25 January, 1845), 571.

5. Bird H. Young of Dadeville, Tallapoosa County, Alabama, was the prototype for Simon Suggs.

6. "Daddy Biggs's Scrape at Cockerell's Bend," *Spirit*, 15 (15 March, 1845), 27.

3.  TC, 15 (8 March, 1845), 9.

"Phil," a Baltimore correspondent,[7] writes us: — "Do ask 'Johnson Hooper' to give you some reminiscences of a certain 'Muscat Club,' belonging to a town in the Old North State, in days 'Lang Syne' when we were boys, and he was the honored poet of said Club.[8] He could dress you up something rich of its doings, in his happy style." Much obliged to "Phil" for the suggestion. As soon as we receive "Daddy Bigg's Scrape at Cockerell's Bend," which he has promised to write out for the "Spirit," we will call on him for the sayings and doings of the "Muscat Club."

4.  TC, 15 (15 March, 1845), 21.

J.J.H. — of course you are at liberty to make any disposition you choose of your sketches published in this paper. A copy of this week's "Spirit" will be forwarded to the address you named. We are greatly obliged for "Daddy Biggs's Scrape," and though we do not exactly cotton to the idea of Capt. Suggs' flogging you "on sight," we are still anxious to hear more of him, and also "How Fish-Trap Johnson got his name."[9]

5.  "Another Crack Original Story," 15 (15 March, 1845), 21.

*"Daddy Biggs's Scrape at Cockerell's Bend."* — On another page will be found the original story under this head, promised us some weeks since by J. J. Hooper, Esq., of East Alabama, the author of "Taking the Census," "Simon Suggs," etc. We have read nothing superior to it for many a day, and doubt not our readers will agree with us in our estimate of the writer's extraordinary ability. His keen perception of the ludicrous and the comic, is only equalled by the

7.  The identity of "Phil" is not known, as Porter indicates in item 7.

8.  The Muscat Club was a group of boys who played together in Wilmington, North Carolina, Hooper's boyhood home. As the 15-year-old club poet, Hooper made his first notable contribution to journalism by writing a poem, "Anthony Milan's Launch," for his father's *Cape Fear Recorder*. This poem commemorates humorously the launching of a ship and the drenching of Anthony Milan, the British Consul at Wilmington. For the text of the poem, see W. Stanley Hoole, *Alias Simon Suggs: The Life and Times of Johnson Jones Hooper* (University, Ala.: The University of Alabama Press, 1952), pp. 6-8.

9.  The existence of a sketch entitled "How Fishtrap Johnson Got His Name" has not been verified. The title is mentioned again in item 5, and the name appears as "Fish Trap Saunders" in item 7.

facility with which he displays in bold relief, striking features in character or incident. His style is forcible, playful or ornate, by turns, and he possesses, in an eminent degree, the happy faculty of rendering his portraitures instinct with life. We can readily imagine the characteristics of "Simon Suggs," or "Daddy Biggs," as if we had seen the one "scare up a Jack," or "fished for cat," with the other.

Mr. Hooper, in a very courteous private letter to us, needlessly apologized for what he is pleased to term his "miserable performance" in the original sketch of *"Daddy Biggs,"* which we publish to-day. "Incessant interruptions, and not feeling 'i' the vein' " for writing, he assigns as the reason. He is kind enough to add,

"I have a long time wished to write for the 'Spirit.' During the summer I hope to have time to write regularly — that is if this sketch does not disgust you."****"If you will send the next 'Spirit' to Capt. ---------, of ---------, Tallapoosa County, Alabama,[10] "Suggs" will believe — else not, 'though one should rise from the dead.' If he catches and flogs me next week at Court — he swears he will — the 'Spirit' shall have the particulars, as well as *"How Fish-Trap Johnson got his name."*

6. NP, 15 (29 March, 1845), 45.

The same publishers [Carey & Hart] have in press *"The Life and Adventures of SIMON SUGGS, the Shifty Man,"*[11] complete in one volume, with a portrait of *Simon*, taken on the spot, and numerous illustrations by Darley.[12] We have *a-sort-of-a-promise* on the part of both Hooper, the author, and of his courteous publishers, of a sketch or two in advance, for the especial gratification of the readers and correspondents of the "Spirit."

7. TC, 15 (5 April, 1845), 57.

J.J.H. — We have no idea who "Phil." of Baltimore is. It may be your old crony, Bill W_g_e. We may as well say to "Phil." — whoever he is — that the author of "Simon Suggs" does recollect some-

10. Possibly another reference to Bird H. Young. See note 5 above.

11. *Some Adventures of Captain Simon Suggs, Late of the Tallapoosa Volunteers; Together with "Taking the Census," and Other Alabama Sketches. By a Country Editor.* Philadelphia: Carey & Hart, 1845. This collection of sketches was dedicated to William T. Porter.

12. F. O. C. Darley was the illustrator of *Some Adventures of Captain Simon Suggs* as well as many other volumes in the Humorous American Works series.

thing about the "Muscat Club," but if he is not mistaken, a reward of $200 was offered for the perpetrator of their principal exploit!! Though twelve or fifteen years have elapsed since, we are desired to ask "Phil." if he can tell us anything about the statute of limitations in "sich" cases? We don't care how often you cheat "that old vilyan," Uncle Sam; he has ruinated us fifty times by over-postage. "Daddy Biggs" was "some," and we shall be delighted to hear from him, or "Fish Trap Saunders," or any other of the "characters" in your wooden country.

We have seen several of Darley's illustrations of the forthcoming issue. They are immense.

8. TC, 15 (12 April, 1845), 69.

   J.J.H. – You shall have a "dog-ra-type minnichure."[13] We have seen several of D.'s[14] designs for the forth-coming memoir of Capt. S.S. All are exceedingly spirited, but the full length portrait of the Captain on his crop-eared "hoss," is amazing. We have never seen a more characteristic portrait.

9. TC, 15 (19 April, 1845), 81.

   J.J.H. – A South Carolina subscriber writes that you have "set him back smartly," in the way of economizing his tailor's bill; "buttons on his jacket clean gone," he says.

10. TC, 15 (19 April, 1845), 81.

   F. C. Jones, Esq:, of the "Mississippi Democrat," will oblige us by giving the rightful credit, *occasionally*, to this paper, otherwise we will oblige him. "Jones's Fight"[15] and other original stories in this paper he appropriates with no acknowledgement whatever, and we see that he announces "Daddy Biggs's Scrape." He will be made to "holler" as loud as his name-sake Colonel Dick Jones, if we ever get him with a sharp stick.

11. TC, 15 (28 June, 1845), 201.

    J.J.H. – Will make the necessary enquiries, and write you at length. Shall be a thousand times obliged for the three chapters.

13. Daguerreotype miniature.

14. Another reference to Darley. See note 12 above.

15. Thomas Kirkman, "Jones Fight," *Spirit*, 9 (25 January, 1840), 559. Kirkman was a planter and humorist who lived in northwest Alabama.

12.  TC, 15 (30 August, 1845), 309.

> J.J.H. – Your Mr. M. called on us for a moment, and promised to look in again, since which we have not seen him, but hope to do so in a day or two.

13.  TC, 15 (13 September, 1845), 333.

> J.J.H. – Please send us the back numbers of the "Whig"[16] from the date you have been connected with it. The first paper we have received is that for the 2d inst. The "dog-ra-type" is ready, but your friend J.S.M. has incontinently "stept out."

14.  NP, 15 (13 September, 1845), 344.

> J. J. Hooper, of Alabama, has "Simon Suggs," etc.; the latter will be published in a few days. By the way Hooper has left "The East Alabamian" and now occupies the editorial chair of the "Wetumpka Whig," in the same State, – a very capital paper, reflecting the highest credit on the country press of Alabama.

15.  NP, 15 (20 September, 1845), 356.

> *"Adventures of Capt. Simon Suggs,"* late of the Talapoosa Volunteers, together with 'Taking the Census,' and other Alabama sketches, by a Country Editor; – with a portrait of 'Simon' from life, and ten humorous illustrations by Darley. This is the best half dollar's worth of genuine humor, ever enclosed between two covers! The writer is so well known to our readers as a correspondent, that we are confident there are very few of them who are not "snatching and eager" to secure a copy. Hoosier[17] has done us the honor to dedicate his first essay as a book maker, to the editor of the "Spirit of the Times" – a compliment quite as unmerited, as unexpected, but which we gratefully appreciate. Aside from the peculiarly interesting and amusing character of the contents of the volume, Mr. Darley has vastly increased the interest, with which one reads of Simon Suggs, Mrs. Stokes, Daddy Biggs, and others, by his inimitable illustrations. The work may be obtained here, of Burgess, Stringer & Co., Graham's, and W. H. Taylor's.

16. *The Wetumpka Whig,* Wetumpka, Alabama, was a weekly newspaper edited by Hooper 1844-1846.

17. "Hoosier" is evidently a misprint which should read "Hooper."

16. TC, 15 (4 October, 1845), 369.

J.J.H. — Have seen the "notice." The "dog-ra-type" shall be forwarded "sure," with many thanks.

17. TC, 15 (11 October, 1845), 381.

J.J.H. — Received the note enclosed in the "C.H."[18] and cheerfully comply with your request.

18. TC, 15 (1 November, 1845), 417.

"The Chicken Man." — Do send us an account of the Deer Hunting party from Montgomery, respecting which we have received a letter from a friend of yours which will appear next week.[19]

19. TC, 15 (29 November, 1845), 465.

J.J.H. — We regret very much that an attack of "dumb ague," or anything else, should have prevented your participation in the Coosa County Hunt. You shall have the "Dog-ra-type."

20. TC, 16 (28 March, 1846), 49.

"E. Grec,"[20] now at N. O. [First portion not pertaining to Hooper omitted.] By the way, Hooper, in the last Wetumpka Whig, warns you off in the following terms: —

"W.T.P. — Wish you would keep 'E. Grec' off 'this unfortunate.' We thought we knew where Caddo Lake was — we camped on it once for five months, and saw in the lake during the winter, almost as many ducks as 'E. Grec' kills of a morning."

21. "Editorial Changes, Etc." 16 (23 May, 1846), 145.

Our old correspondent, J. J. Hooper, Esq., the author of "Simon Suggs," etc., has retired from the Wetumpka Whig, and associated himself with our friends Bates & Sayre, of the Montgomery Journal.[21] He has few equals in his peculiar style. Why in the

18. *The Chamber County Tribune*, La Fayette, Alabama, was a weekly newspaper edited by Hooper 1849-1854. Porter refers to it as *The Chambers Herald* in this item and in item 43.

19. "Sporting Epistle from Alabama," *Spirit*, 15 (8 November, 1845), 436. This letter, signed "Reader," mentions "Chicken Man" and "the author of 'Simon Suggs' " as a member of a hunting party.

20. "E. Grec." was a *Spirit* contributor of sporting news.

21. *The Alabama Journal*, Montgomery, Alabama, was a successively weekly, tri-weekly, and daily newspaper edited by Hooper 1846-1849.

world doesn't he write more? He has done nothing worthy of his reputations for months, that we have seen; it may be though, that he is at work on some "Sketches of the Alabama Legislature," which we talked of last winter.

22. TC, 16 (30 May, 1846), 157.

> J.J.H. — much obliged for your letter, to which we will reply by the "Great Britain" steamer, if the offer is entertained.

23. TC, 16 (25 July, 1846), 253.

> J.J.H. — We wrote you on Saturday relative to your orders of the 9th and 10th, for Paper, etc., etc. Have not been able to find a printing machine yet, of the size required.

24. TC, 16 (31 October, 1846), 421.

> J.J.H. — Your bills amounted to something over $300; we intended to charge you 5 per cent commission for filling the orders, but quite promiscuously forgot it, until reminded by your letter of the fact of your indebtedness. An X and a V remitted to us will make it all right. ***If you enquire of Mr. B. — your excellent postmaster — he will probably inform you that one of your partners, or some good natured friend, is in the habit of taking your paper from the office.

25. TC, 16 (2 January, 1847), 529.

> J.J.H. — Shall be very glad to receive the original song you alluded to. We have heard "Query" sing the published one deliciously, but have never seen a copy.[22] If you will refer to the "Spirit" of the 31st Oct. you will find an answer to the question proposed in a previous letter.

26. NP, 16 (9 January, 1847), 552.

> "*The Rose of Alabama.*" — We are indebted to Mr. Bouliemet, of Mobile, and Mr. Mayo, of New Orleans, for a copy of this popular melody, with *new words*, by the Hon. A. B. Meek, of Ala., which are "respectfully dedicated to Mrs. J. J. Hooper, of Montgomery," — the

22. "The Rose of Alabama," in Alexander Beaufort Meek, *Songs and Poems of the South* (New York; Mobile, Ala.: S. H. Goetzel and Co., 1857), pp. 23-24. A copy of this volume is in the Alabama Collection of the University of Alabama Library. See also item 26.

accomplished lady of our occasional correspondent, the author of "Capt. Simon Suggs," etc., etc., who is now an associate editor of the Alabama Journal. The "new words" were originally published in the "Planter"of Mobile, the editor of which, like ourselves, considers the composition as charming as the music which is full of pathos. Married as it now is, to immortal verse, this simple air we trust will find a resting place among the native melodies of the land.

27. TC, 17 (24 April, 1847), 97.

J.J.H. — The report was published two weeks since. There is no one at work on the American Stud Book that we are aware of. We have ordered the English Books through Messrs. Wiley & Putnam, who have a branch house in London.

28. TC, 17 (23 October, 1847), 405.

J.J.H. — The books have not been received yet, but are daily expected. They will be transhipped, on their arrival, to J.B.S.

29. TC, 17 (4 December, 1847), 477.

J.J.H. — We have ordered for you an exercise and three race saddles, with two suits of clothes, complete, of Gibson, and shall be able to ship them next Saturday, probably.

30. TC, 18 (4 March, 1848), 13.

J.J.H. — Will send you the Dorkings[23] next week. The books ordered from London have not been received.

31. TC, 18 (27 May, 1848), 157.

J.J.H. — The books were ordered long since through Wiley & Putnam, who have advertised for them in the London "Publisher's Journal" — thus far without success. Will send you some Dorkings as soon as we can find some fine ones.

32. TC, 18 (1 July, 1848), 217.

"An old Subscriber." — Now that the author of "Simon Suggs' has become a neighbor of your's, why don't you "stir him up" for that new story?[24] What is he doing at C? Shall publish the order next week.

23. A dorking is an edible domestic fowl.
24. "The Muscadine Story: The Unwritten Chapter in the Biography of 'Captain Simon Suggs,' " *Spirit*, 19 (24 March, 1849), 55.

33. TC, 18 (19 August, 1848), 301.

> J.J.H. – Have ordered your letters to be forwarded to L. Will write you as soon as we hear from the owners of T.

34. TC, 18 (19 August, 1848), 301.

> P.H.B. – Much obliged for your letter. Do stir up J.J.H., from whom and yourself we should be gratified to hear frequently.

35. TC, (10 February, 1849), 601.

> J.J.H. – The owners of T. have not made up their minds where to place him this season. We shall be glad to hear from "Takeba" and yourself frequently.

36. TC, 19 (10 March, 1849), 25.

> We have half a dozen very capital original articles on hand, for which we have no space this week. Our readers will be gratified to learn that the author of "Simon Suggs" has sent us that "Muscadine Story," which beats "Daddy Biggs's at Cockerell's Bend." We have the pleasure to state that no less than eight new correspondents have sent original communications this week.

37. TC, 19 (24 March, 1849), 49.

> J.J.H. – We have received the package, but have yet to see your friend M., the bearer. Sent you two copies of F.S. Will keep an eye out for you. Write as frequently as you can.

38. TC, 19 (24 September, 1849), 361.

> J.J.H. – Have met your friend M. Will fix your matter with C. of the K. Why don't you sent the T. to us.

39. TC, 19 (24 November, 1849), 469.

> J.J.H. – Neither A. nor B. wins; the bet is off as neither was right. The stakeholder's pronunciation was correct. Giraffe (pronounced Jeraff,) is a French work, and the stakeholder's decision is expressed as well as it could be, probably, in type, in your 'place.'

40. NP, 21 (17 May, 1851), 150.

> "Captain Simon Suggs. Some Adventures of Captain Simon Suggs, late of the Tallapoosa Volunteers, together with 'Taking the Census,' and other Alabama Sketches; with a portrait of the Author, and other Illustrations by Darley." – These Tales have appeared, at

intervals, in the "Spirit," but now collected and formed into a handsome little book, illustrated with excellent woodgravings, and published at the small charge of 50 cts., by Getz & Buck, Philadelphia, and Stringer & Townsend, Broadway, New York.[25]

41. TC, 21 (13 December, 1851), 505.

J.J.H. — As A. bet on Lady Fillmore against the field (which included Spot,) after she had won two heats, he loses. If Lady F. was 2d in either the 1st or 2d heats won by Spot, she is entitled to the purse, as Spot was disqualified. [He had previously trotted for money.][26] If not, Lewiston Bay wins, if he was 2d in the 4th and 5th heats. Send us the exact placing.

42. TC, 21 (7 February, 1852), 601.

J.J.H. — We ordered your Gun from London, two weeks since.

43. TC, 22 (3 March, 1852), 37.

A.C.N. — Send your paper to J.J.H., Lafayette, Ala. The name of the paper there is "The Chambers Herald."

44. TC, 23 (16 July, 1853), 253.

J.J.H. — Can get you a first-rate Gun, made to order here, for $150. A well-broken Pointer or Setter will cost you $75. Will do the best we can for you.

45. TC, 23 (30 July, 1853), 277.

J.J.H. — Have given your order to Mullin, who will fill it in time.

46. TC, 23 (24 September, 1853), 373.

J.J.H. — Have handed your letter to Mullin, who will write you. Of course we charge you no commission, but one of these days we will take a chew of tobacco or a mint-julep with you, while we enquire for "Simon Suggs" and "Daddy Biggs!"

25. Getz & Buck of Philadelphia and Stringer & Townsend of New York published reissues of *Some Adventures of Captain Simon Suggs* in 1851.

26. Porter's brackets.

47. TC, 23 (19 November, 1853), 469.

> A.H.B. (of C. Ala.) — You can have either Pointer or Setter for $75. How is J.J.H. and his friend Capt. Suggs?

48. TC, 24 (1 April, 1854), 73.

> J.J.H. — We shall mail a copy to the "M.M."[27] and also one to your address, "for your private tooth."

49. TC, 24 (8 April, 1854), 85.

> J.J.H. — The Scotch Terrier puppies you describe can be had for $25, to you. It will cost $5 to send them to M.

50. TC, 24 (8 July, 1854), 254.

> A.H.B. — Have received a Daguerreotype of the author of "Simon Suggs" — so represented, but "have our doubts" as to the identity. Will "Jonse"[28] be good enough to inform? It came from Dr. G., of Crawford and is a pretty good likeness of "N. of Arkansas."[29] "No tricks upon travellers" mind.

51. TC, 24 (9 December, 1854), 505.

> J.J.H. — Regret that we cannot permit ourselves to furnish your friend S.S. with the information desired. Mr. H. (F.F.)[30] will write for the S.M.G.,[31] if properly remunerated.

52. TC, 25 (16 June, 1855), 205.

> J.J.H. — Will you be kind enough to ask Mr. S.S. to send us a copy of the "Military Gazette" from its commencement. Also enquire why the "Mail" does not reach us?

27. *The Montgomery Mail*, Montgomery, Alabama, was successively a weekly, tri-weekly, and daily newspaper edited by Hooper 1854-1861.

28. "Jonse" was Hooper's nickname and the name of a racehorse named for Hooper.

29. Charles F. M. Noland was an Arkansas humorist who wrote under the pseudonyms "Pete Whetstone" and "N. of Arkansas."

30. Henry William Herbert was a *Spirit* correspondent and sportsman who wrote under the pseudonym "Frank Forrester." Hooper dedicated *Dog and Gun: A Few Loose Chapters on Shooting* (New York: C. M. Saxton & Co., 1856) to Frank Forrester.

31. *The Southern Military Gazette* was published in Birmingham, Alabama, and Atlanta, Georgia, ca. 1855. All 13 chapters of *Dog and Gun* appeared in this periodical publication. See Hoole, *Alias Simon Suggs*, p. 105.

COSTERUS. Essays in English and American Language and Literature.

Volume 1. Amsterdam 1972. 240 p. Hfl. 40.—
GARLAND CANNON: Sir William Jones's Translation-Interpretation of Sanskrit Literature. SARAH DYCK: The Presence of that Shape: Shelley's *Prometheus Unbound.* MARJORIE ELDER: Hawthorne's *The Marble Faun:* A Gothic Structure. JAMES L. GOLDEN: Adam Smith as a Rhetorical Theorist and Literary Critic. JACK GOODSTEIN: Poetry, Religion and Fact: Matthew Arnold. JAY L. HALIO: Anxiety in *Othello.* JOHN ILLO: Miracle in Milton's Early Verse. F. SAMUEL JANZOW: De Quincey's "Danish Origin of the Lake Country Dialect" Republished. MARTIN L. KORNBLUTH: The Degeneration of Classical Friendship in Elizabethan Drama. VIRGINIA MOSELY: The "Dangerous" Paradox in Joyce's "Eveline". JOHN NIST: Linguistics and the Esthetics of English. SCOTT B. RICE: Smollett's *Travels* and the Genre of Grand Tour Literature. LISBETH J. SACHS and BERNARD H. STERN: The Little Preoedipal Boy in Papa Hemingway and How He Created His Artistry.

Volume 2. Amsterdam 1972. 236 p. Hfl. 40.—
RALPH BEHRENS: Mérimée, Hemingway, and the Bulls. JEANNINE BOHLMEYER: Mythology in Sackville's "Induction" and "Complaint". HAROLD A. BRACK: Needed — a new language for communicating religion. LEONARD FEINBERG: Satire and Humor: In the Orient and in the West. B. GRANGER: The Whim-Whamsical Bachelors in Salmagundi. W. M. FORCE: The What Story? or Who's Who at the Zoo? W. N. KNIGHT: To Enter lists with God. Transformation of Spencerian Chivalric Tradition in Paradise Regained. MARY D. KRAMER: The Roman Catholic Cleric on the Jacobean Stage. BURTON R. POLLIN: The Temperance Movement and Its Friends Look at Poe. SAMUEL J. ROGAL: Two Translations of the Iliad, Book I: Pope and Tickell. J. L. STYAN: The Delicate Balance: Audience Ambivalence in the Comedy of Shakespeare and Chekhov. CLAUDE W. SUMERLIN: Christopher Smart's A Song to David: its influence on Robert Browning. B.W. TEDFORD: A Recipe for Satire and Civilization. H. H. WATTS: Othello and the Issue of Multiplicity. GUY R. WOODALL: Nationalism in the Philadelphia National Gazette and Literary Register: 1820—1836.

Volume 3. Amsterdam 1972. 236 p. Hfl. 40.—
RAYMOND BENOIT: In Dear Detail by Ideal Light: "Ode on a Grecian Urn". E. F. CALLAHAN: Lyric Origins of the Unity of 1 Henry IV. FRASER DREW: John Masefield and Juan Manuel de Rosas. LAURENCE GONZALEZ: Persona Bob: seer and fool. A. HIRT: A Question of Excess: Neo-Classical Adaptations of Greek Tragedy. EDWIN HONIG: Examples of

Poetic Diction in Ben Jonson. ELSIE LEACH: T. S. Eliot and the School of Donne. SEYMOUR REITER: The Structure of 'Waiting for Godot'. DANIEL E. VAN TASSEL: The Search for Manhood in D. H. Lawrence's 'Sons and Lovers'. MARVIN ROSENBERG: Poetry of the Theatre. GUY R. WOOD-ALL: James Russell Lowell's "Works of Jeremy Taylor, D.D.'

Volume 4. Amsterdam 1972. 233 p. Hfl. 40.–
BOGDDY ARIAS: Sailor's Reveries. R. H. BOWERS: Marlowe's 'Dr. Faustus', Tirso's 'El Condenado por Desconfiado', and the Secret Cause. HOWARD O. BROGAN: Satirist Burns and Lord Byron. WELLER EMBLER: Simone Weil and T. S. Eliot. E. ANTHONY JAMES: Defoe's Autobiographical Apologia: Rhetorical Slanting in 'An Appeal to Honour and Justice'. MARY D. KRAMER: The American Wild West Show and "Buffalo Bill" Cody. IRVING MASSEY: Shelley's "Dirge for the Year": The Relation of the Holograph to the First Edition. L. J. MORRISSEY: English Street Theatre: 1655–1708. M. PATRICK: Browning's Dramatic Techniques and 'The Ring and the Book': A Study in Mechanic and Organic Unity. VINCENT F. PETRONELLA: Shakespeare's 'Henry V' and the Second Tetralogy: Meditation as Drama. NASEEB SHAHEEN: Deriving Adjectives from Nouns. TED R. SPIVEY: The Apocalyptic Symbolism of W. B. Yeats and T. S. Eliot. EDWARD STONE: The Other Sermon in 'Moby–Dick'. M. G. WILLIAMS: 'In Memoriam': A Broad Church Poem.

Volume 5. Amsterdam 1972. 236 p. Hfl. 40.–
PETER G. BEIDLER: Chaucer's Merchant and the Tale of January. ROBERT A. BRYAN: Poets, Poetry, and Mercury in Spenser's Prosopopia: Mother Hubberd's Tale. EDWARD M. HOLMES: Requiem For A Scarlet Nun. E. ANTHONY JAMES: Defoe's Narrative Artistry: Naming and Describing in Robinson Crusoe. MICHAEL J. KELLY: Coleridge's "Picture, or The Lover's Resolution": its Relationship to "Dejection" and its Sources in the Notebooks. EDWARD MARGOLIES: The Playwright and his Critics. MURRAY F. MARKLAND: The Task Set by Valor. RAYMOND S. NELSON: Back to Methuselah: Shaw's Modern Bible. THOMAS W. ROSS: Maimed Rites in Much Ado About Nothing. WILLIAM B. TOOLE: The Metaphor of Alchemy in Julius Caesar. PAUL WEST: Carlyle's Bravura Prophetics. GLENA D. WOOD: The Tragi-Comic Dimensions of Lear's Fool. H. ALAN WYCHER-LEY: "Americana": The Mencken – Lorimer Feud.

Volume 6. Amsterdam 1972. 235 p. Hfl. 40.–
GEORG W. BOSWELL: Superstition and Belief in Faulkner. ALBERT COOK: Blake's Milton. MARSHA KINDER: The Improved Author's Farce: An Analysis of the 1734 Revisions. ABE LAUFE: What Makes Drama Run? (Introduction to Anatomy of a Hit). RICHARD L. LOUGHLIN: Laugh and Grow Wise with Oliver Goldsmith. EDWARD MARGOLIES: The American Detective Thriller & The Idea of Society. RAYMOND S. NELSON: Shaw's Heaven, Hell, and Redemption. HAROLD OREL: Is Patrick White's Voss the Real Leichhardt of Australia? LOUIS B. SALOMON: A Walk With Emerson On The Dark Side. H. GRANT SAMPSON: Structure in the Poetry of Thoreau. JAMES H. SIMS, Some Biblical Light on Shakespeare's Hamlet.

ROBERT F. WILLSON, Jr.: Lear's Auction. JAMES N. WISE: Emerson's "Experience" and "Sons and Lovers". JAMES D. YOUNG: Aims in Reader's Theatre.

Volume 7. Amsterdam 1973. 235 p. Hfl. 40.—

HANEY H. BELL Jr.: Sam Fathers and Ike McCaslin and the World in Which Ike Matures. SAMUEL IRVING BELLMAN: The Apocalypse in Literature. HALDEEN BRADDY: England and English before Alfred. DAVID R. CLARK: Robert Frost: "The Thatch" and "Directive". RALPH MAUD: Robert Crowley, Puritan Satirist. KATHARINE M. MORSBERGER: Hawthorne's "Borderland": The Locale of the Romance. ROBERT E. MORSBERGER: The Conspiracy of the Third International. "What is the metre of the dictionary?" — Dylan Thomas. RAYMOND PRESTON: Dr. Johnson and Aristotle. JOHN J. SEYDOW: The Sound of Passing Music: John Neal's Battle for American Literary Independence. JAMES H. SIMS: Enter Satan as Esau, Alone; Exit Satan as Belshazzar: *Paradise Lost*, BOOK (IV). MICHAEL WEST, Dryden and the Disintegration of Renaissance Heroic Ideals. RENATE C. WOLFF: Pamela as Myth and Dream.

Volume 8. Amsterdam 1973. 231 p. Hfl. 40.—

SAMUEL I. BELLMAN: Sleep, Pride, and Fantasy: Birth Traumas and Socio-Biologic Adaptation in the American-Jewish Novel. PETER BUITEN-HUIS: A Corresponding Fabric: The Urban World of Saul Bellow. DAVID R. CLARK: An Excursus upon the Criticism of Robert Frost's "Directive". FRANCIS GILLEN: Tennyson and the Human Norm: A Study of Hubris and Human Commitment in Three Poems by Tennyson. ROBERT R. HARSON: H. G. Wells: The Mordet Island Episode. JULIE B. KLEIN: The Art of Apology: "An Epistle to Dr. Arbuthnot" and "Verses on the Death of Dr. Swift". ROBERT E. MORSBERGER: The Movie Game in Who's Afraid of Virginia Woolf and The Boys in the Band. EDWIN MOSES: A Reading of "The Ancient Mariner". JOHN H. RANDALL: Romeo and Juliet in the New World. A Study in James, Wharton, and Fitzgerald "Fay ce que vouldras". JOHN E. SAVESON: Conrad as Moralist in Victory. ROBERT M. STROZIER: Politics, Stoicism, and the Development of Elizabethan Tragedy. LEWIS TURCO: Manoah Bodman: Poet of the Second Awakening.

Volume 9. Amsterdam 1973. 251 p. Hfl. 40.—

THOMAS E. BARDEN: Dryden's Aims in *Amphytryon.* SAMUEL IRVING BELLMAN: Marjorie Kinnan Rawling's Existentialist Nightmare *The Yearling.* SAMUEL IRVING BELLMAN: Writing Literature for Young People. Marjorie Kinnan Rawlings' "Secret River" of the Imagination. F. S. JANZOW: "Philadelphus," A New Essay by De Quincey. JACQUELINE KRUMP: Robert Browning's Palace of Art. ROBERT E. MORSBERGER: The Winning of Barbara Undershaft: Conversion by the Cannon Factory, or "Wot prawce selvytion nah?" DOUGLAS L. PETERSON: Tempest-Tossed Barks and Their Helmsmen in Several of Shakespeare's Plays. STANLEY POSS: Serial Form and Malamud's Schlemihls. SHERYL P. RUTLEDGE: Chaucer's Zodiac of Tales. CONSTANCE RUYS: John Pickering—Merchant Adventurer and Playwright. JAMES H. SIMS: Death in Poe's Poetry: Variations on a Theme. ROBERT A. SMITH: A Pioneer Black Writer and the Problems of Discrimination and Miscegenation. ALBERT J. SOLOMON: The Sound of Music in "Eveline": A Long Note on a Barrel-Organ. J. L. STYAN: Goldsmith's Comic Skills. ARLINE R. THORN: Shelley's *The Cenci* as Tragedy. E. THORN: James Joyce: Early Imitations of Structural Unity. LEWIS TURCO: The Poetry of Lewis Turco. An Interview by Gregory Fitzgerald and William Heyen.

New Series. Volume 1. Edited by James L. W. West III. Amsterdam 1974. 194 p. Hfl. 40.—

D. W. ROBERTSON, Jr.: Chaucer's Franklin and His Tale. CLARENCE H. MILLER and CARYL K. BERREY: The Structure of Integrity: The Cardinal Virtues in Donne's "Satyre III". F. SAMUEL JANZOW: The English Opium-Eater as Editor. VICTOR A. KRAMER: Premonition of Disaster: An Unpublished Section for Agee's *A Death in the Family*. GEORGE L. GECKLE: Poetic Justice and *Measure for Measure*. RODGER L. TARR: Thomas Carlyle's Growing Radicalism: The Social Context of *The French Revolution*. G. THOMAS TANSELLE: Philip Gaskell's *A New Introduction to Bibliography*. Review Essay. KATHERINE B. TROWER: Elizabeth D. Kirk's *The Dream Thought of Piers Plowman*. Review Essay. JAMES L. WEST III: Matthew J. Bruccoli's *F. Scott Fitzgerald a Descriptive Bibliography*. Review Essay. JAMES E. KIBLER: R. W. Stallman's *Stephen Crane: A Critical Bibliography*. Review. ROBERT P. MILLER: Jonathan Saville's *The Medieval Erotic Alba*. Review.

New Series. Volume 2. THACKERY. Edited by Peter L. Shillingsburg. Amsterdam 1974. 359 p. Hfl. 70.—

JOAN STEVENS: *Vanity Fair* and the London Skyline. JANE MILLGATE: History *versus* Fiction: Thackeray's Response to Macaulay. ANTHEA TRODD: Michael Angelo Titmarsh and the Knebworth Apollo. PATRICIA R. SWEENEY: Thackeray's Best Illustrator. JOAN STEVENS: Thackeray's Pictorial Capitals. ANTHONY BURTON: Thackeray's Collaborations with Cruikshank, Doyle, and Walker. JOHN SUTHERLAND: A *Vanity Fair* Mystery: The Delay in Publication. JOHN SUTHERLAND: Thackeray's Notebook for *Henry Esmond*. EDGAR F. HARDEN: The Growth of *The Virginians* as a Serial Novel: Parts 1–9. GERALD C. SORENSEN: Thackeray Texts and Bibliographical Scholarship. PETER L. SHILLINSBURG: Thackeray Texts: A Guide to Inexpensive Editions. RUTH apROBERTS: Thackeray Boom: A Review. JOSEPH E. BAKER: Reading Masterpieces in Isolation: Review. ROBERT A. COLBY and JOHN SUTHERLAND: Thackeray's Manuscripts: A Preliminary Census of Library Locations.

New Series. Volume 3. Edited by James L. W. West III. Amsterdam 1975. 184 p. Hfl. 40.—

SAMUEL J. ROGAL: Hurd's Editorial Criticism of Addison's Grammar and Usage. ROBERT P. MILLER: Constancy Humanized: Trivet's Constance and the Man of Law's Custance. WELDON THORNTON: Structure and Theme in Faulkner's *Go Down, Moses*. JAYNE K. KRIBBS: John Davis: A Man For His Time. STEPHEN E. MEATS: The Responsibilities of an Editor of Correspondence. Review Essay. RODGER L. TARR: Carlyle and Dickens *or* Dickens and Carlyle. Review. CHAUNCEY WOOD: Courtly Lovers: An Unsentimental View. Review.

New Series. Volume 4. Edited by James L. W. West III. Amsterdam 1975. 179 p. Hfl. 40.–
JAMES L. W. WEST III: A Bibliographer's Interview with William Styron. J. TIMOTHY HOBBS: The Doctrine of Fair Use in the Law of Copyright. JUNE STEFFENSEN HAGEN: Tennyson's Revisions of the Last Stanza of "Audley Court". CLIFFORD CHALMERS HUFFMAN: *The Christmas Prince*: University and Popular Drama in the Age of Shakespeare. ROBERT L. OAK-MAN: Textual Editing and the Computer. Review Essay. T.H. HOWARD-HILL: The Bard in Chains: *The Harvard Concordance to Shakespeare*. Review Essay. BRUCE HARKNESS: Conrad Computerized and Concordanced. Review Essay. MIRIAM J. SHILLINGSBURG: A Rose is a Four-Letter Word; or, The Machine Makes Another Concordance. Review Essay. RICHARD H. DAMMERS: Explicit Statement as Art. Review Essay. A. S. G. EDWARDS: Medieval Madness and Medieval Literature. Review Essay. NOEL POLK: Blotner's Faulkner. Review.

New Series. Volume 5–6. **GYASCUTUS. Studies in Antebellum Southern Humorous and Sporting Writing. Edited by James L. W. West III.** Amsterdam 1978.
NOEL POLK: The Blind Bull, Human Nature: Sut Lovingood and the Damned Human Race. HERBERT P. SHIPPEY: William Tappan Thompson as Playwright. LELAND H. COX, Jr.: Porter's Edition of *Instructions to Young Sportsmen*. ALAN GRIBBEN: Mark Twain Reads Longstreet's *Georgia Scenes*. T. B. THORPE's Far West Letters, ed. Leland H. Cox, Jr. An Unknown Tale by GEORGE WASHINGTON HARRIS ed. William Starr. JOHNSON JONES HOOPER's "The 'Frinnolygist' at Fault" ed. James L. W. West III. SOUTH CAROLINA WRITERS in the *Spirit of the Times* ed. Stephen E. Meats. A NEW MOCK SERMON ed. James L. W. West III. ANOTHER NEW MOCK SERMON ed. A. S. Wendel. The PORTER-HOOPER Correspondence ed. Edgar E. Thompson.

New Series. Volume 7. **SANFORD PINSKER: The Languages of Joseph Conrad.** Amsterdam 1978. 87 p. Hfl. 20.–
*Table of Contents:* Foreword. Introductory Language. The Language of the East. The Language of Narration. The Language of the Sea. The Language of Politics. *Victory* As Afterword.

New Series. Volume 8. **GARLAND CANNON: An Integrated Transformational Grammar of the English Language.** Amsterdam 1978. 315 p. Hfl. 60.–
*Table of Contents:* Preface. 1) A Child's Acquisition of His First Language. 2) Man's Use of Language. 3) Syntactic Component: Base Rules. 4) Syntactic Component: Lexicon. 5) Syntactic Component: Transformational Rules. 6) Semantic Component. 7) Phonological Component. 8) Man's Understanding of His Language. Appendix: the Sentence-Making Model. Bibliography. Index.

New Series: Volume 9. GERALD LEVIN: Richardson the Novelist: The Psychological Patterns. Amsterdam 1978. 172 p. Hfl. 30.—

*Table of Contents:* Preface. Chapter One. The Problem of Criticism. Chapter Two. "Conflicting Trends" in *Pamela.* Chapter Three. Lovelace's Dream. Chapter Four. The "Family Romance" of *Sir Charles Grandison.* Chapter Five. Richardson's Art. Chapter Six. Richardson and Lawrence: the Rhetoric of Concealment. Appendix. Freud's Theory of Masochism. Bibliography.

New Series: Volume 10. WILLIAM F. HUTMACHER: Wynkyn de Worde and Chaucer's Canterbury Tales. A Transcription and Collation of the 1498 Edition with Caxton[2] from the General Prologue Through the Knights Tale. Amsterdam 1978. 224 p. Hfl. 40,—

*Table of Contents:* Introduction. Wynkyn's Life and Works. Wynkyn De Word's Contribution to Printing. Significance of Wynkyn's *The Canterbury Tales.* Significance of Wynkyn's Order of the Tales. Scheme of the Order of *The Canterbury Tales.* Wynkyn's Variants from CX[2]. Printer's Errors. Spelling. Omissions in Wynkyn's Edition. Additions in Wynkyn's Edition. Transpositions in Wynkyn's Edition. Miscellaneous Variants in the Reading. Bibliography. Explanation of the Scheme of the Transcription and Recording of the Variants. The Transcription and Collation.

New Series: Volume 11. WILLIAM R. KLINK: S. N. Behrman: The Major Plays. Amsterdam 1978. 272 p. Hfl. 45,—

*Table of Contents:* Introduction. *The Second Man. Brief Moment. Biography. Rain From Heaven. End of Summer. No Time for Comedy. The Talley Method. But For Whom Charlie.* Language. Conclusion. Bibliography.

Editions Rodopi N.V., Keizersgracht 302-304, Amsterdam, the Netherlands.